World Cultures Through Art Activities

WORLD CULTURES THROUGH ART ACTIVITIES

Dindy Robinson

Illustrations by Rebecca Estes

1996
Teacher Ideas Press
A Division of
Libraries Unlimited, Inc.
Englewood, Colorado

This book is dedicated to my husband
Bill
who did not know what he was getting into
when he married a teacher.

TEACHER IDEAS PRESS
A Division of
Libraries Unlimited, Inc.
P.O. Box 6633
Englewood, CO 80155-6633
1-800-237-6124

Production Editor: Kevin W. Perizzolo
Copy Editor: Tama J. Serfoss
Design and Layout: Pamela J. Getchell

Library of Congress Cataloging-in-Publication Data

Robinson, Dindy.
    World cultures through art activities / Dindy Robinson ;
illustrations by Rebecca Estes.
    xix, 222 p. 22x28 cm.
    Includes bibliographical references.
    ISBN 1-56308-271-3
    1. Art--Study and teaching (Elementary)--United States.
2. Multicultural education--Activity programs--United States.
3. Project method of teaching. I. Title.
N362.R629 1996
372.5'044-dc20   96-5023
                                                          CIP

CONTENTS

PREFACE

This book was written to enable those who work with students in an educational setting (primary teachers, art teachers, preschool and kindergarten teachers, and day care providers) to recreate aspects of a culture within the classroom so that students might better understand and appreciate other peoples. It is essential that today's students receive a multicultural education as they will be the leaders of tomorrow's global community. The more understanding they have of the many different peoples that make up our world, the better they will be able to handle the problems that our generation will leave them. This book is intended as a supplement for the classroom social studies curriculum. The activities described are most appropriate for elementary-age students, K-3, although preschool and post-primary students will find many of the activities enjoyable and worthwhile.

I wish to thank Jane Bellion, formerly headmistress of St. Andrews Episcopal School in Grand Prairie, Texas, for allowing me the freedom to design my own social studies curriculum and for not complaining too loudly about the messiness of our many creative works in progress.

I would also like to thank my students, too numerous to list by name, who tried many of the activities in this book and through their enthusiasm, encouraged me to develop more activities.

I wish to thank my mother, Martha Naugle, the teacher who originally inspired me, and my students' parents, who did not so much as raise an eyebrow at the many unusual requests that came home and willingly contributed items for classroom displays.

Finally, my deepest appreciation and love for my husband, Bill, and my daughters, Fritha and Jaala. Over the years they have been remarkably tolerant of sharing me with the kids in my class and have provided many helpful ideas and enormous support.

INTRODUCTION

In recent years, there has been a welcome movement away from fill-in-the-blank style teaching and workbooks as schools have implemented thematic learning and whole language curriculums. In teaching art, we have become aware that the process of doing is more important than the end product, and that the child learns more from picking up a gray crayon and drawing an elephant freehand than by coloring in between the lines in a coloring book.

In keeping with that philosophy, the activities in this book are freehand activities, designed to encourage the child's creativity and development, wherever possible. Students should be encouraged to use their imaginations and ideas to improve on a design. Some patterns are provided, but these are reduced to the minimum number necessary.

While this book attempts to introduce children to cultures from all over the world, space limitations make it impossible to include every country, or even every culture within each country. Countries were selected on the basis of their importance in world history and with an attempt to represent many regions of the world. The chapters are arranged roughly by continent. Asian countries are covered first, then Australia, and then African, European and American countries.

Each chapter covers a different country and is broken down into subsections such as home and family life or geography. Topics were chosen on the basis of identification with a particular country, uniqueness, and suitability of artistic representation. Given that an entire library could be written about each country presented, many important and interesting topics were omitted due to space limitations. This book is not intended to be a complete guide to any culture, but, rather, is an overview of many different cultures.

Factual information introduces each activity idea to aid the teacher in presenting the activity to the students. Teachers are strongly encouraged to use additional books and pictures of each country when presenting the material. A list of reference books is provided at the end of each chapter, and in many cases, teachers are referred to a particular book that has pictures appropriate for each activity.

Children's literature is one of the most rapidly growing fields in publishing today. New high-quality children's books about different parts of the world and different cultures appear in bookstores almost every day. Teachers are encouraged to browse through the children's section of their local library or bookstore to acquire a library of literature to go along with their cultural units.

A complete list of materials is provided for each activity. For the most part, materials are inexpensive and easy to obtain. In some cases, several variations of an activity are given to allow for different age levels or classroom environments. In many cases, the activities in one chapter could easily be applied to another chapter, for instance, the technique used to make a relief map described in chapter 1, could be used in any one of the other chapters.

My intent has been to make this book as easy as possible for teachers, even non-artists, to use. The most important thing to remember is to let the child be the artist. All you have to do is provide the materials and the initial idea and let the child take over from there.

1 CHINA

Capital: Beijing
Government: People's Republic
Population: 1,165,800,000
Area: 3,691,515 square miles

China, home of the world's oldest living continuous civilization, is a land filled with beauty, tradition, and history. It is a mountainous country; lands 3,281 feet or more above sea level make up more than 68 percent of the total area of the country. These mountains have in the past served to protect China from the rest of the world. Although within the boundaries, different ruling families often struggled against each other for control, China was free from conquest until the invasion of the Mongols in 1234.

This isolation left the people of China free to develop their unique culture without much outside influence. Art has always been an important part of Chinese culture. The early Chinese worshipped the spirits of their ancestors and created artifacts to accompany the dead in their tombs. Their art is dominated by spirits and legends. The ancient Chinese believed that a spirit in nature breathed life into all things and art must capture this spirit to give it life.

One of the major religions in China is Taoism, which teaches that people are of little importance compared to nature. Therefore, Chinese artists often included small figures to show that humans are just a minor part of the forms and patterns of the natural world. Some of the works of jade, porcelain, bronze, and silk created by the ancient Chinese have never been equaled.

A unit on China will introduce students to the beauty of nature and the importance of tradition, as well as many amusing legends.

HOME

The Ancient Chinese Home

The Chinese culture stresses respect for the elderly. Because of this and strong family ties, several generations of one family often lived together in the same house. The homes of the most wealthy Chinese were surrounded by walls. Bright tiles and ornaments decorated these buildings, while gently curving roofs with upturned eaves protected the homes from the rain. Show students pictures of Chinese homes. A picture of a house such as that owned by a wealthy Chinese family can be found in *The Art of China* by Shirley Glubok.

Refrigerator Box House

Materials:

- Refrigerator box
- Red posterboard (six pieces)
- Red and black paint
- Paintbrushes
- Glue or tape

Turn the refrigerator box on its side. Cut out windows and a door and paint the sides of the box red. When the paint is dry, add black lines to simulate bricks. Attach one piece of posterboard to the top of each end of the box and two pieces of posterboard to the top of each side. Cut inward curves from the edges of the posterboard that are on each of the box's four corners to simulate the curved eaves of the roof of the house.

Milk Carton House

Materials:

- Cardboard milk cartons, any size
- Cardboard
- Construction paper, various colors, especially red
- Glue
- Scissors

Cut a door and window out of the milk carton. Cut red paper into small rectangles and glue them to the sides of the carton to form brick walls. Glue large red rectangles to tops of cartons, with edges turned up to form a curved roof. Glue the bottom of the milk carton to the cardboard base and add a banner cut from construction paper and decorated with Chinese characters, samples of which can be found in *Long Is a Dragon: Chinese Writing for Children* by Peggy Goldstein and *Chinese Writing: An Introduction* by Diane Wolff. Add flowers cut from paper for the garden.

Door Seals

The Chinese decorate their homes with papercuts and line the doors of their homes with red paper covered with inscriptions or philosophies for life such as "May you find wealth on your path of life" or "Glory with honor and wealth." Many Chinese families today make up their own inscriptions for the red seals around their doors.

Door Seal Picture

Materials:

- Red paper
- Black or gold felt-tip markers

Make up your own philosophy of life and write it on red paper to hang around the classroom door.

Fans

Many Chinese use fans to keep cool and fan cooking fires, although the exquisitely decorated fans used for centuries are now mostly reserved for export. Chinese fans often contain scenes from nature that are hand-painted, embroidered, or burned into sandalwood.

Construction Paper Fan

Materials:

- Watercolors
- Paintbrushes
- White construction paper (12 by 18 inches)
- Tape or a stapler
- Ribbons

Paint a scene on white paper. Favorite subjects of the Chinese are flowers, birds, or butterflies. When dry, fold the paper accordion style and gather at the bottom. Staple or tape the bottom. Tie a ribbon at the bottom to serve as a handle.

Posterboard Fan

Materials:

- Paintbrushes
- Watercolors
- Stiff paper such as posterboard or tagboard
- Yarn
- Glue
- Craft sticks
- Scissors

Cut the paper into an oval shape. Paint a scene on the surface of the paper. Favorite subjects of Chinese art are flowers, birds, or butterflies. Punch holes around the edge and lace yarn through the holes. Glue a craft stick to the bottom as a handle.

Fish Banners

China is one of the world's leading fishing nations. Fish is a main food for the Chinese, even in the inner parts of the mainland. Fish is transported inland on boats along the Yangtze and Yellow Rivers. The Chinese often hang fish banners outside their homes as a symbol of the importance of the fishing industry.

Construction Paper Fish Banner

Materials:

- Tempera, various colors
- Newspaper
- White construction paper (12 by 18 inches)
- Yarn
- Stapler
- Scissors
- Paintbrushes

Trace a large fish shape on the white paper. Cut out through a double layer of paper. Staple the cutouts together, leaving an opening at the end, and stuff crumpled newspaper inside. Paint the outside of the fish with tempera. Attach yarn to the top of the fish near the head and tail and hang from ceiling.

Painted Screens

The Chinese use painted screens to separate areas of their homes. These screens come in many sizes and are finely decorated, often with pictures of landscapes or animals.

Cardboard Box Screen

Materials (this is a whole class project):

- Large box, unfolded with top and bottom flaps cut off
- Watercolors
- Paintbrushes

- Black construction paper or black crepe paper streamers
- White butcher paper
- Glue or tape

To create a screen for the classroom, cover the box with the white butcher paper. Tape or glue a narrow band of black paper around all the edges to create a border. Use watercolors to paint scenes of trees or houses on the white paper.

Farmer's Hat

For protection from the sun and rain, farmers in China wear wide-brimmed hats made from woven bamboo.

Paper Hat

Materials:

- Crayons or paints and paintbrushes
- Scissors

- Stapler
- Shirtboard or brown or yellow construction paper

Cut an 18-inch circle from the shirtboard. Cut a line from the edge of the paper to the center. Overlap the edges to form a cone and staple the edges. Decorate with colors or paints as desired.

NATURE IN CHINA

Silkworms

Silkworms, the source of silk, one of China's most traditional industries, have been raised by the Chinese for centuries and have been so completely domesticated that they depend on humans to supply their every need, including prodigious amounts of mulberry leaves. Silkworms can be raised in the classroom, and children will enjoy making models of each of the stages in the silkworm life cycle. Girls in China often raise silkworms as pets. A ton of unprocessed cocoons yields about 240 pounds of raw silk. *A Silkworm Is Born* by Ann Stepp tells of the life of a silkworm: egg, larva, cocoon, and moth stages.

Silkworm Eggs

Materials:

- Gray construction paper
- Hole punch
- Green paper

- Glue
- Scissors
- Mulberry leaf pattern (see fig. 1.1)

Punch holes in the gray paper. Trace and cut mulberry leaves from green paper. Glue "holes" from gray paper on the leaves to form the silkworm eggs.

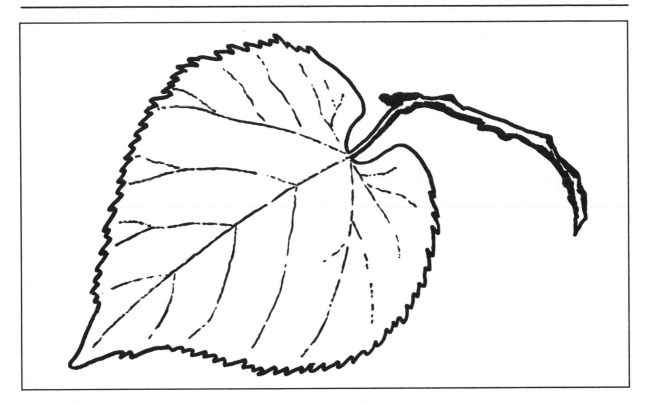

Fig. 1.1.

Stocking Silkworm Larvae

The larva of a silkworm looks like a large, fat, gray worm. At maturity, it is 2½-to 3-inches long. The larvae has large, black "false eyes" on its head, and when it is ready to spin its cocoon, it will lift the front part of its body off the surface of the mulberry leaf and sway back and forth.

Materials:

- White or cream colored socks
- Material for stuffing
- Felt scraps
- Glue
- Scissors

Fill the sock with stuffing material. Add features with felt scraps. If you want, leave out the stuffing and make a silkworm puppet.

Egg Carton Silkworm Larvae

Materials:

- Colored felt-tip markers
- Egg carton, cut in half down middle, leaving one row of six compartments
- Twist ties

Draw features on egg carton and add twist ties for antennae.

Yarn Silkworm Cocoon

Materials:

- White or yellow yarn or thread
- Cotton ball
- Stick

Wrap yarn or thread around cotton ball and then wrap it all around a stick, forming an elongated oval cocoon about 2 inches long.

Tissue Paper Silkworm Moth

Materials:

- Clip clothespins
- White or pale yellow tissue paper
- Tape
- Colored felt-tip markers

Bunch a square of tissue paper tightly in the middle, fanning sides out. Tape around the middle and fasten with the clothespin. Draw features on the clothespin.

Bamboo

This versatile grass, used for baskets, mats, hats, and fish traps, is so strong that it can also be used in building houses and bridges. Young bamboo shoots are eaten as a vegetable; the grain is also a food. The plants range from 3 to 164 feet in height, and can have a diameter of up to 12 inches at the base. The main shoot does not produce leaves; it is the secondary or tertiary branches, growing from buds on the main stem, that produce the leaves.

Paper Bamboo

Materials:

- Green butcher paper, 3 to 6 feet long
- Green and yellow construction paper
- Scissors
- Stapler and glue

Roll the butcher paper into a cylinder 2 to 4 inches in diameter to form the main shoot of the bamboo. Cut yellow stripes from construction paper and glue around the main shoot. Roll green construction paper into cylinders, 1 inch in diameter. Glue yellow stripes around the smaller cylinders. Trace leaves on green paper. Cut out and glue these leaves to the tops of small cylinders. Staple the cylinders to the main shoot to form a leafy bamboo plant.

THE HISTORY OF CHINA

The Great Wall of China

The Great Wall of China, which stretches from the Pacific coast to central Asia, was built during the Chou Dynasty (1027–256 B.C.). It was begun in 500 B.C. as a means to repel Mongol invaders. Most of this incredible monument still stands today. Although it is said to be the only human artifact that can be seen from space this is actually a myth stemming from a vision dreamed by the First Emperor, Shihuangdi. It is 1,880 miles long, and was built entirely by hand. Two good books about the wall are *The Great Wall of China* by Leonard Everett Fisher and *Early China and the Wall* by Peter Nancarrow. A good picture of the wall can be found in *The Man-Made Wonders of the World* by Dorothy Turner.

Paper Bag Wall

Materials:

- Paper grocery bags
- Newspaper
- Gray paint
- Masking tape
- Paintbrushes

Stuff paper grocery bags with crumpled newspaper. Fold the tops of the bags over and tape shut. Paint the bags gray and arrange them against the classroom wall to form a copy of the Great Wall of China.

Cardboard Carton Wall

Materials:

- Black and gray paint
- Large carton, unfolded
- Paintbrushes

Paint the sides of the carton gray. After the paint dries, add black lines to form bricks.

Picture of the Great Wall

Materials:

- Gray and white construction paper
- Crayons or colored pencils
- Glue
- Scissors

Cut small rectangles from gray paper and glue them onto the white paper to represent the Great Wall. With crayons or pencils, draw a scene of the Chinese laborers working to build the wall, or perhaps a battle scene centering around the wall.

Kites

According to Chinese tradition, the first kite was invented in 549 by an emperor besieged within a walled city. He sent a kite into the air so that his soldiers would know he was in trouble, but the kite was shot down. Kites in China are of different shapes, depending on the region of the country. Northern kites are large and strong, shaped like animals or common geometric shapes. Kites from the South are lighter and often butterfly shaped. Pictures of Chinese kites can be found in *Journey Through China* by Philip Steele.

Construction Paper Kite

Materials:

- Construction paper
- Crepe paper streamers
- Paints
- Paintbrushes
- String
- Glue
- Scissors

Design your own kite. The Chinese often layer their kites, for example, a kite might have three butterflies, one above the other. Decorate your kites with paints and connect the layers by stapling the bottom of the top layer to the top of the middle layer and the bottom of the middle layer to the top of the bottom layer. Staple colored streamers to the sides and attach a string for flying.

THE GEOGRAPHY OF CHINA

The Topography of China

China is a mountainous country, with only about one-tenth of its surface classified as plains. The remainder of the surface is filled with hills, plateaus, and mountains. The mountain ranges contain vast water and mineral resources. Students should refer to an atlas when doing this activity.

Topographical Relief Map
Materials:

- Large map of China
- Paintbrushes and pencil
- Puff paint (made from equal parts flour, salt, and water)
- Tracing paper and carbon paper
- Large sheet of heavy cardboard
- Tempera (brown, yellow, green, and blue)

Trace the outline of China from the large map. Use the carbon paper to transfer this outline to heavy cardboard. Mix the puff paint with different colors of tempera and use it to form the highlands and lowlands. Use brown paint for high mountains, yellow for other highlands, green for lowlands, and blue for water. Allow to dry thoroughly.

The Yangtze River

At 3,915 miles long, the Yangtze River is the world's third longest river. It serves as a major transportation route into central China. Have students find a map of the river in an atlas. A photo of the river can be found in *People's Republic of China* from the Enchantment of the World series by Valjean McLenighan.

Yangtze River Mural
Materials:

- Long piece of yellow roll paper
- Construction paper, various colors
- White butcher paper
- Paintbrushes
- Scissors and glue
- Crayons and watercolors

Hang the white butcher paper on the wall or bulletin board. Cut a gently curving strip from the yellow paper and glue to the center of the white paper to form the Yangtze River. Make trees, rice fields, and a city along the banks of the Yangtze with crayons, watercolors, and construction paper. A typical city would have a wall separating the city from the river with a gate and boat docks. Don't forget to put in junks and sampans, as well as ducks and other water animals.

TRANSPORTATION IN CHINA

Chinese Junks

Chinese junks are big cargo boats with sails that travel up and down the Yangtze and Yellow Rivers in China. They are used to transport goods and people, as fishing boats, and even as homes for people. People often paint two big eyes on the prow of their junk so the ship can find its way in the ocean. Pictures of junks can be found in *Journey Through China* by Philip Steele.

Styrofoam Tray Junks

Materials:

- Found materials such as: Styrofoam trays, aluminum foil, straws, pipe cleaners, paper towels, and so on
- Glue

Using a Styrofoam tray as a base, construct a Chinese junk from found materials. See if you can create a junk that will actually float.

THE ARCHITECTURE OF CHINA

Arches

Arches are a major component of Chinese architecture, decorating temples, houses, and gateways to cities.

Posterboard Arch

Materials:

- Red posterboard or cardboard
- Gold metallic paint
- Paintbrushes
- Scissors

Design your own arch on the posterboard. Then cut it out and decorate it with gold metallic paint.

THE ART OF THE CHINESE

Block Printing

The Chinese invented the art of printing in 868. The technique is called block printing. Today, block printing is considered an artform.

Paper Towel Block Prints
(For children ages three to seven)

Materials:

- Powdered tempera
- Paper
- Various items for printing (select items with interesting shapes and textures, such as utensils, carved vegetables, blocks, and so on)
- Pie tins
- Paper towels

Place a folded, wet paper towel in the bottom of each pie tin and sprinkle a different color of powdered tempera over each. Allow this to stand for five minutes till moistened. Press items onto the paper towel pad and then press the object onto the paper, making any design you choose.

Rubber Block Prints

Materials:

- Pie tins
- Wooden blocks
- Scraps of rubber, obtainable from a junkyard or old inner tubes
- Rubber cement
- Powdered tempera
- Paper
- Paper towels

Cut a shape out of rubber. Cover one entire surface of the wooden block with rubber cement. Put the rubber shape on this side and allow to dry. Printing procedure is the same as that described in "Paper Towel Block Prints" (see p. 9).

Mole Skin Block Prints

Materials:

- Paint and jar lids
- Adhesive-backed moleskin or corn pads (located in the foot care section of the pharmacy.)
- Paper

Cut desired shape from the foot care product and stick the shape to top of jar lid. Dip the block in paint and press onto paper.

Calligraphy

The characters that make up the written Chinese language were developed 4,000 years ago. These characters began as pictures of the objects they represented. Over the centuries, the characters have been simplified. In some cases, two or more characters have been combined to form a new character with an entirely different meaning, for example, the character for "woman" and the character for "child" have been combined to make the character for "good." To read a common Chinese newspaper, a person must be able to read 2,000 to 3,000 characters. Discuss with students the differences between Chinese writing, which is based on pictures, and our own alphabet, which is based on sounds. Why would this lead to a greater number of symbols in the Chinese writing? There are many examples of Chinese calligraphy available. Obtain as many samples as possible from the library for students to examine. Two good books for children are *Long Is a Dragon: Chinese Writing for Children* by Peggy Goldstein and *Chinese Writing: An Introduction* by Diane Wolff.

Calligraphy Picture

Materials:

- Black paint
- Small paintbrushes
- White paper
- Samples of Chinese calligraphy

Paint Chinese characters on your paper. Begin by simply copying the different symbols. If you want, try combining them to form simple sentences or tell stories.

Paper Cutting

Paper cutting is an artform that Chinese children learn at a very young age. Chinese designs are intricate, detailed and sometimes used in shadow plays. Some papercuts are used for a single special occasion and then thrown away. Others are kept as works of art. Papercuts can be created with knives or scissors and are often painted. *The Book of Paper Cutting* by Chris Rich and *Chinese Folk Designs* by W. M. Hawley are books of papercut designs.

Papercuts

Materials:

- Tracing paper
- Scissors
- Glue
- Pencils
- Thin, brightly colored paper (colored photocopy paper works well)
- Simple design to trace (black and white magazine pictures are good). See figures 1.2 and 1.3 for examples.

Lay the tracing paper over your chosen design and trace around the outside edges to create your pattern. Put small drops of glue on the back of the pattern just outside the drawing, being careful not to get glue inside the outline. Press the tracing paper onto the colored paper and let it dry firmly in position. Working slowly and carefully, cut around the traced outline. As you cut, the tracing paper will fall away. When you are finished, you can glue your papercut to another piece of paper of a contrasting color. Complete the picture with additional papercuts and add a simple border design.

Jade Carvings

Jade is a precious stone that the Chinese have been using in their art for centuries. It comes in many colors, but the most valuable color is dark green. Jade carving is a revered art in China and the techniques have been passed down through the generations. Ancient jade carvings are some of the most beautiful and prized artifacts of the ancient Chinese.

Cornstarch Clay Beads

Materials:

- Cornstarch (½ cup)
- Flour (¾ cup)
- Salt (½ cup)
- Green tempera (mixed 1:1 with white glue)
- Warm water (½ to 1 cup)
- Paintbrushes
- Large needle
- Thread or fishing line

Have the teacher prepare the clay by mixing cornstarch, flour, and salt in a bowl. Add water gradually till the mixture forms a shape.

Knead the clay and shape it into beads. Have the teacher poke holes through the centers of the beads with a large needle and let sit overnight to harden. (This can be shortened by baking at 200° for one hour.) Once the beads are hard, paint them with the glue-paint mixture and then string them together with thread or fishing line.

Watercolors

Painting with watercolors is a popular artform in China. The art is understated, with light strokes of the brush defining the painting. Chinese art is impressionistic, with the "spirit" of the subject being more important than what the subject looks like in reality, so artists try to use the fewest number of brush strokes possible to define their subject. Discuss with students how this style of painting is in keeping with the Chinese tradition of honoring the spirits of their ancestors and in nature. Some samples of Chinese paintings can be found in *Far Eastern Antiquities* by Michael Ridley, *History of Far Eastern Art* by Sherman E. Lee, and *The Art of China* by Shirley Glubok.

(Text continues on page 14.)

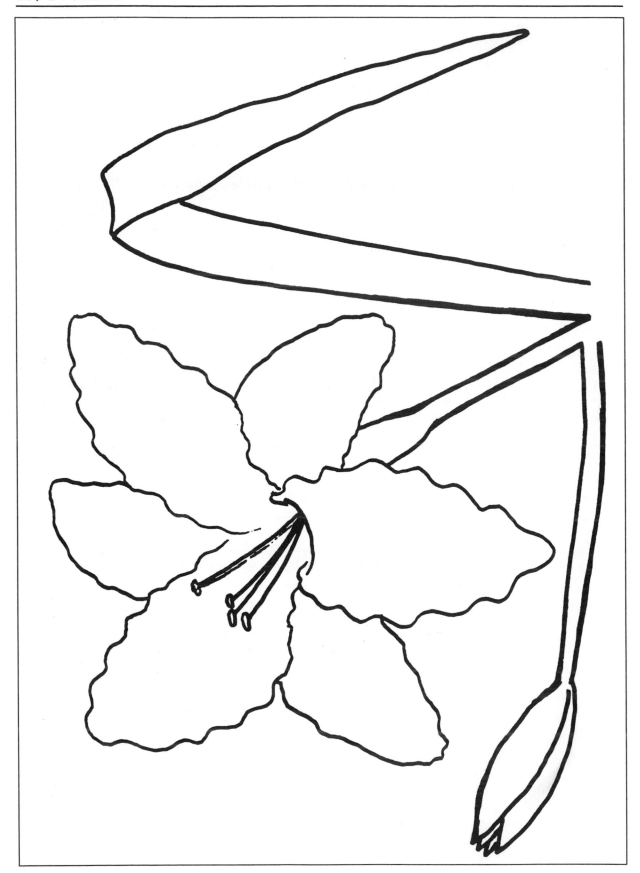

Fig. 1.2.

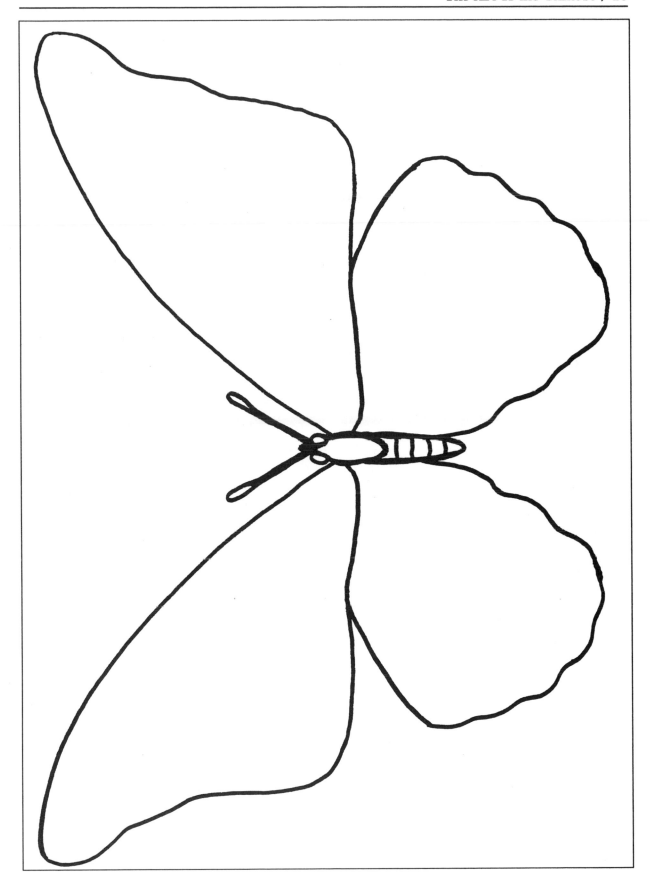

Fig. 1.3.

Painted Scroll

Materials:

- Paintbrushes
- Wooden dowels
- Long, narrow sheets of white paper (shelf paper is good)
- Watercolors
- Glue

Study samples of Chinese watercolors and then create your own watercolor masterpiece on long, narrow sheets of white paper, painting down the long paper, not across. Try to use the fewest number of strokes possible. Glue the top and bottom of the paper to the wooden dowels to create a Chinese painted scroll.

Silk Screen Painting

This activity requires a lot of time and patience, but produces spectacular results!

Silk Screen Picture

Materials:

- Clear Plexiglas (12 by 18 inches)
- Watercolors
- Thick sheet of cloth paper (12 by 18 inches)
- Thick dowel
- Vividly colored picture of any type (pages from magazines are good)
- Tub of water
- Small paintbrushes
- Liquid soap
- Blow dryer

Lay the Plexiglas over the picture and cover it with a light layer of soap. Paint on the Plexiglas with watercolors, tracing over the color and design of the picture as closely as possible. Meanwhile, the cloth paper should be soaking in a tub of water. When the Plexiglas has been painted completely, dry the paint with a blowdryer and lay the Plexiglas, paint side up, on a flat surface. Take the wet paper and lay over the painted surface. Roll the dowel over the back of the paper, pressing hard. When the paper is lifted, the design will be transferred, in reverse, from the Plexiglas to the paper.

CHINESE DRAMATIC ARTS

Shadow Plays

Shadow plays, in which a play is performed behind a lighted screen so the audience sees only the shadows of the performers, are very popular in China. According to legend, shadow plays date back to 100 B.C. when a priest claimed to have brought the emperor's dead wife back to life and cast a woman's shadow onto a white screen with a lamp as proof. Shadow plays can be performed by living actors, but they are more often performed using puppets made from translucent leather and colored with transparent dyes so they cast colored shadows on the screen. Pictures of shadow plays can be found in *The Chinese Knew* by Tillie S. Pine and Joseph Levine.

Shadow Play Mural

Materials:

- Strong light source
- White and black butcher paper
- Pencils
- Scissors and tape

Tape white butcher paper to wall. Shine light on the paper and have a student strike a pose between the light and the paper. Trace around the student's shadow. Lay this white sheet on top of a black sheet of paper and cut through both sheets around the traced shape. Arrange several students' "shadows" on the wall to create a scene from a shadow play.

Shadow Play Picture

Materials:

- Scissors and glue
- Colored construction paper
- Black construction paper (9 by 11 inches or 11 by 18 inches)
- White tissue paper, cut the same size as the black construction paper

Cut shapes of people, animals, and plants from your colored paper and glue them onto the black paper to make your own scene from a shadow play. Lay a sheet of white tissue paper over the scene and glue it into place. The colored cutouts under the white tissue paper will mimic the effect of colored shadows projected on a screen. The whole class may cooperate with each student creating one scene from a favorite Chinese legend so that an entire play may be displayed on the wall.

Chinese Opera

The opera is as popular in China as it is in Italy. It began in the T'ang Dynasty under the Emperor Ming Huang (713–756). The plots are simple dramatizations of popular tales or historical incidents. They generally end on a moral note, and virtue is almost always triumphant.

The audience in China goes to hear, not see, the opera. There is no scenery, but the players are dressed in rich, vibrant colors and have bright, colorful make-up or masks. The colors are symbolic—red for loyalty, black for boldness, white for treachery. The performance is a combination of acrobatics, pantomime, dance, and song. Samples of Chinese operas can be found in volumes 1 through 3 of *Traditional Chinese Plays*, translated by A. C. Scott. Pictures of masks can be found in *Journey Through China* by Philip Steele. Opera masks are often available in Chinese import stores and can be displayed in the classroom.

Chinese Opera Masks

Materials:

- Paper plates and construction paper
- Tempera and paintbrushes
- Crepe paper streamers
- Cotton balls colored by rolling in powdered tempera
- Yarn
- Glue
- Scissors and stapler

Paint facial features on your paper plate with bright, vivid colors. Attach a construction paper hat to the top of the plate. Decorate the hat with colored cotton balls, and plumes and feathers cut from construction paper. Crepe paper streamers can be attached to the bottom of the mask for a beard and yarn can be added for hair. You may want to create a mask for a character from an actual opera or from a favorite Chinese folk tale.

CHINESE HOLIDAYS

Chinese New Year

There are many important holidays in the Chinese calendar. The most important is the Chinese New Year, which marks the beginning of the year in the Chinese lunar calendar. A good book about this holiday is *The Chinese New Year* by Cheng Hou-tien.

The Chinese New Year falls between January 20 and February 20 each year and is made up of several smaller festivals. One of these is the Lantern Festival, held on the last day of the New Year celebration, in which Chinese families all join in a parade, carrying lighted lanterns, seeking the spirits of their ancestors. The Lion Dance, in which several dancers join together under a long lion costume and dance down the street, is another well-known tradition of the Chinese New Year celebration. A picture of the Lion Dance can be found in *Journey Through China* by Philip Steele. As part of the New Year's celebration, the Chinese decorate their homes with papercuts and line the doors of their homes with red paper covered with inscriptions or philosophies for life such as "May you find wealth on your path of life" or "Glory with honor and wealth." Many Chinese families today make up their own inscriptions for the red seals around their doors. The Chinese invented fireworks and rockets centuries before the Western world learned about gunpowder. Colorful fireworks displays highlight Chinese New Year celebrations.

Chinese Lanterns

Materials:

- Construction paper (12 by 18 inches)
- Scissors
- Yellow or orange tissue paper (12 by 18 inches)
- Crepe paper streamers
- Stapler or glue

Cut a 1-inch strip off the short end of the paper to serve as the handle. Fold the construction paper lengthwise (hot dog style). Place the paper with the fold at the bottom. Draw a line across the paper 1 inch from the top. Make cuts from the fold to the line, about 1 inch apart. Unfold. Staple or glue the short sides together. Staple or glue the handle across the top. Crumple tissue paper and staple or glue it inside to make a light. Attach crepe paper streamers to the bottom of the lantern.

Fireworks Picture

Materials:

- Black construction paper
- Straws
- Glue
- Tempera (bright colors)
- Glitter

Spoon drops of tempera paint onto the black paper and blow on the drop through the straws, swirling the paint across the paper to create a starburst of color. When the paint dries, trace around the color with glue and shake glitter over the paper. Shake off the excess glitter when the painting has dried.

Paper Bag Lion

Materials:

- Paper grocery bag
- Construction paper
- Crepe paper streamers
- Long piece of cloth

- Colored felt-tip markers
- Glue
- Scissors

Decorate the paper bag with construction paper so that it will be the head of the lion. Cut features and a mane and glue them onto the front of the bag. Attach crepe paper streamers to the bottom of the bag. Color the cloth with markers and attach it to the back of the bag. Attach crepe paper streamers to the bottom edge of the cloth. Have one student wear the head of the lion. The other students can dance behind underneath the cloth as the "lion" parades around the room.

The Dragon Boat Festival

This festival is held every June and is the most important holiday in the summer. The story goes that once an emperor spurned a wise statesman's advice. The statesman felt he was not wanted and drowned himself. The emperor soon realized that he should have listened to the statesman and sent boats out seeking the wise man's spirit, and the tradition is repeated every June. The boats used for this festival are specially built with carved dragons on the prows.

Large Paper Dragon

Materials:

- Scissors and glue
- Bottle caps, juice can lids, packing peanuts, and other beautiful junk

- Large sheets of green butcher paper

Cut a dragon shape out of green paper. Glue pieces of your "beautiful junk" to the dragon to create his scales. Use orange tissue paper to create the dragon's flames.

Paper Dragon

Materials:

- Green construction paper
- Orange tissue paper

- Glue
- Scissors

Cut a 2 inch-wide strip of construction paper and accordion fold it in the middle, leaving about 3 inches unfolded at the front and 2 inches unfolded at the back. Cut a triangular tail at the back end and a blunt triangular head at the front. Glue a small piece of orange tissue paper extending from the mouth for the flames.

REFERENCES

Fisher, Leonard Everett. *The Great Wall of China*. New York: Macmillan, 1986.

Glubok, Shirley. *The Art of China*. New York: Macmillan, 1973.

Goldstein, Peggy. *Long Is a Dragon: Chinese Writing for Children*. San Francisco: China Books & Periodicals, 1991.

Hou-tien, Cheng. *The Chinese New Year*. New York: Holt, Rinehart & Winston, 1976.

Lee, Sherman E. *History of Far Eastern Art*. New York: H. N. Abrams, 1982.

McLenighan, Valjean. *People's Republic of China*, Enchantment of the World series. Chicago: Childrens Press, 1984.

Nancarrow, Peter. *Early China and the Wall*. Minneapolis: Lerner, 1978.

Pine, Tillie S., and Joseph Levine. *The Chinese Knew*. New York: McGraw-Hill, 1958.

Rich, Chris. *The Book of Paper Cutting*. New York: Sterling, 1993.

Ridley, Michael. *Far Eastern Antiquities*. Chicago: Henry Regner, 1972.

Scott, A. C., trans. *Traditional Chinese Plays*, vols. 1–3. Madison: University of Wisconsin Press, 1967.

Steele, Philip. *Journey Through China*. Mahwah, NJ: Troll, 1991.

Stepp, Ann. *A Silkworm Is Born*. New York: Sterling, 1972.

Turner, Dorothy. *The Man-Made Wonders of the World*. Minneapolis, MN: Dillon, 1986.

Wolff, Diane. *Chinese Writing: An Introduction*. New York: Holt, Rinehart & Winston, 1975.

FURTHER READING

Boehn, Max. *Dolls and Puppets*. New York: Cooper Square, 1966.

Bram, Leon L., ed. *Funk & Wagnalls New Encyclopedia*, vol. 12. New York: Funk & Wagnalls, 1986.

China. Amsterdam: Time-Life, 1984.

Clayton, Robert. *China*, Finding Out About Geography series. New York: John Day, 1971.

Coldrey, Jennifer. *The Silkworm Story*. London: André Deutsch, 1983.

Danforth, Kenneth C., et al., eds. *Journey into China*. Washington, DC: National Geographic Society, 1982.

Feinstein, Stephen C. *China in Pictures*, Visual Geography series. Minneapolis, MN: Lerner, 1989.

Hammond, Jonathan. *China*, The Land and Its People series. Morristown, NJ: Silver Burdett, 1974.

Hawley, W. M. *Chinese Folk Designs*. New York: Dover, 1949.

Kang, Lai Po. *The Ancient Chinese*. Morristown, NJ: Silver Burdett, 1980.

Latourette, Kenneth Scott. *The Chinese: Their History and Culture*. New York: Macmillan, 1986.

McHenry, Robert, ed. *The New Encyclopaedia Britannica*, vols. 1–3, 6, 9, 10, 12, 17. Chicago: Encyclopaedia Britannica, 1992.

Murowchick, Robert E., ed. *China*, Cradles of Civilization series. Norman: University of Oklahoma Press, 1994.

Ringgren, Helmer, and Åke V. Ström. *Religions of Mankind: Yesterday and Today*. Philadelphia: Fortress Press, 1967.

Schafer, Edward H. *Ancient China*. New York: Time-Life Books, 1967.

Spencer, Cornelia. *The Land and People of China*, Portraits of the Nations series. Philadelphia: J. B. Lippincott, 1972.

Stefoff, Rebecca. *China*, Places and Peoples of the World series. New York: Chelsea House, 1991.

Thomas, Peggy. *City Kids in China*. New York: HarperCollins, 1991.

2
JAPAN

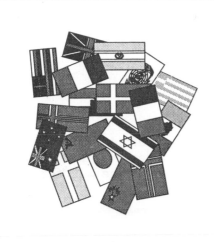

Capital: Tokyo
Government: **Constitutional monarchy**
   (Executive power is vested in a cabinet
   headed by a prime minister)
Population: **123,692,000**
Area: **145,883 square miles**

Japan is a land of seeming contradictions. Although Japan has been home to some of the world's most ferocious warriors, the Japanese have also always been devoted to flowers, poetry, and art. Japanese culture and art finds beauty in everyday objects.

Japan has lived throughout its history in semi-isolation. At times there was a free exchange of ideas and knowledge from China, at other times Japan was completely shut off from the mainland. During these times, the Japanese adapted cultural ideas that came from China to suit their own unique tastes.

Nature has not been kind to Japan. Although the land is beautiful, it is also violent. Japan lies on the volcanic "Ring of Fire" that encircles the Pacific Ocean, so earthquakes are common, there are some active volcanoes, and the island experiences an average of one major typhoon a year. Despite this, the people of Japan cherish their land and protect it. A unit on Japan will introduce students to a land not only rich in tradition and history, but to a people who strive to live in harmony with nature and with each other.

THE JAPANESE HOME

The Japanese home is efficient, yet harmonious and pleasing to the eye. The Japanese use every bit of space, and because homes are small, areas often serve more than one function.

Paper Walls

In many Japanese homes, the walls are made of paper because it is economical and helps keep the home cool during the hot summers. Discuss with students how paper walls serve as a space saver. A room with paper walls can be created in the classroom.

Paper Walls

Materials:

- White butcher paper
- Scissors
- Tape

Set this up in a corner of the classroom. Attach the end of the butcher paper to one wall. Stretch it out into the room and loop it around a chair or a desk before attaching the free end to the other wall to form an enclosure. Cut a door in the wall. Scatter cushions inside for seating, and add a low table for dining.

Tatami Mats

Tatami mats, Japanese floor coverings, are woven from rice straw. The size of the room is determined by the area covered by the mats. Students can weave tatami mats to put on the floor of their Japanese room.

Paper Tatami Mats

Materials:

- Yellow or brown construction paper
- Yellow or brown strips of paper ($\frac{3}{4}$ by $9\frac{1}{2}$ inches)
- Scissors
- Stapler

Fold the construction paper sheets widthwise (hamburger style) and make cuts about 1 inch apart from the folded edge to within 1 inch of the outside edges of the paper. Weave the strips of paper through the slits. When finished, staple each strip of paper at the edge to hold the weave in place.

JAPANESE ARCHITECTURE

Pagodas

Pagodas, Buddhist memorial reliquaries, are found throughout Japan. Their designs are often copied and placed in Japanese gardens. Pictures of pagodas can be found in *Take a Trip to Japan* by Gwynneth Ashby, *A Samurai Warrior* by Anne Steel, *Japan's Cultural History: A Perspective* by Yutaka Tazawa, et al., and *Japan* by Peter Spry-Leverton and Peter Kornicki.

Milk Carton Pagoda

Materials:

- Half-pint milk cartons with tops cut off
- Red and yellow construction paper
- Poster paints and paintbrushes
- Scissors
- Glue
- Metallic gold paint (optional)

Cover the milk carton with red paper. Paint doors and windows with poster paints. Cut four trapezoids from yellow paper, measuring 4 inches wide on the bottom edge, 3 inches high, and 3 inches wide on the top edge. Cut an inward curve from corner to corner on each of the 3 inch sides (but not the top edge) and glue trapezoids to the top of the milk carton, one on each side. If you want, paint trim on your pagoda with metallic gold paint.

JAPANESE CLOTHING

Kimono

The word *kimono* means "a thing worn." The basic kimono design is always the same, whether formal or casual. Men's and women's are similar, except the hemline and sleeves of women's kimonos are slightly longer and the hem may be quilted. Look in *Count Your Way Through Japan* by Jim Haskins or *Japan*, from the National Costume Reference series by Marion Sichel for pictures of kimonos.

Kimono

Material:

- Man's dress shirts (one that can be cut up)
- Long, wide scarves
- Scissors

Cut the collar and cuffs off the dress shirt and tie the scarf around the waist for a kimono-style garment.

JAPANESE ART

Ikebana

Ikebana, the Japanese art of flower arranging, in its purest form represents Japanese world philosophy, with flowers representing heaven, the earth, and the moon, in the Japanese scheme of the universe. This artform developed from the custom of offering flowers to the Buddha. In the seventh century, Ono No Imoko, the Japanese ambassador to China, introduced this art into Japan from China. If possible, invite an ikebana practitioner to the class to demonstrate their art or let the students practice ikebana with actual flowers. Florist shops will often donate day-old flowers for such an activity. If this is not possible, students can make an ikebana picture. Discuss with students the history of ikebana and its relationship to the Buddhist philosophy.

Ikebana Picture

Materials:

- Black tempera, mixed thinly
- White construction paper
- Colored tempera, mixed thickly
- Drinking straws
- Sponges, cut into small shapes such as squares or circles

Spoon the black tempera onto the paper and blow on the paint through the straw to create branches. When the paint dries, dip the sponges into various colors of paint and press them on the branches to create blossoms (see figure 2.1). Keep in mind that Ikebana is an art form with meaning. What do you want your picture to mean? How can you show it?

Fig. 2.1.

Origami

The Japanese art of paper folding, origami, was originally practiced nearly a thousand years ago at the Japanese Imperial Court, where it was considered an amusing and elegant means of passing time. In ancient Japan, the paper was thought to contain a spirit, therefore, paper could not be cut lest the spirit be harmed. Rather, the paper was folded to maintain the spirit's safety. Over the centuries, the skill was passed down to ordinary people who took it up with enthusiasm and made it into a folk art. There are many books in the library with innumerable origami designs. Obtain as many books as possible and experiment with copying the patterns. Some good books are: *The ABC's of Origami: Origami for Children* by Claude Sarasas, and *Origami in Color: Paperfolding Fun* and *The Great Origami Book*, both by Zülal Aytüre-Scheele.

Ceramics

The Japanese have created ceramic products for thousands of years. Although the art originated in China, the Japanese have developed their own unique style and are known throughout the world for the beauty of their ceramics. Many examples of Japanese pottery can be found in import stores and can be displayed to students, or pictures of Japanese pottery can be found in *From Gold to Porcelain: The Art of Porcelain and Faïence* by Ruth Berges.

Clay Bowls

Materials:

- Self-hardening clay
- Red, green, blue, and gold metallic paint
- Paintbrushes

Study examples of Japanese vases and bowls. Then form your own bowls out of clay and paint designs on the sides. Flowers are a popular motif in Japanese pottery.

Plaster-of-Paris Plate

Materials:

- Plaster of paris
- Pie tins
- Poster paints and paintbrushes
- Drinking straws
- Scissors
- String or yarn

Mix plaster of paris until it is thick and smooth, like pancake batter. Pour into pie tin. Cut a small section from a drinking straw and stick it into the plaster of paris near the top of the circle. Let harden about an hour then remove from the pan. Pull the straw section out, leaving a hole behind. Decorate the plate with poster paints. Hang it with string or yarn tied through the hole in the top.

THE MUSIC OF JAPAN

Taiko Drums

Taiko drums, the traditional drums of the Japanese, come in many different sizes. The Japanese have elevated the Taiko drums to one of their highest forms of art. Groups of drummers perform together, creating compositions solely for the drum. The act of beating the drum becomes an artform in and of itself, with the drums being rearranged on stage for different compositions.

Tin Can Drum

Materials:

- Glue
- Manila paper
- Large cans or cylindrical containers (e.g., tin cans, oatmeal boxes, salt boxes)
- Paint and paintbrushes or colored felt-tip markers
- Brown construction paper
- Scissors

Cut the brown paper to a width equal to the height of the can. Glue the paper around the can. Cut a large circle from the manila paper and glue it to the top of the can, pulling the overhanging edges down and gluing to the sides of the can. Paint or draw Japanese symbols or scenes on the sides of the drum.

GARDENS

Rock and Sand Gardens

The art of rock and sand gardens was introduced into Japan by Zen monks who arranged large rocks surrounded by tiny rocks in patterns. Traditional Japanese rock gardens use rocks in earth colors such as brown, gray, black, and sometimes white. Some patterns simulate storms, others represent cascades or ocean waves. Still others are abstract, leaving the viewer to contemplate the scene and derive individual meaning from it. Pictures of rock gardens can be found in *Early Japan* by Jonathan Norton Leonard, *Japan's Cultural History: A Perspective* by Yutaka Tazawa, et al., and *Japan* by Peter Spry-Leverton and Peter Kornicki.

Garden in a Box

Materials:

- Shallow boxes or Styrofoam meat trays
- Rocks ranging from gravel to 2 inches
- Pencils
- Combs

Decide on what your rock garden is to represent. Then place your larger rocks. Arrange your small rocks in patterns around the large rocks. Create lines by drawing a pencil or comb through the small rocks.

3-D picture

Materials:

- Sturdy cardboard
- Dried beans and peas or gravel
- Styrofoam packing peanuts
- Gray paint
- Glue

Dip the packing peanuts in gray paint and allow them to dry. Glue painted packing peanuts in place to simulate large rocks. Then arrange the dried beans on the cardboard, creating waves or lines, and glue them in place.

Garden in a Wading Pool

Materials:

- Rake
- Large rocks
- Plastic childrens swimming pool (one for the entire class)
- Gravel

Pour gravel into plastic swimming pool. Place one or two large rocks inside the pool according to your design. Then rake the gravel into waves and patterns around the larger rocks.

Bonsai

Bonsai, the art of deliberately dwarfing plants and shrubs, originated in China more than a thousand years ago, but was pursued and developed primarily by the Japanese under the encouragement of the Ashikagu Shogunate, some 800 years ago. A bonsai plant may live for a century or more and can be passed down from generation to generation as a family treasure. Obtain a bonsai plant for the class to examine.

Bonsai Picture

Materials:

- Brown tempera, mixed thinly
- Feathers or leaves from evergreen shrubs
- White construction paper (4 by 5 inches)
- Green tempera
- Straws

Drop spoonfuls of brown paint onto the paper and use a straw to blow the paint across the paper, creating curving, twisting designs. Allow this paint to dry, then dip the feathers or leaves in green paint and press them over the brown lines, creating green leaves on brown stems.

Cherry Blossoms

The cherry tree is the national tree of Japan, and the flowering of the cherry trees in the spring is marked with festivals. People perform dances and compose poems in honor of the cherry blossoms, attaching the poems to the branches of the trees.

Tissue Paper Cherry Tree

Materials:

- Clay flower pots
- Sand
- Small branches
- Pink tissue paper

Fill each clay pot with sand and stick a branch in the sand. Cut the tissue paper into narrow strips and tie them around the branch to simulate cherry blossoms.

JAPANESE DRAMA

Bunraku

Bunraku is a classical form of puppet theater named for an eighteenth-century Japanese puppet master, Vemura Bunrakuken. Puppets can be as much as 5 feet tall, are richly costumed, and can require up to three people to operate. The puppet operators remain in full view of the audience. Pictures of Bunraku puppets can be found in *Take a Trip to Japan* by Gwynneth Ashby, *Japan*, from the Enchantment of the World series by Carol Greene, *Japan*, from the Places and Peoples of the World series by Rebecca Stefoff and Time-Life's *Japan*.

Tagboard Bunraku Puppet

Materials:

- Tagboard
- Pipe cleaners
- Paint, scraps of construction paper, or fabric
- Glue
- Scissors
- Brass paper fasteners (optional)

Cut the body of the puppet from tagboard and decorate it with paints, paper, and fabric. Cut arms, legs, and head from tagboard and decorate. Attach the limbs to the body with small strips of construction paper, folded accordion style, or by metal fasteners. Attach pipe cleaners to arms, legs, and head to use for manipulating puppet. With other students, put on a puppet show of your favorite Japanese story.

No Theatre

Classic No drama arose in the fourteenth century and was performed primarily for the upper classes. The performers were all men, and the costumes have been handed down for centuries within families. One No play still performed today is *Komachi and the Hundred Nights*. This play tells the story of Shii no Shosho, a ninth century poet, and the famous beauty, Ono No Komachi. Shii no Shosho courted Ono No Komachi, who promised to marry him if he would sleep one hundred consecutive nights before her house on a bench used to support the shafts of her carriage. Shosho came for 99 nights, each time making a mark on the bench, but when his father died he had to forego the last night. Komachi wrote a poem for him, offering to make the hundredth mark herself. This play and others can be found in *Twenty Plays of the No Theatre* by Donald Keene. *Japan*, from the National Costume Reference series by Marion Sichel contains pictures of No masks.

Paper Plate No Masks

Materials:

- Paper plates
- Paints
- Construction paper or fabric
- Black yarn
- Metallic gold paint
- Glue
- Scissors
- Paintbrushes

The mask for a female character can be created by painting expressionless features onto a paper plate—black eyebrows, red lips, eyes, and a nose. Glue black yarn to the top and sides of the mask for hair.

The mask for a male character is made the same way as that for a female character, but a yarn mustache and goatee may be added and features may be given an expression.

THE HISTORY OF JAPAN

Samurai Warriors

The elite class of Japanese warriors, the Samurai, first appeared in Japan in 794. The sword was the symbol of the Samurai class, and until the 1870s, the warriors were permitted to wear two swords in public. The Samurai's armor was made from metal and bamboo (see fig. 2.2). Pictures of Samurai warriors can be found in *A Samurai Warrior* by Anne Steel or *Japan*, from the National Costume Reference series by Marion Sichel.

Paper Bag Samurai Armor

Materials:

- Paper grocery bags
- Aluminum foil
- Scissors
- Glue

Cut holes for arms and head from grocery bag. Cover with 1-inch strips of aluminum foil. Glue these horizontally across the chest of the armor. Add rectangular flaps of aluminum foil along the bottom of the bag.

Aluminum Foil Samurai Helmet

Materials:

- Construction paper
- Aluminum foil
- Scissors
- Glue

Cut a 10-inch circle from construction paper. Cut a slit from the edge to the center and overlap edges, stapling them to form a high domed hat. Cover the hat with aluminum foil and attach a sheet of aluminum foil at the back to hang down over shoulders. Form aluminum foil into a crest or spikes and attach these decorations to the top of the helmet.

Tagboard Samurai Sword

Materials:

- Tagboard or posterboard
- Aluminum foil
- Crayons or colored felt-tip markers
- Glue
- Scissors

Cut a long, curved sword from the tagboard. Cut a 3-inch circle with a slit in the middle and slide it over one end of the sword to form the handle. Cover the blade with aluminum foil. Decorate the handle with crayons or markers.

Fig. 2.2.

Samurai Pictures

Materials:

- Construction paper
- Aluminum foil
- Scissors and glue
- Crayons or colored felt-tip markers

Draw a picture of a Samurai warrior on paper and glue pieces of aluminum foil in place for the warrior's armor, helmet, and sword. Add additional features with crayons.

Daruma Dolls

Daruma dolls are named after Bodidharma (Dharma), a sixth-century Indian Buddhist who is credited as the founder of Zen Buddhism. The Daruma toy symbolizes Dharma's elevated position in Japanese life, for no matter how the doll is pushed, it rolls about till it lands in an upright position. According to legend, Dharma meditated without moving for nine years, resulting in the permanent loss of the use of his arms and legs. Stories say he rolled all the way from India to Japan to spread his teachings.

Plastic Egg Daruma Doll

Materials:

- Bottom half of a plastic Easter egg
- Construction paper
- Modeling clay
- Glue or tape
- Scissors
- Colored felt-tip markers or crayons

Fill the egg half with modeling clay. Cut a large (4 by 6 inch) triangle from construction paper, curving the bottom of the triangle outward. Fold the triangle into a cone, gluing overlapping edges. Draw facial features on the cone and glue or tape it onto the open half of the egg.

FESTIVALS

Koi Festival

The Koi Festival is celebrated each year on May 5. The word *koi* means carp, which is a symbol of strength and endurance to the Japanese. It was originally a festival in which little boys celebrated their journey into manhood. The name derives from the hope that boys would be as strong as the carp when they climb the waterfall to return to their spawning grounds. Today, all children take part, and banners shaped like carp, symbolizing strength and determination, are suspended from poles.

Paper Lunch Bag Koi

Materials:

- Paper lunch sack
- Colored felt-tip markers
- Crepe paper streamers
- Yarn or string
- Scissors
- Glue

Cut a large circle from the bottom of the sack to form the mouth of the fish. Draw scales and fins on the sides of the bag with the markers and glue crepe paper streamers along the open end of the bag. Punch two holes in the sack above the mouth and loop a piece of yarn through the holes to make a handle.

Tanabata Matsuri (The Star Festival)

This festival, celebrated on July 7, commemorates the legend of Princess Shokujo and the shepherd boy Kinju who became stars in the heavens. Princess Shokujo was weaving cloth for a coat for her father when she fell in love with Kinju. They made plans to be married, but Shokujo forgot to weave the cloth. The angry king sent them to live at opposite ends of the Milky Way but permitted them to meet one day each year. Because there is no bridge over the Milky Way, Shokujo and Kinju had no way to reach each other until the birds made a bridge with their wings. A variation of this legend can be found in *A Song of Stars* by Tom Birdseye.

Tanabata means "weaving loom" and for the Tanabata Festival, the streets are festooned with huge banners imitating the stars of the Milky Way. Bamboo branches decorated with paper dolls and prayer strips are placed in front of each house. At the end of the holiday, the branches are taken down and floated away on the river.

Paper Tanabata Banners
Materials:

- Tissue paper
- Construction paper
- Yarn

- Scissors
- Glue or tape

Crumple the tissue paper into a ball. Hang several pieces of yarn from the ball. Cut triangles from construction paper and glue or tape them onto the yarn, one above the other. Hang the banners from the ceiling.

ANIMALS IN JAPAN

Crickets

Singing crickets are kept by the Japanese as pets in small bamboo cages. Some of the cages are small enough to hang from their belts so the Japanese can hear songs as they move around.

Clothespin Cricket
Materials:

- Plastic fruit boxes
- Old-fashioned clothespins
- Pipe cleaners

- Colored felt-tip markers
- Black paint
- Paintbrushes

Draw a face on the knob end of the clothespin. Wrap three pipe cleaners around the prongs of the clothespin for legs, with both ends of the pipe cleaner pointing down for a total of six legs. Paint the clothespin black. Place the cricket inside two fruit boxes held together, top to top, then wire the boxes together with pipe cleaners.

Goldfish

Goldfish were domesticated by the Chinese 1,000 years ago and have been bred by the Japanese into many beautiful forms and colors. Originally pets for the aristocracy, they are now sold on streets around temples, shrines, and resort beaches.

Goldfish Picture

Materials:

- White construction paper
- Tissue paper of various colors
- Sponges cut into small circles

- Tempera, mixed thinly
- Scissors
- Glue

Cut a fish shape from the white paper. Choose a color and sponge paint scales over the body surface. Let dry. Cut large fins with feathered edges from colored tissue paper and glue them to the fish.

Oysters and Pearls

Japanese pearls are admired worldwide and are grown on pearl farms. Thirteenth-century China is said to have discovered the art of cultivating pearls, but the modern pearl industry in Japan was started in the 1890s by Mikimoto Kokichi. Kokichi discovered that the most successful stimulant for pearl production was small mother-of-pearl beads inserted into the oyster's tissue.

Today, immature pearl oysters are stored in barrels for two to three years until they mature. Then they are irritated with mother-of-pearl beads and suspended in wire nets from floating rafts in the ocean. There the oysters are tended by divers until they are ready for harvesting, a process that can take up to three years.

Paper Plate Oyster

Materials:

- Two paper plates
- Gray construction paper
- Thinly mixed black or purple watercolors

- Paintbrushes
- Stapler
- Glue

Paint the bottoms of both paper plates with concentric half circles, starting at one end and moving outward, increasing in size. Staple the two plates, bottoms outward, together at the end where the circles begin. Roll a small piece of gray construction paper into a ball and glue inside the oyster at the stapled end to represent the pearl.

GEOGRAPHY

Mount Fuji

At 12,388 feet, Mount Fuji is Japan's highest mountain. According to legend it was formed in 280 B.C. by an earthquake, but in actuality it was formed by volcanic eruption more than 600,000 years ago. It is a dormant volcano that last erupted in 1707. The name *Fuji* means "everlasting life." It is famous for its beauty and symmetry and is a sacred symbol of Japan. Every summer, thousands of Japanese climb to the peak as a pilgrimage. Fuji is surrounded by temples and shrines, even at the edges and bottom of the crater.

Picture of Mount Fuji

Materials:

- Gray and blue construction paper
- White tempera, mixed thinly
- Straws
- Scissors
- Glue

Study a picture of Mount Fuji, then cut its shape from gray paper and glue it onto blue paper. Drop a spoonful of white paint at the top of the mountain and blow through the straw onto the paint puddle, pushing paint down the mountain sides to create a snowcapped peak.

JAPANESE TECHNOLOGY

Automobiles

Japan is the leading car manufacturer in the world. Its vehicles are models of fuel economy, quality, and efficiency.

Japanese Car Collage

Materials:

- Magazines
- Posterboard
- Scissors
- Glue

Clip pictures of Japanese cars from magazines and glue them to posterboard to create a Japanese car collage.

Robotics

The Japanese auto industry was the first to introduce robotics and automation into factories. Japan is the world leader in making and using robots for industry. The robots are operated by microcomputers, can work faster than people, and are programmed to never make mistakes.

Cardboard Box Robot

Materials:

- Masking tape
- Paint
- Paintbrushes
- Wood glue
- Found materials such as cardboard boxes, tubes, paper cups, egg cartons, pipe cleaners, straws, buttons, and so on

Use glue and tape to combine items that you have found to create your own robot model. Paint your creation.

REFERENCES

Ashby, Gwynneth. *Take a Trip to Japan.* New York: Franklin Watts, 1980.

Aytüre-Scheele, Zülal. *The Great Origami Book.* New York: Sterling, 1987.

———. *Origami in Color: Paperfolding Fun.* New York: Gallery Books, 1986.

Berges, Ruth. *From Gold to Porcelain: The Art of Porcelain and Faïence.* New York: Thomas Yoseloff, 1963.

Birdseye, Tom. *A Song of Stars.* New York: Holiday House, 1990.

Greene, Carol. *Japan,* Enchantment of the World series. Chicago: Childrens Press, 1983.

Haskins, Jim. *Count Your Way Through Japan.* Minneapolis: Carolrhoda Books, 1987.

Keene, Donald, ed. *Twenty Plays of the No Theatre.* New York: Columbia University Press, 1970.

Leonard, Jonathan Norton. *Early Japan.* New York: Time-Life, 1968.

Sarasas, Claude. *The ABC's of Origami: Origami for Children.* Rutland, VT: Charles E. Tuttle, 1964.

Sichel, Marion. *Japan,* National Costume Reference series. New York: Chelsea House, 1987.

Spry-Leverton, Peter, and Peter Kornicki. *Japan.* New York: Facts on File, 1987.

Steel, Anne. *A Samurai Warrior.* Vero Beach, FL: Rourke, 1988.

Stefoff, Rebecca. *Japan,* Places and Peoples of the World series. New York: Chelsea House, 1988.

Tazawa, Yutaka, Saburo Matsubara, Shunsake Okuda, and Yasunori Nagahata. *Japan's Cultural History: A Perspective.* Japan: Ministry of Foreign Affairs, 1973.

FURTHER READING

The Arts of Mankind: Painting, Architecture and Music. Englewood Cliffs, NJ: International Geographic Society, 1962.

Bring, Mitchell, and Josse Wayembergh. *Japanese Gardens: Design and Meaning.* New York: McGraw-Hill, 1981.

Gibson, Michael. *The Samurai of Japan.* London: Wayland, 1973.

Gustafson, Herb L. *The Bonsai Workshop.* New York: Sterling, 1994.

Joseph, Joan. *Folk Toys Around the World and How to Make Them.* New York: Parents Magazine Press, 1972.

King, Constance Eileen. *The Collector's History of Dolls.* New York: Bonanza Books, 1977.

Kittel, Mary Badham. *Japanese Flower Arrangements for American Homes.* New York: Bonanza Books, 1960.

McHenry, Robert, ed. *The New Encyclopaedia Britannica,* vols. 2, 3, 5, 9-11, 17, 26. Chicago: Encyclopaedia Britannica, 1992.

Pipe, Ann Kimball. *Bonsai: The Art of Dwarfing Trees.* New York: Appleton-Century, 1964.

Slesin, Suzanne, Stafford Cliff, and Daniel Rozensztroch. *Japanese Style.* New York: Potter, 1987.

Smith, Lawrence, Victor Harris, and Timothy Clark. *Japanese Art: Masterpieces in the British Museum.* New York: Oxford University Press, 1990.

Spicer, Dorothy Gladys. *The Book of Festivals.* Detroit: Gale Research, 1969.

White, Gwen. *Antique Toys and Their Background.* New York: Arco, 1971.

3
INDIA

Capital: New Delhi
Government: Federal Republic
Population: 853,373,000
Area: 1,222,559 square miles

India is one of the world's earliest centers of civilization. It is the birthplace of two major religions, Buddhism and Hinduism. Ancient Hindu scholars invented the system of numbers we use today, including the decimal system. The Indians were also the first to weave cotton into cloth and domesticate chickens. Two popular games, chess and badminton, come from India, as well as gambling with dice.

India has been a united nation only since 1947, when it gained its independence from Britain. Prior to that, it was composed of hundreds of separate empires, kingdoms, and princedoms. Even now, India is a fragmented land where hundreds of languages are spoken. Many people cannot understand their fellow citizens from another part of the country. Throughout India's history, Hinduism has been the tie that binds the people together, one of the few things that most Indians have in common.

Hinduism has greatly influenced the artwork of India, much of which is religious in nature. Even after the Muslim conquest in 1193, Hinduism continued to influence the arts, blending with Muslim influences to produce some of the world's most beautiful architectural monuments.

A unit on India will introduce students to a curious blend of modernity and tradition, and will give students an appreciation for Indian culture, as well as facilitate an awareness of different religious and cultural beliefs.

HOMES IN INDIA

Most homes in India are the simple one or two room huts occupied by the poor, who make up the majority of the population. Middle-class families often live in apartments and well-to-do families live in large homes. Pictures of Indian homes can be found in *We Live in India* by Veenu Sandal and *Let's Travel in India*, edited by Darlene Geis.

Mud Huts

Many people in India live in homes made of homemade brick. These homes are built slowly, allowing time for the clay bricks to dry in the sun. When the home is finished, the walls are lined with mud and cow dung, then painted white, though often the owners also paint pictures of birds and animals on their outside walls. The furniture is very simple; people sit on woven mats and sleep on mats slung across a wooden frame. An example of a painted house can be found in *The Arts of Mankind: Painting, Architecture and Music* from the International Geographic Society or *India*, from The Land and Its People series by Natasha Talyarkhan.

Clay House

Materials:

- Cardboard
- Modeling clay
- Paints and paintbrushes
- Straw or grass

Using cardboard for the base, form the walls of a round, one-room hut from the modeling clay. When the clay is dry, paint inside and outside with white paint. When the paint dries, paint birds or animals on the outside walls. Pile the grass in a dome for a thatched roof.

Courtyard

Most homes have a walled courtyard that serves as a kind of family room. The courtyard is where the children play and adults sit to pass the time of day or work on crafts. The family cow may even live here. The floor is usually made of pressed earth and is painted daily with bright designs.

Painted Walls

Materials:

- Paints and paintbrushes
- Modeling clay

With the modeling clay, add a walled courtyard to the clay hut described in the previous activity. Paint the wall white, then paint a design on the floor of the courtyard with bright colors.

INDIAN CLOTHING

Indian clothes are very colorful. The styles vary across the many regions of the country. Girls often put a little round dot called a *bindi* in the middle of their foreheads, often choosing a color that matches their clothes. The bindi is for decorative purposes and is made with paint or dye.

Sari

Most Indian women wear some form of the sari, a dress made by wrapping material around the body and over the shoulder (see fig. 3.1). The sari can be adjusted to any size or shape of body and can be made from any material: cotton, silk, or nylon. Many pictures of saris can be found in *India: An Ancient Land, A New Nation* by Amita Vohra Sarin and *India*, from the Library of Nations series from Time-Life Books.

Cloth Sari

Materials:

- 6 yards of fabric
- Safety pins

Wrap the fabric around your waist two or three times, tucking it in securely (pin with safety pins if desired). Drape one end across your chest and over one shoulder.

Fig. 3.1.

Turbans

Most Indian men wear turbans. It takes much practice to learn to wrap a turban as quickly as they do.

Cloth Turban

Materials:

- Three yards of fabric

Hold one end of the fabric in your teeth. Wrap the fabric around the top of your head, tucking the ends under when finished.

INDIAN SPICES

Indian food is very spicy! Indian cooks blend their spices carefully for effect, sometimes using as many as 15 spices in a single dish.

Spice Book

Materials:

- Stapler
- Glue (edible)
- Paintbrushes for glue
- Powdered Indian spices: curry, ginger, turmeric, cumin, coriander, cinnamon, cloves, and so on
- Construction paper
- Pencils
- Scissors

Cut several squares (4 by 4 inches) from construction paper. Select as many squares as there are spices, plus one more square for the cover. Label the cover "My Spice Book." Brush glue on each page and sprinkle a different spice on each page. If you want, make extra pages by blending spices together. When pages are dry, staple the pages together. Now you have your own "Sniff Book" of Indian spices.

HOLIDAYS AND FESTIVALS IN INDIA

There are hundreds of gods and goddesses in the Hindu religion. Therefore, because of the prominence of religion in Indian life, on any given day there will be a religious festival going on somewhere.

Dussehra

The festival of Dussehra commemorates when Prince Rama fought the giants Ravana, Kumbhakarma, and Meghad, who had stolen his bride. Rama was successful and won his bride back. The festival, which has been celebrated for more than 2,000 years, lasts for 10 days. During the festival, 30-foot models of the giants, made of paper and wood and stuffed with firecrackers, stand in the town square. On the tenth day at sunset, the giants are set on fire and explode. A picture of these giants can be found in *India in Pictures* by Elizabeth Katz and *The Hindu World* by Patricia Bahree.

Large Paper Giant

Materials:

- Butcher paper
- Paints and paintbrushes

Cut a long piece of butcher paper, long enough to stretch from floor to ceiling, and, as a group, paint a giant on the paper.

Muharram

Muharram is a Muslim festival that takes place in February, and commemorates Mohammed's grandson, al Husayn ibn Ali, a Shiite martyr who was killed in battle in Iraq in 680. After a period of fasting, groups of Muslims carry representations of the tomb of Husayn, called *tazia*, in a procession. These tazias are in the form of a domed and minaretted building and are several feet high, made from light wood and covered in tissue paper, tinsel, and colored stripes. The tazias are taken to the closest body of water and immersed to the accompaniment of prayers and chanting.

Craft Stick Tazia

Materials:

- Craft sticks
- Tissue paper
- Crepe paper streamers
- Tinsel
- Construction paper
- Glue
- Scissors
- Cardboard

Glue the craft sticks together into a boxlike frame. Cut strips of cardboard and arch them over the top of the frame. Decorate the model with the tissue, crepe paper, and tinsel, imitating the domes and minarets of Muslim buildings.

Holi

This festival symbolizes the downfall of the evil Holika. According to legend, Prahlada was a demon's son who persisted in worshipping Vishnu, the Hindu ruler of the world. A female demon, Holika, carried Prahlada into fire in revenge, but Vishnu intervened. Prahlada emerged from the flames unharmed while Holika was burned to ashes. The celebration of Holi is considered an opportunity to let off steam. Young people throw brightly colored powders and water on each other, resulting in happy, walking rainbows.

Holi Picture

Materials:

- Coffee filters
- Food coloring

Dampen the coffee filters. Squeeze drops of food coloring onto the filters, using as many colors as possible, creating bright bursts of color.

Painted T-Shirt

Materials:

- Plain white T-shirt
- Acrylic paint in squeezable bottles

Squirt paint onto the T-shirt, allowing the colors to drip and run down.

ART IN INDIA

Indian art through the ages has been inspired by religion. The colors are rich and vibrant and the designs intricate. Nature is a common motif with gold predominating. A good children's book about Indian art is *The Art of India* by Shirley Glubok.

Bas Relief

Much Indian artwork is bas relief, partially three-dimensional figures carved in stone on flat surfaces such as buildings, monuments, and in caves.

Plaster-of-Paris Bas Relief
Materials:

- Plaster of paris, mixed thickly
- Pie tins
- Craft sticks

Pour the plaster of paris into a pie tin. Use the craft stick to shape a picture in the plaster. Animal motifs are popular in India. Let the bas relief sit for at least an hour to harden, then remove from the pie tin.

Jewelry

Indians wear much jewelry, from dangle bracelets to necklaces to rings in their noses and ears. The finest jewelry is passed on to the next generation and preserved as a tie to the past.

Homemade Jewelry
Materials:

- Metal wire, string, thread, or yarn
- Aluminum pie tins
- Shiny, colorful beads, shells, or small stones with holes cut through them
- Heavy-duty scissors
- Aluminum foil or gold foil paper

String the beads, shells, and stones on the wire. Form small ornaments from the aluminum foil or gold foil or cut shapes from the pie tins and string those shapes alongside the beads.

Indian Religious Paintings

Most Indian paintings are religious in nature. The color gold is heavily used.

Indian-Style Picture
Materials:

- Tempera paint
- Paintbrushes
- Metallic gold paint
- Paper

Examine several samples of Indian paintings and attempt to re-create the style in your own paintings. Hindu gods are a popular subject. Read about the elephant-headed Ganesh, the god of luck and success; the monkey god Hanuman; the warrior goddess Durga, who protects against evil with her eighteen arms; and Kali, the goddess of death, who is surrounded by snakes and skulls. Pictures of these Hindu gods and others can be found in *India: An Ancient Land, A New Nation* by Amita Vohra Sarin, *The Hindu World* by Patricia Bahree, *India*, from The Land and Its People series by Natasha Talyarkhan, and *India*, from the Library of Nations series from Time-Life Books.

Kathakali

Kathakali, Indian dance theater, was developed in the sixteenth and seventeenth centuries. Based on myths and legends of the Hindu religion, the dramas contains gods, demons, warriors, sages, villains, and ladies. Boys must train for six years to become Kathakali dancers, and dancers wear elaborate masks (see fig. 3.2). Pictures of Kathakali dancers can be found in *Let's Travel in India,* edited by Darlene Geis; *India,* from The Land and Its People series by Natasha Talyarkhan; and *India,* from the Library of Nations series from Time-Life Books.

Paper Kathakali Mask

Materials:

- Glue
- Paints and paintbrushes
- Colored yarn, rick-rack, and edging material
- Construction paper: white and other miscellaneous colors
- Gold foil paper
- Scissors

To create the face of the mask, cut an oval from the construction paper. Paint black lines above and below the eyes, a yellow shield shape in the center of the forehead, and red lips. Paint the rest of the face green. Cut a short, white beard from white paper and attach to the bottom of the face.

Then cut large round circles from the gold foil paper and attach them to the side of the face for earrings.

Finally, cut two bell shapes from paper, one smaller than the other. Turn them so the flat edge is at the top, and glue the curved edge of the smaller bell to the flat edge of the larger bell. Cut a large circle to glue behind the two bell shapes. Glue lines of colored yarn and rickrack over the surface of the headdress, and glue the headdress, curved side down, on top of the Kathakali mask.

INDIAN ARCHITECTURE

Taj Mahal

The Taj Mahal, believed by many to be the most beautiful building in the world, was built in the seventeenth century by the Shah Jehan as a memorial for his most beloved wife, Mumtaz, who died during childbirth. It took 20,000 daily builders 22 years to complete. It is made of bricks, covered with white marble inside and out, and inlaid with semiprecious stones. The inlay work is so fine that the joints between the pieces cannot be seen, even with a magnifying glass. Pictures of the Taj Mahal can be found in *We Live in India* by Veenu Sandal, *The Man-Made Wonders of the World* by Dorothy Turner, and *India: An Ancient Land, A New Nation* by Amita Vohra Sarin.

Memorial Picture

Materials:

- Scissors
- Glitter and sequins
- Finely embossed wrapping paper in single colors
- Construction paper
- Glue

Create a building as a memorial to yourself or someone you love. Cut the basic shape from wrapping paper and glue onto construction paper, then decorate with glue and sequins. How does your design reflect your culture? How did Shah Jehan's?

Fig. 3.2.

THE GEOGRAPHY OF INDIA

Indian geography ranges from mountains to deserts to swamps. Some parts of India get so little rain that the children are surprised to see water come from the sky. Other parts of India hold the record for the world's heaviest rainfall.

The Himalayas

The Himalayas are the world's tallest mountains. They form an almost impassable barrier between the Tibetan plateau and the plains of India. The Himalayas are characterized by steep, jagged peaks; deep chasms where rivers run; and large valley glaciers. Nanda Devi, India's highest peak, is more than 4 miles high. The word *himalaya* means "abode of the snows." The snow from the mountains melts and feeds the Ganges River, India's largest waterway.

Clay Model of the Himalayas

Materials:

- Modeling clay
- White, blue, brown, and green paint
- Paintbrushes
- Cardboard

Study relief maps or topographical maps of the Himalayas. Then using the cardboard as a base, form a mountain range from modeling clay. Let the clay harden, then paint the mountain range.

The Ganges River

The Ganges is not just a river; for Hindus, it is a holy river. Hindus believe that bathing in the Ganges washes away their sins. In towns and villages along the Ganges, steps lead right down to the river, and pilgrims can be seen bathing in the holy waters. In some parts of the river, people create floating gardens. In other parts, people fish from basket-shaped fishing boats. Pictures of the Ganges can be found in *Let's Travel in India*, edited by Darlene Geis, and *India*, from the Library of Nations series from Time-Life Books. Students can also refer to an atlas during the following activities.

Ganges River Mural

Materials:

- Roll of brown paper
- Construction paper
- Crayons and colored felt-tip markers
- Scissors
- Glue

Cut a long, curving strip from the brown paper to represent the Ganges and hang it on the wall. Add details along the river, such as steps, pilgrims bathing, rural countryside, or village buildings, by drawing them in or cutting them out of construction paper. Create floating gardens from green paper and basket-shaped fishing boats by cutting circles from yellow paper, cutting a line from one edge to the center of the circle, and overlapping the edges slightly to make a cone.

Climactic Map of the Ganges

Make a model of the climactic changes the Ganges exhibits from one season to the next. Before the rainy season begins in May, the Ganges water level is so low that in some places across the Uttar Pradesh and the Bihar, it scarcely flows at all. Once the monsoon season starts, though, the Ganges becomes a raging torrent, 3,000 feet wide, sweeping across the land. As the rains stop for the year, the river slowly diminishes in size until it is restored nine months later by the new monsoon season.

Materials:

- Roll of white paper
- Paint and paintbrushes
- Construction paper
- Sandpaper
- Brown yarn

- Polyester fiberfill
- White tissue paper
- Sand
- Glue
- Scissors

Refer to an atlas or other reference books for information about the seasonal changes in the Ganges. Roll the white paper out on the floor for easy access. Cut it to the length desired. At one end, paint a picture of the Ganges during the monsoon season. Glue clumps of polyester fiberfill on black paper for rain clouds. Use gray paint for a torrent of rain. Cut a wide sheet of brown paper for the Ganges River and glue clumps of shredded white tissue paper on top for frothy waves.

Gradually narrow the river and lessen the rain until you are representing the drought conditions at the end of the paper. Use brown yarn for the narrow, muddy trickle of the Ganges. Use sandpaper for the land around this end of the river and sprinkle sand in the air above the ground for a sandstorm.

THE ANIMALS IN INDIA

Indians have great respect for animals, largely because of the Hindu religion, in which so many of the gods are associated with animals. Cows are sacred to the Hindus and are allowed to roam freely through the towns and villages. The Indians were the first to domesticate the chicken, and have nurtured a culture of living side by side with the creatures who share their land.

Peacock

The beautiful peacock, native to India, is the national bird. The Shah Jehan in the seventeenth century had a famous "Peacock Throne," so called because of the richly bejeweled peacocks that stood behind it, their magnificent tail feathers spread wide.

Peacock Picture

Materials:

- Peacock pattern (see fig. 3.3)
- Glue and brushes for glue
- Paints, crayons, or colored felt-tip markers

- Glitter
- Paintbrushes

Spread glue over the peacock pattern and sprinkle with glitter. Let dry, then fill in details with paint, colors, or markers.

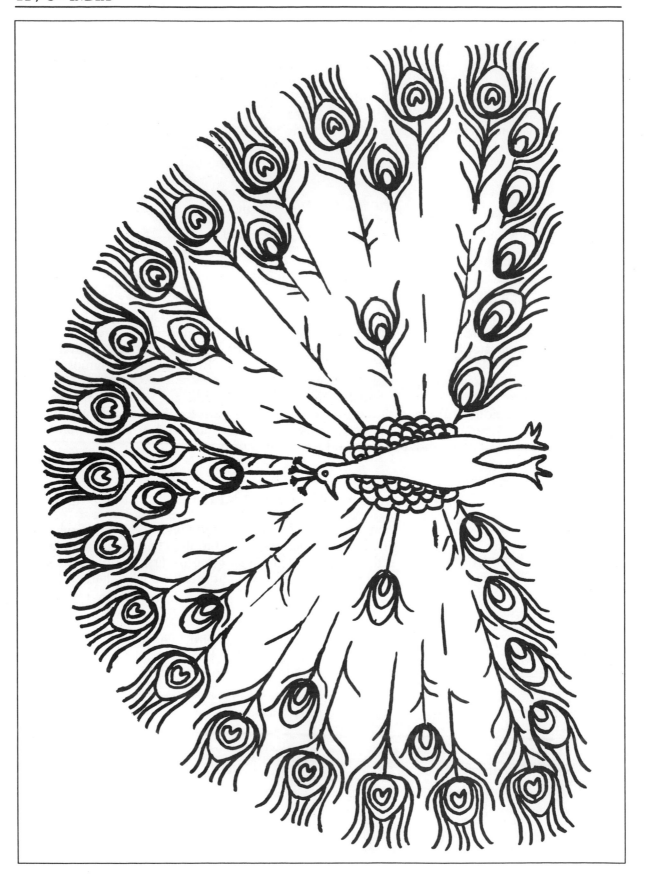

Fig. 3.3.

Elephants

At one time, elephants provided a major source of labor and transportation in India. Elephants used for transporting nobility were richly bedecked with jewels. These beasts were truly a sight to behold.

Elephant Mask

Materials:

- Brown paper grocery bags
- Gray and white paper
- Paintbrushes
- Paint, gray and one additional color
- Sequins and glitter
- Glue
- Scissors

Cut 5 or 6 inches off the top of a grocery bag so that it will fit over your head comfortably. Cut a rectangle in the front for eyes. Paint the front and sides of the bag gray. Use another color to paint the top and back of the sack. Continue painting with this color on the front of the sack, making a triangle that extends down from the top of the bag to a point between the eyes. Decorate the top, back, and triangle on the front of the bag with glitter and sequins. When the paint is dry, cut two large circles from gray paper and attach them to sides of bag for ears. Cut a tapering strip of gray paper 18 inches long and fold it accordion style for the nose. Cut two triangles from white paper for tusks.

TREES IN INDIA

Trees in India seem to always have leaves and be in flower. The people of India plant many trees, largely because of the shade they provide. In the country, trees are an important crop. The fruit, fiber, leaves, bark, and trunk of certain trees are all harvested to support the family.

Mangrove Trees

Mangrove trees trap salt and flotsam with the spidery clumps of roots at their base (see fig. 3.4). These trapped materials decay to provide a rich soil. Because of their ability to trap soil, the mangroves have created much rich delta farmland for India.

Mangrove Picture

Materials:

- Paper (12 by 18 inches)
- Brown paint
- Green paint
- Straws

Create the trunk of a mangrove tree by straw-painting brown paint across the paper, making lots of spidery roots at the bottom. Make leaves by finger-painting green paint on the branches.

Fig. 3.4.

Banyan Tree

This unusual-looking tree drops aerial roots from its branches to the ground (see fig. 3.5). These roots thicken into trunks which support the tree's branches. An old tree may grow as tall as 100 feet and spread out across several acres of land. It forms a miniature forest from one single tree. The banyan tree is considered sacred in India.

Banyan Picture

Materials:

- White, brown, and green construction paper
- Yellow yarn or twine
- Scissors
- Glue

Cut a trunk and branches from brown paper and glue it onto the white paper. Tear small pieces of green paper for the leaves. Extend strips of yellow yarn or twine from the branches onto the ground to represent aerial roots.

REFERENCES

The Arts of Mankind: Painting, Architecture and Music. Englewood Cliffs, NJ: International Geographic Society, 1962.

Bahree, Patricia. *The Hindu World.* Morristown, NJ: Silver Burdett, 1985.

Geis, Darlene, ed. *Let's Travel in India.* Chicago: Childrens Press, 1960.

Glubok, Shirley. *The Art of India.* Toronto: Macmillan, 1969.

India, Library of Nations Series. Alexandria, VA: Time-Life, 1987.

Sandal, Veenu. *We Live in India.* New York: Bookwright, 1984.

Sarin, Amita Vohra. *India: An Ancient Land, A New Nation.* Minneapolis, MN: Dillon, 1985.

Talyarkham, Natasha. *India*, The Land and Its People Series. Morristown, NJ: Silver Burdett, 1977.

FURTHER READING

Ahsan, M. M. *Muslim Festivals.* Vero Beach, FL: Rourke, 1987.

Bram, Leon L., ed. *Funk & Wagnalls New Encyclopedia*, vol. 13. New York: Funk & Wagnalls, 1986.

Lee, Sherman E. *History of Far Eastern Art.* New York: Harry N. Abrams, 1982.

McHenry, Robert, ed. *The New Encyclopaedia Britannica*, vols. 4, 6, 11. Chicago: Encyclopaedia Britannica, 1992.

Powell, Andrew. *Living Buddhism.* New York: Harmony Books, 1989.

Ridley, Michael. *Far Eastern Antiquities.* Chicago: Henry Regner, 1972.

Schulberg, Lucille. *Historic India.* New York: Time-Life, 1968.

Spicer, Dorothy Gladys. *The Book of Festivals.* Detroit: Gale, 1969.

Turner, Dorothy. *The Man-Made Wonders of the World.* Minneapolis, MN: Dillon, 1986.

Fig. 3.5.

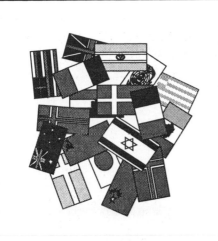

4
AUSTRALIA

Capital: **Canberra**
Government: **Federal Parliamentary State
(Republic with bicameral parliament)**
Population: **17,075,700**
Area: **2,966,200 square miles**

Australia. A country. A continent. A place like no other on earth. It was the last continent, next to Antarctica, to be discovered and explored by the Western world. Europeans first landed in Australia in 1616. However, the aborigines had arrived 25,000–40,000 years before, possibly crossing ancient land bridges; moving from island to island from Indonesia, Sri Lanka, or India; or maybe even migrating by boat or canoe from Malaysia.

Because of the country's geographic isolation, Aboriginal culture and the animals of Australia are unique in the world. Aboriginal art tends to be of a practical nature—symbolic paintings, carved message sticks, body ornamentation. The Aboriginal culture also contains a wealth of legend and symbolism. A unit on Australia will introduce students not only to unique natural wonders but to the richness and beauty of the Aboriginal culture.

ABORIGINES

The earliest archaeological evidence of Australian aborigines are tools dated from 38,000 years ago. Aborigines are hunter-gatherers who live in balance with their environment. They make tools from local materials, and lead a rich spiritual and artistic life, worshipping the land and their ancestors.

Aborigine Grave Carvings

These wooden carvings, similar to totem poles, honor ancestral spirits and are used to mark grave sites. Pictures of grave carvings can be found in *Australia* from the Countries of the World series by Andrew Kelly and *Down Under—Vanishing Cultures* by Jan Reynolds.

Oatmeal Box Grave Carvings

Materials:

- White or manila construction paper
- Paint
- Boxes: oatmeal, round ice cream boxes, shoeboxes, and so on
- Wood glue
- Paintbrushes

Choose a selection of five or six shoeboxes. If any are not solid in color, cover with white or manila paper. Glue boxes together end to end, alternating round and square boxes. Paint a repetitive design on each box, a different design for each box. Aborigine artwork is very geometric, and uses mostly earth colors—whites, browns, golds, and dark red. Stripes and rectangles are popular motifs. How do these grave carvings compare with tombstones in our culture?

Bark Baskets

These long baskets are woven from string bark and are used when an aborigine goes on a walkabout, meaning a long journey. The bark basket is hung from a thick stick slung over the shoulder. Pictures of these can be found in *Down Under—Vanishing Cultures* by Jan Reynolds and *The Australian Aborigines* by Eleanor Z. Baker.

Burlap Baskets

Materials:

- Brown burlap
- Large-eyed sewing needles
- Paint and paintbrushes
- Yarn
- Sticks

Cut two strips of burlap 36 by 12 inches. Stitch them together, rolling the bottom seam up and leaving the top end open. With the yarn, sew patterned columns running the length of the bag all the way around the bag, making each pattern different. Alternatively, paint the columns. Attach a length of yarn to the top and hang the basket over the stick.

Construction Paper Basket

Materials:

- Brown construction paper
- Paint
- Sticks
- Glue
- Sponges
- Film canisters
- Scissors
- String or yarn

Glue two sheets of brown construction paper together around the edges, leaving the top open. Cut the sponges into shapes and glue the shapes to the bottom of the film canisters. Dip the shapes in paint and press them onto the paper, creating patterned columns all the way around the paper, extending the columns from top to bottom. Attach the bag to the stick with a string.

Hand Spear

The hand spear is an aborigine's most important weapon. It is usually about 12 feet long with a throwing range of 50 to 70 yards, and is made from a hollow or lightwood wooden shaft, fitted with a hardwood head.

Paper Spear

Materials:

- Brown construction paper (12 by 18 inches)
- Tape or stapler
- Glue

Roll the construction paper lengthwise into a tight cylinder and tape securely. Make two or three cylinders and attach them end to end. At one end, tape or staple a flattened triangle for the head of the spear.

Boomerang

The boomerang, a crescent-shaped throwing weapon unique to Australia, comes in two types: the returning and the nonreturning. The returning boomerang, while most familiar to the Western world, was never very popular in Australia and was used only for play or ceremonial purposes, or as a hawk decoy to drive flocks of game into nets strung from trees. The nonreturning boomerang is crescent-shaped with a shallower curve than that of the returning boomerang. It can weigh as much as $1\frac{1}{2}$ pounds, and is used for hunting, fighting, and demonstrating disapproval.

Cardboard Boomerang

Materials:

- Cardboard
- Brown paint

Cut the cardboard into a shallow crescent shape and paint it brown for a nonreturning-style boomerang.

ABORIGINAL ART

Australian aborigines attribute their painting skills and designs to mythical ancestors. The custom of painting is commonplace among the aborigines and the designs have many uses: sacred, historical, and communicative.

Rock Paintings

Many rock sites in the Australian Outback contain remarkable galleries of aboriginal paintings. The subjects include ancestor spirit figures that cast good magic over the landscape and X-ray-style renderings of fish and other animals, showing the animals' internal organs and skeletal structure. Pictures of aboriginal paintings can be found in *Down Under—Vanishing Cultures* by Jan Reynolds, *Australia*, from the Enchantment of the World series by Emilie U. Lepthien, *Understanding Primitive Art* by Peter Pollack, and *Let's Travel in Australia* by Gordon Currie.

X-Ray Pictures

Materials:

- Sandpaper or brown construction paper
- Paint (earth colors: black, white, brown, orange, yellow, red)
- Paintbrushes

Study pictures of aboriginal rock paintings, then paint a design of your choice. Try to duplicate the X-ray style of the aborigines by painting an animal and showing its skeletal structure and internal organs along with the external body markings.

Bark Paintings

Bark paintings were used to detail the history of a tribe or to convey messages from one tribe to another. Artists were considered the owners of their designs and handed them down through the generations, only using someone else's design by permission. Pictures of bark paintings can be found in *The Australian Aborigines* by Eleanor Z. Baker and *Passport to Australia* by Susan Pepper.

Bark Paintings

Materials:

- Paintbrushes
- Paint
- Flat pieces of wood or brown construction paper

Study pictures of Australian bark paintings and then create your own paintings on the wood or paper using earth colors.

Message Sticks

Message sticks—small, carved, wooden tablets—are used by many aborigine tribes as reminders of debts, passports for safe passage, and invitations.

Cardboard Tube Message Sticks

Materials:

- Paper towel tubes
- Scissors and glue
- Brown paper
- Black felt-tip markers

Cut the brown paper to fit the length of the tube and cover the tube with the paper, gluing it into place. Make up pictograph symbols to create a message, and draw the symbols on the message stick with the marker. How does the message stick compare to the ways we send messages in the United States?

Cat's Cradle

Aborigines use string made from bark fibers to create more than 400 cat's cradle designs for fun and storytelling. Women make string designs most often, but men will occasionally make designs for ceremonial purposes. Some of the figures are realistic representations but many are abstract. *String Magic: String Designs and How to Make Them* by Pat Brigandi is a fun book with many different cat's cradle designs.

Cat's Cradle Picture

Materials:

- Yarn or string
- Paper
- Glue

Study pictures and books on cat's cradles. Try to produce an authentic cat's cradle. Then arrange the yarn or string on a piece of paper and glue it into place.

THE ANIMALS OF AUSTRALIA

Because Australia has been completely separated from other continents for so long, its native life is unique. There are more than 100 different marsupial and monotreme species that are found nowhere else on earth. A good book on Australian animals is *Strange Animals of Australia* by Toni Eugene.

The Kangaroo

A newborn kangaroo is only 1 inch long and grows to be as much as 7 feet tall in some species. The kangaroo is a marsupial, or pouched mammal. It is the most recognized animal of Australia, and images of it appear on airplanes, coins, and the Australian coat of arms.

Paper Bag Kangaroo Costume

Materials:

- Paper grocery bags
- Paper lunch bags
- Brown construction paper
- Kangaroo pattern (see figs. 4.1a, 4.1b, and 4.2)
- Scissors
- Glue, stapler or double-backed tape

Cut the bottom off of one grocery bag and cut a 3-inch strip from the top. Cut the strip in half lengthwise resulting in two 1½-inch strips. Attach them, suspender style, to one end of the grocery sack, crisscrossing in the back and cutting to fit the child's body. Cut another grocery bag in half and attach to the front of the first bag, forming the kangaroo's pocket. Cut and measure a paper strip to fit the circumference of the child's head and attach large, triangular ears to each side. Trace the baby kangaroo's head, figure 4.1, out of heavy brown paper and glue to the folded bottom of a paper lunch bag. Cut two paws from a double thickness of brown paper and glue onto the sides of the bag. Cut two legs from a double thickness of brown paper and glue onto the sides of the bag about halfway up from the bottom. Cut two tails. Glue together along the top edge only. Fold back at the dotted lines and use glue or double-backed tape to glue on the back of the bag about 2½ inches from the bottom. Put the baby kangaroo in the pouch with the paws hanging over the edge.

Koalas

The koala is probably the most charming Australian mammal. It looks like a large, fluffy teddy bear, and spends most of its life either eating eucalyptus leaves or sleeping.

(Text continues on page 57.)

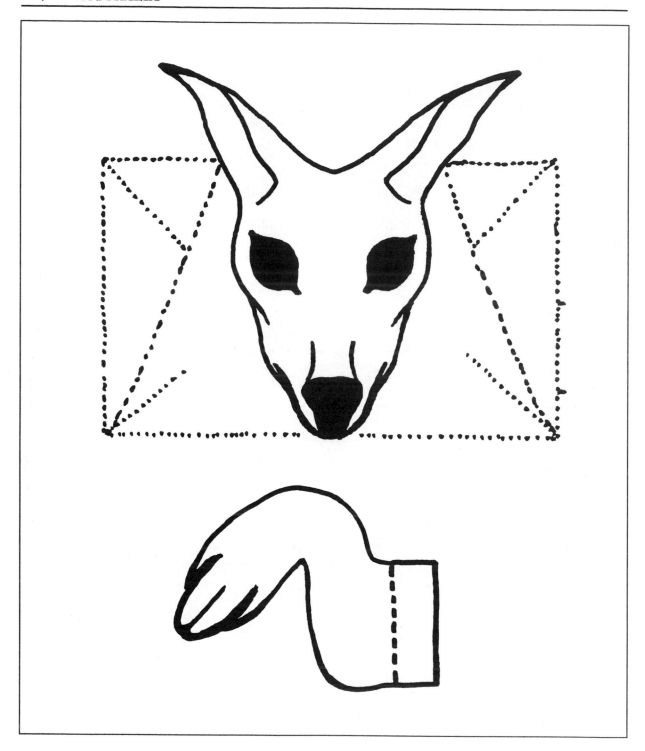

Fig. 4.1a.

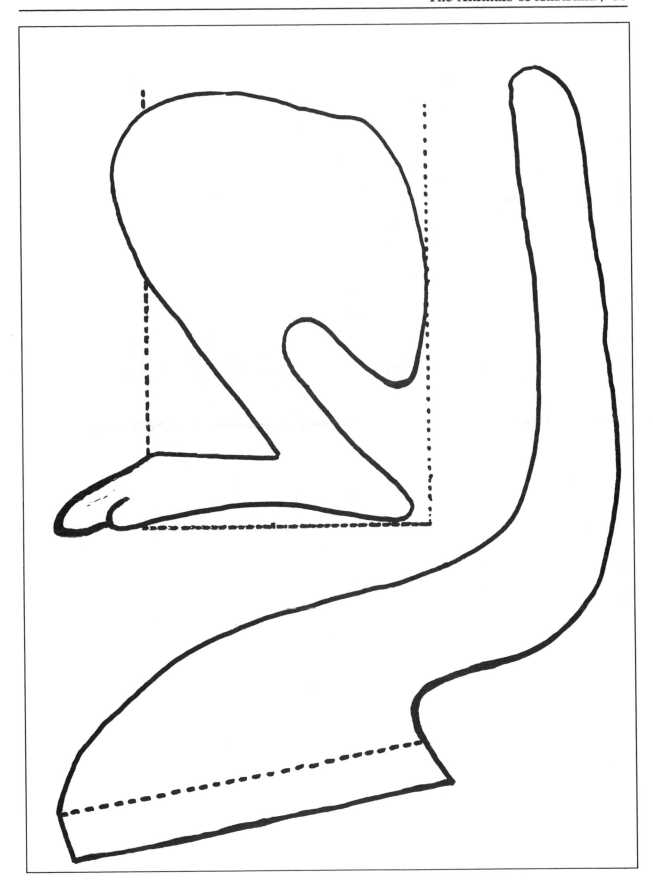

Fig. 4.1b.

Fig. 4.2.

Koala Picture

Materials:

- Construction paper
- Brown yarn
- Coffee grounds
- Koala bear pattern (see fig. 4.2 on page 56)
- Glue
- Scissors
- Stapler

Trace and cut out the koala bear pattern on construction paper. Cover the cutout with glue and sprinkle coffee grounds on top. Glue strands of yarn on the ears for fuzzy hair.

Parrots

There are 60 different species of parrots in Australia. These brightly colored birds have evolved to fill just about every available niche in Australia's ecosystem. There are nectar-sipping parrots, seed eaters, bulb and root eaters, and insect and grub eaters. There are parrots that eat fruit, some that eat nuts, and even a type that eats the flesh of live sheep.

Parrot Picture

Materials:

- Colored felt-tip markers
- Paper

Consult reference books such as encyclopedias and bird guides to find pictures of the many varieties of Australian parrots. Choose one parrot to research, then draw the parrot and color it with markers.

Tissue Paper Parrot

Materials:

- Liquid starch and brushes for the starch
- Parrot pattern (see fig. 4.3)
- Scissors
- Colored tissue paper

Cover the parrot pattern with thin layer of starch. Then lay colored tissue paper over the pattern, arranging it in bright patterns of color.

Echidna

The echidna, or spiny anteater, is an egg-laying mammal or *monotreme*. It looks like a ball with quills, and has a long snout and sticky tongue to catch ants and termites (see fig. 4.4). When the young hatch, they crawl into a pouch that the mother develops only during breeding season.

Echidna Picture

Materials:

- Toothpicks
- Paper
- Crayons
- Glue

Draw a flattened circle on the paper. Glue toothpicks onto the circle. Then draw a long snout at one end.

(Text continues on page 60.)

Fig. 4.3.

Fig. 4.4.

The Sea Life of the Great Barrier Reef

The Great Barrier Reef, a complex of reefs, lagoons, and islands that stretches 1,200 miles along the Queensland coast, was discovered by the Europeans in 1770 when Captain James Cook ran his ship aground on it. It is composed of more than 400 types of corals and contains countless species of sea life, among them the humpback whale and the sea turtle. A good book about the reef is *The Great Barrier Reef: A Treasure in the Sea* by Alice Gilbreath.

Reef Picture

Materials:

- Colored tempera
- Yarn
- Salt
- Paper
- Tissue paper
- Sponges cut in small shapes
- Construction paper
- Glue

Mix two or three spoonfuls of salt into each color of tempera. Dip a piece of yarn into the paint and draw it across the paper. Repeat this several times then let the paper dry. When dry choose another color and repeat the process. The salt helps make the paint sparkle when dry. After several colored lines have been crisscrossed on the paper, add fish and other sea animals by sponge-painting them onto the reef or by cutting them out from tissue paper and gluing them onto the paper.

PLANTS IN AUSTRALIA

Australia contains a rich variety of plant life, covering the entire range from rain forests to desert. The rain forests of North Queensland have been called "the cradle of the flowering plants" and scientists have found many primitive plants there. Rare and beautiful plants grow in the alpine meadows above the snow line, and even in the desert, a rainfall results in splashes of color as beautiful flowers spring to life.

Mulla Mulla

The Mulla Mulla, a perennial flower, is about 2 feet tall and made up of a multitude of tightly packed flowerets growing on top of thin stalks. This flower is found in the Outback and comes in many colors.

Mulla Mulla Picture

Materials:

- Paper
- Crayons
- Colored cotton balls (Many different colors. These can be bought, or made by shaking white cotton balls with colored powdered tempera.)
- Glue

With green crayon, draw several long stalks on paper. Glue one colored cotton ball at top of each stem.

Kingias

Kingias are also known as grass trees or drumheads. This plant is distantly related to the lily, and consists of a trunk topped by grassy leaves 3 or more feet long. Spikes with white flowers extend from the top of the tree, usually after fires (See fig. 4.5).

Kingias Picture

Materials:

- White, blue, and brown paper
- Grass (real or plastic Easter grass)
- Glue
- Scissors

Cut a long, thin trunk from brown paper and glue it onto a blue background. Glue grass in a bushy clump at the top of the trunk. Select some long grass blades to extend from the top of the clump. Tear tiny pieces of white paper and glue them to the ends of the stalks to create flowers.

Wattle Trees

Early settlers wove the limbs of wattle, or acacia, trees into the walls of their mud huts. These trees are related to the pea plant, which also produces seed pods. There are about 600 species of wattle, which is one of the few hardwoods to grow in the desert.

Wattle Tree Picture

Materials:

- Blue and brown paper
- Colored tempera (green plus any one color)
- Scissors and glue

Cut a trunk and branches from brown paper and glue them onto the blue paper. Wattle trees come in many varieties and shapes, so the branches can be arranged however you want. Dip the tip of one finger into the green paint and press it along the branches of the tree to form the leaves. Let the paint dry, then repeat the procedure with the colored paint, covering the branches with colored blossoms.

THE GEOGRAPHY OF AUSTRALIA

Australia is the flattest, the driest, and the smallest of continents. It is flat because there have been no recent episodes of mountain building. The land has been gradually eroded by the forces of wind, rain, and sun over millions of years. Nevertheless the land has many beautiful and exotic features.

Ayers Rock

Ayers Rock is a strange, lonely rock rising above the desert in the center of Australia. It is 2.2 miles long, more than 1.5 miles wide, and 1,100 feet high. Made of red sandstone, it changes color with the light of day. Ayers Rock dates back 230 million years, and it has been greatly weathered by the wind. There are basins on the top, and the base is riddled with caves that the ancient aborigines covered with cave paintings. Pictures of Ayers Rock can be found in *Australia*, from the Enchantment of the World series by Emilie U. Lepthien and *Let's Travel in Australia* by Gordon Currie.

Fig. 4.5.

Paper Bag Rock

Materials:

- Brown butcher paper
- Dark orange tempera
- Newspaper

- Paintbrushes
- Paper grocery bags
- Yellow masking tape

Create a representation of Ayers Rock by filling at least four (you can use more depending on how large the rock is to be) paper grocery bags with crumpled newspaper. Fold the top of each bag over and tape it securely. Arrange the filled bags into a rectangular shape and cover it with brown butcher paper. The lines and creases that the butcher paper makes naturally will simulate the creases of Ayers Rock. Paint over the butcher paper with orange paint to simulate the red sandstone.

REFERENCES

Baker, Eleanor Z. *The Australian Aborigines*. Austin, TX: Steck-Vaughn, 1968.

Brigandi, Pat. *String Magic: String Designs and How to Make Them*. New York: Scholastic, 1993.

Currie, Gordon. *Let's Travel in Australia*. Chicago: Childrens Press, 1968.

Eugene, Toni. *Strange Animals of Australia*. Washington, DC: National Geographic Society, 1981.

Gilbreath, Alice. *The Great Barrier Reef: A Treasure in the Sea*. Minneapolis, MN: Dillon, 1986.

Kelly, Andrew. *Australia*, Countries of the World series. New York: Bookwright, 1989.

Lepthien, Emilie U. *Australia*, Enchantment of the World series. Chicago: Childrens Press, 1982.

Pepper, Susan. *Passport to Australia*. New York: Franklin Watts, 1987.

Reynolds, Jan. *Down Under—Vanishing Cultures*. San Diego: Harcourt Brace Jovanovich, 1992.

FURTHER READING

Arnold, Caroline. *Australia Today*. New York: Franklin Watts, 1957.

Bergamini, David, et al. *The Land and Wildlife of Australia*. New York: Time-Life, 1964.

McHenry, Robert, ed. *The New Encyclopaedia Britannica*, vols. 1, 2, 4–6, 9. Chicago: Encyclopaedia Britannica, 1992.

Palmer, Laurence. *Fieldbook of Natural History*, 2d ed. New York: McGraw-Hill, 1975.

Pollack, Peter. *Understanding Primitive Art*. New York: Lion Press, 1972.

Samachson, Dorothy, and Joseph Samachson. *The First Artists*. Garden City, NY: Doubleday, 1970.

Scheffel, Richard L., ed. *ABC's of Nature*. Pleasantville, NY: Reader's Digest Association, 1984.

5
AFRICA

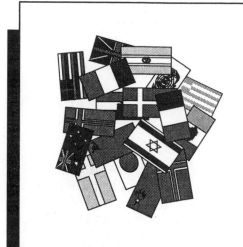

Population: 647,518,000
Area: 11,667,000 square miles

Africa is the world's second largest continent, containing 22 percent of the world's total land area and 12½ percent of the world's population. Human beings are widely thought to have originated in Africa 300,000 to 500,000 years ago. Remains of *Australopithecus*, the oldest known hominid, have been found in southern Africa and are estimated to be as much as 8 million years old.

To build a curriculum unit around Africa can be misleading, as this implies that Africa is a single large nation and that the culture is the same throughout. In actuality, of course, Africa is composed of more than 3,000 distinct ethnic groups which speak, among them, 800 to 1,000 different languages.

In general, though, art is a very important part of the African heritage and is expressed through sculpture, architecture, furniture, pottery, textiles, jewelry, body ornamentation, and paintings. African artwork, after being ignored for years or derided as primitive, is emerging in the modern era as an important influence on Western artists, who admire the African emphasis on abstraction and their freedom from realism.

A unit on Africa should take elements from many different African cultures to show students the diversity of African culture and to help them develop an appreciation for and respect for life in the "Cradle of Civilization."

HOMES IN AFRICA

For the most part, homes in Africa, especially in rural or undeveloped areas, are simple and built for hot days and cool nights. The styles and materials vary from one region to another, based on local resources.

Stilt Houses

The African stilt houses found in the country of Benin in West Africa have floors made of bamboo raised on wooden stilts. The raised floors help keep animals out of the house and allow cooling breezes to flow beneath the house. A picture of a stilt house can be found in *The Arts of Mankind: Painting, Architecture and Music* from the International Geographic Society.

Stilt House Picture

Materials:

- Toothpicks
- Construction paper
- Glue
- Crayons

Glue toothpicks onto construction paper in the shape of a stilt house. Add details of an African village with crayons.

Mud Houses

The mud houses found in central Africa are circular in shape, with thick, pointed straw roofs designed to absorb the heat of the sun. The roofs look like straw hats sitting on top of the house. See *The Village of Round and Square Houses* by Ann Grifalconi for pictures.

Clay House

Materials:

- Modeling clay
- Grass or straw
- Paper
- Glue
- Scissors
- Cardboard

Using modeling clay, form the walls of a circular house. Set the house on a cardboard base. Cut a semicircle from a piece of paper and roll it into a cone. Put the cone on top of the clay house for the roof and glue grass or straw onto it.

Decorated Mud House

The outside walls of mud houses in northern Nigeria (in West Africa) are brightly painted with bold, geometric shapes.

Decorated Paper House

Materials:

- Construction paper
- Grass or straw
- Tempera
- Scissors
- Glue
- Paintbrushes

Roll a sheet of construction paper into a wide tube. This is the house. Cut a cone shape from another piece of paper and glue grass or straw to the cone. This will go on top of the house for the roof. Cut doors and windows from the side of the house. Paint the walls with tempera. Use bright colors and large, bold, geometric shapes.

CLOTHING IN AFRICA

The clothing of Africa is colorful and varies greatly from region to region. In general, though, it is designed for hot weather and to attract attention.

Nigerian Tie-Dye

The traditional Nigerian tie-dye technique produces beautifully colored clothes. This technique is still used today to make clothing.

Tie-Dyed T-Shirt or Handkerchief

Materials:

- White T-shirt or handkerchief
- Rubber bands
- Clothing dye (one color recommended)

Gather the cloth into clumps all over the garment and tie them into knots or twist them tightly and secure with rubber bands. The more knots, the prettier the results. Prepare clothing dye according to package directions. Dip the cloth into the dye and then rinse in cold water. Dry thoroughly before removing the knots.

Ashanti Printed Cloth

The Ashanti tribe of Ghana are known worldwide for their beautifully printed cloth. It is printed with vivid colors, using a geometric-shaped motif.

Printed T-Shirt or Handkerchief

Materials:

- White T-shirts or handkerchiefs
- Acrylic paints
- Sponges or wooden blocks cut into geometric shapes

Press the block or sponge into the paint and then onto the cloth. Use a variety of colors, making a bright pattern on the cloth.

Raffia Grass Dance Skirts

These traditional dance skirts are still worn in ceremonial dances by several tribes, including the Dogon of Mali, the Masai of Kenya, and the Zulu of Swaziland and South Africa.

Paper Grass Skirt

Materials:

- Green or yellow butcher paper
- Paper clips or tape
- Scissors

Cut a piece of paper big enough to fit around your waist. Then cut a fringe from the bottom to within 4 inches of the top. Fasten the skirt around your waist with paper clips or tape.

AFRICAN ART

African art varies from region to region, although geometric shapes are a common motif. There are many books demonstrating the art of Africa, both ancient and modern, including wood carvings, cloth, pottery, and drawings.

Stone Paintings

These are the oldest examples of historical African art. Some may be 5,000 years old, but others are fairly recent. The artists use mainly primary colors and the spiral is a frequent motif. Examples of African stone art can be found in *The First Artists* by Dorothy and Joseph Samachson and *The Art of Africa* by Shirley Glubok.

Stone Paintings

Materials:

- Sandpaper
- Watercolors
- Paintbrushes

Study pictures of ancient African stone paintings. Then use primary watercolors to paint on the sandpaper, focusing on the spiral motif.

Charcoal Drawings

This ancient art is still practiced frequently today. Much African portraiture is done in charcoal.

Charcoal Drawing

Materials:

- Charcoal (ideally burnt wood chips, but commercial charcoal pencils are available from art supply stores)
- Construction paper

Draw a portrait using charcoal.

Pottery

Pottery is one of the most common types of African art and occurs in many shapes. Bowls and vessels are often formed from clay, along with figurines, both human and animal. Pictures of African pottery can be found in *South Africa in Pictures*, from the Visual Geography series by Peter English and *The Art of Africa* by Shirley Glubok.

Clay Pottery

Materials:

- Modeling clay
- Paints
- Paintbrushes

After looking at pictures of African pottery, create a clay form trying to imitate one of the African styles you studied. Then paint your piece if you want.

Skin Pottery

Some Africans made beautiful pottery from animal skins. They covered clay molds with small, thin pieces of scraped animal skins. When the pottery was dry, they dug out the clay and painted designs on the skin. These pots were used to hold food and water.

Clay and Paper Pottery

Materials:

- Soft modeling clay or Play Doh
- Vaseline
- Paintbrushes
- Paints
- Paper strips

Form the clay into the shape you want, preferably a bowl or a wide-mouthed vase. Coat the outside of the clay with Vaseline and cover the clay with five or six layers of thin paper strips, which will stick to the Vaseline. Let the jar dry for several days. Carefully dig the clay out with a spoon or knife and paint a design on the paper pottery.

Coil Baskets

Tribes in Zambia (in southern Africa) use woven grass fiber to make a coiled basket. These beautiful baskets are often painted.

Yarn pottery

Materials:

- Styrofoam soup bowls
- Thin cotton rope or yarn
- White glue
- Paint
- Paintbrushes

Dip yarn into the glue and coil it inside the bowl, starting in the center and building up the sides. When the bowl is completely covered, squirt glue in between the layers and let it dry. When the yarn basket is completely dry, carefully remove it from the Styrofoam and paint it with bright colors using a mixture of one part paint to one part glue.

Calabash Carvers

The Calabash carvers of the Yoruba tribe of Nigeria (in West Africa) have an artistic tradition that goes back to the sixth century. Artisans today still make decorative objects from the calabash, a pumpkin-like plant. When the pulp is removed, the gourd can be used as a container or even a musical instrument such as a drum, which resounds beautifully when struck. Calabash carvers will spend an entire day carving and decorating a single gourd. *The Art of Africa* by Shirley Glubok contains pictures of this African gourd art.

Balloon-and-Masking-Tape Bowl

Materials:

- Large balloons
- Masking tape
- Paintbrushes
- Paints
- Glue

Blow up the balloon and tie it shut. Cover the bottom half of the balloon with two layers of masking tape. Paint the tape with glue and allow it to dry. Pop the balloon and paint the inside surface of the masking tape with glue. Let dry. When the glue dries, designs can be painted on the outside of the bowl.

Gourd Pottery

Materials:

- Paintbrushes
- Vinegar and water mixture
- Butter knife
- Steel wool pad
- Soft rag
- Turpentine
- Paints (oil paints are strongly recommended as they will best adhere to the gourd's surface)
- Ornamental gourds (suggested varieties are Crown of Thorns, Pears, Apples, Eggs, Orange, and Warties)

Curing: Wipe gourds with a mixture of vinegar and water and set them on a rack that will allow the air to circulate around them, preferably in an area of low humidity, Turn the gourds occasionally to expose all the surfaces to the air. As the gourds dry, their colors will fade and they will grow a moldy crust. This is normal. It can take several weeks to adequately dry gourds. Gourds that disintegrate or shrivel should be discarded.

Cleaning: When dry, the gourds will have thin, solid shells. They will be light in weight and their seeds will rattle. Remove the mold and crust from the gourds under warm, running water with a butter knife and a steel wool pad. Then dry the gourd with a soft rag.

Cutting (Optional): If you would like, the gourd may be cut to make a bowl or a spoon. This will depend upon the shape of the gourd. Have your teacher cut your gourd for you. After the gourd has been cut, the inner surface needs to be scraped clean.

Decorating: Decorate your gourd with dyes or oil paints applied by brush or by dipping. Clean oil paints from brushes and hands with turpentine.

Ceremonial Masks

The ceremonial masks of many of the tribes of Africa are beautifully colored and highly imaginative. Carved from wood and embellished with dried grass, leaves, and feathers, they depict many different animals and spirits. Pictures of masks can be found in *Understanding Primitive Art* by Peter Pollack and *South Africa in Pictures*, from the Visual Geography series by Peter English.

Paper Plate Masks

Materials:

- Paper plates
- Stapler
- Paints
- Collage materials including feathers and dried grass
- Scissors
- Glue
- Paintbrushes

Paint a face with bold, exaggerated features on the paper plate. Decorate the mask with dried grass, yarn, or feathers. The imagination is the limit here.

Zulu Spear and Shield

A century ago, the Zulu were the most feared warriors in Africa. Today many have adopted more peaceful ways, however, they still preserve their traditions, such as traditional Zulu costumes and the ancient ceremonial dances. Zulu warriors made their own spears and shields, choosing their shape and design. Shields were usually one of the basic geometric shapes—oval, round, or rectangular.

Cardboard Shield

Materials:

- Cardboard
- Brown butcher paper
- Paints
- Tape
- Scissors
- Glue or stapler
- Paintbrushes

Cut cardboard into the size and shape of shield you want. Paint a design on the front. Glue or staple cardboard strips to the back of the shield so you can hold onto it. Make a spear from rolled butcher paper. Tape the edges together and display it with the shield.

AFRICAN JEWELRY

People from Africa, like people all over the world, adorn themselves with beautiful hand made jewelry, making creative use of bones, shells, stones, metal, and wood. Obtain as many pictures as possible of African jewelry so students will have many examples to imitate. Pictures of African jewelry can be found in *South Africa in Pictures*, from the Visual Geography series by Peter English.

Necklaces

Necklaces are made from just about any material, the more varied and colorful, the better. Some necklaces are used as more than decorations. In many African tribes, necklaces made from cowry shells are worn to demonstrate a person's wealth.

Shell or Bead Necklaces

Materials:

- Yarn, string, or thin wire
- Beads, small stones with holes, seashells with holes, seed pods, or poultry neck bones (boiled, soaked in bleach and dried)

Study pictures of necklaces worn in different parts of Africa. Pick a style and, using materials you have collected, create a necklace and bracelet of your own.

Masai Collar Necklaces

Women from the Masai tribe of Kenya wear circles of metal wire that cover the entire chest and are decorated with beads.

Aluminum Foil Necklace

Materials:

- Cardboard
- Beads

- Aluminum foil
- Scissors and glue

Cut a large collar from the cardboard. Cover it with aluminum foil and glue beads to the surface.

AFRICAN PLANT AND ANIMAL LIFE

Who has not dreamed of going on an African safari? With countless varieties of plants and animals, the African continent is a vast treasure trove of life. Africa teems with beautiful flowers and unique vegetation. There are more types of trees on this continent than anywhere else on earth.

Baobab Tree

The baobab tree looks like a bottle with arms stretching in all directions from the top (see fig. 5.1). An ancient African legend says that this tree was created when a giant child of the gods pulled a tree up by the roots and stuck it back in the ground upside down. The trunk of this tree contains a spongy wood saturated with moisture that can hold up to 25,000 gallons of water, so people use this tree as a water source. Elephants have also been known to attack baobab trunks with their tusks to get at the water inside. The trunk (which has hollow spaces) can also serve as a temporary shelter.

Plastic Bottle Baobab Tree

Materials:

- Plastic soda bottles
- Brown and green paper

- Scissors
- Glue

Cover the bottle with brown paper. Cut short branches from the brown paper and attach them to the top of the bottle. Cut leaves from green paper and glue them onto the branches.

Fig. 5.1.

Traveler's Tree

The traveler's tree can grow to a height of 90 feet. Its branches are arranged like a fan, and the leaves, which are shaped like palm leaves, can be 12 to 15 feet long. The base of each leaf forms a cup-shaped reservoir that can hold about a quart of rain water.

Traveler's Tree Picture

Materials:

- Scissors
- Brown, white, and green construction paper
- Glue

Cut a straight trunk from the brown paper and glue it onto white paper. From the green paper, cut branches with palm-like leaves at the end. Glue these branches like a fan at the top of the tree trunk.

The African Jungle

Trees in the African jungle in the Congo River basin of equatorial Africa grow so close together and so tall that the branches meet far overhead, forming an unbroken roof blocking the sky. In addition to the trees, the African jungle is festooned with hanging vines. Many animals, such as snakes, birds, and insects live in the jungle.

An African jungle can be created in the classroom with ordinary art supplies. Obtain tapes of jungle sounds to complete the atmosphere.

Butcher Paper Trees

Materials:

- Brown butcher paper
- Green construction paper
- Scissors
- Glue or stapler

Tear long strips of brown butcher paper and twist together into paper ropes. Bunch several ropes together and hang them on the wall to form tree trunks. Use single ropes for branches. Cut leaves from green paper and attach them to branches.

Butcher Paper Vines

Materials:

- Brown butcher paper
- Scissors
- Tape or glue

Cut the butcher paper into long lengths as desired and roll to form vine. Tape or glue them securely and hang from the ceiling or drape them over the windows.

Jungle Snakes

Africa contains hundreds of different kinds of snakes. Most of these are harmless, but it is the poisonous ones, often the most brightly colored, that attract our attention. Pictures of African snakes can be found in *Living Snakes of the World in Color* by John M. Mehrtens and *Snakes of the World* by Christopher Mattison. Study these pictures and add snakes to your classroom jungle.

Pantyhose Snake

Materials:

- Leg from pantyhose
- Newspaper
- Paints
- Paintbrushes

Crumple the newspaper and stuff it into the leg from the pantyhose. Tie the pantyhose shut and paint designs on the snake. Try to copy the patterns of real snakes as you create your own.

Jungle Insects and Birds

The birds and insects of the African jungle are vividly colored. Make available several books of African wildlife for students to study. Two good books are *Who Comes to the Water Hole?* by Colleen Stanley Bare and *Bugs of the World* by George McGavin.

Bug or Bird Picture

Materials:

- Brightly colored tempera and paintbrushes
- Paper

Choose an African bird or insect to paint, using bright, vivid colors. Cut out your picture and display it in the jungle scene.

ANIMALS OF THE SAVANNAH

A unit on Africa would not be complete without studying the large land mammals found on Africa's savannahs, or plains.

African Elephant

The African elephant is the largest living land mammal. It can weigh up to 8 tons and stand 10 to 12 feet high at the shoulder. The ears of the African elephant are larger than those of the Indian elephant. Both male and female African elephants have ivory tusks, which makes them equally prized by poachers. The only animal the elephant fears is the human. A good book about African elephants is *The Elephant in the Bush* by Ian Redmond.

Elephant Picture

Materials:

- Green and yellow paint
- Paintbrushes
- Gray paper
- Scissors and tape
- Brown butcher paper
- Elephant pattern (see fig. 5.2)

Cut out the elephant shape and tape it onto gray paper, using rolled tape stuck to the back of the cutout. Paint green and yellow stripes across the paper, including over the cutout, with the paintbrush. When the paint is dry, carefully remove the cutout. This makes two pictures, the gray paper will look like an elephant on the savannah and the cutout will be a painted elephant. Display all the pictures on the brown butcher paper for a picture of a herd of elephants on the savannah.

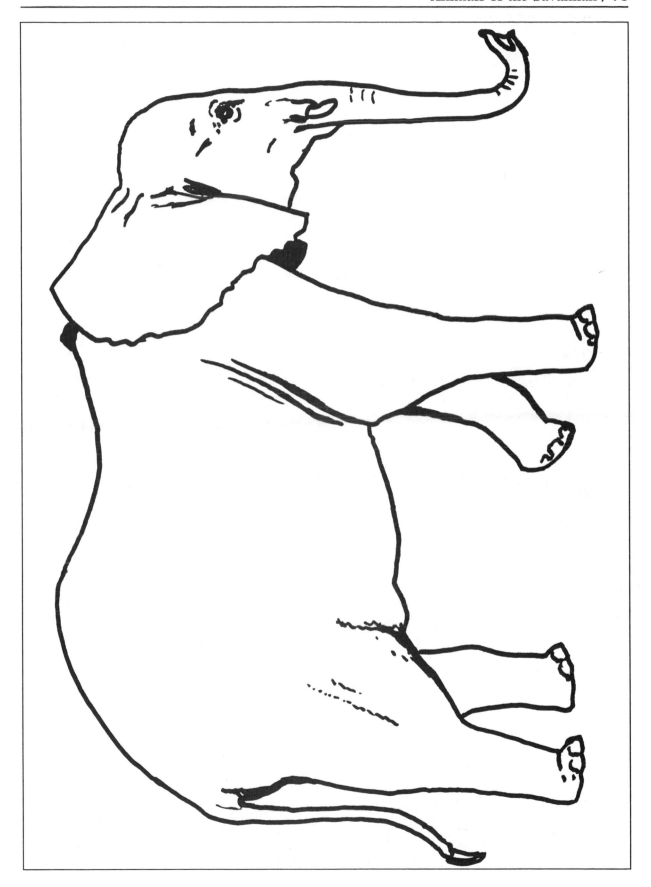

Fig. 5.2.

Zebra

Zebras are the size of large ponies, and no two zebras have the same pattern of stripes. They graze across the plains in great herds often numbering several hundred. Antelope often form mixed groups with zebras, whose alertness provides extra protection from predators, including lions.

Zebra Prints

Materials:

- Corrugated cardboard
- White paper
- Black paint
- Zebra pattern (see fig. 5.3)

- Scissors
- Pencils
- Paintbrushes

Trace the zebra pattern onto a piece of corrugated cardboard. Cut out the shape. Paint black paint on ridged side of cardboard and, while still wet, press onto white paper to make zebra prints.

Giraffes

The giraffe can stand up to 18 or 19 feet tall. They are peaceful creatures but can put up a good fight when attacked. Because they are seldom heard to make noises, it is commonly assumed that they have no vocal cords but in actuality, they are capable of making low calls and moans. *Giraffes: The Sentinels of the Savannahs* by Helen Roney Sattler is a good book about giraffes.

Giraffe Picture

Materials:

- White paper
- Orange and yellow paint
- Cotton balls

- Scissors
- Pencils
- Giraffe pattern (see fig. 5.4)

Cut the giraffe shape from white paper and paint markings onto it with cotton balls dipped in orange and yellow paint.

Large-Scale Picture

Materials:

- Yellow butcher paper
- Orange and brown paint
- Opaque projector

- Scissors
- Pencils

Use the opaque projector to project the giraffe shape onto the butcher paper. Trace around the giraffe and cut it out. As a group, make spots on the giraffe by dipping your hands in orange and brown paint and pressing on the giraffe.

(Text continues on page 79.)

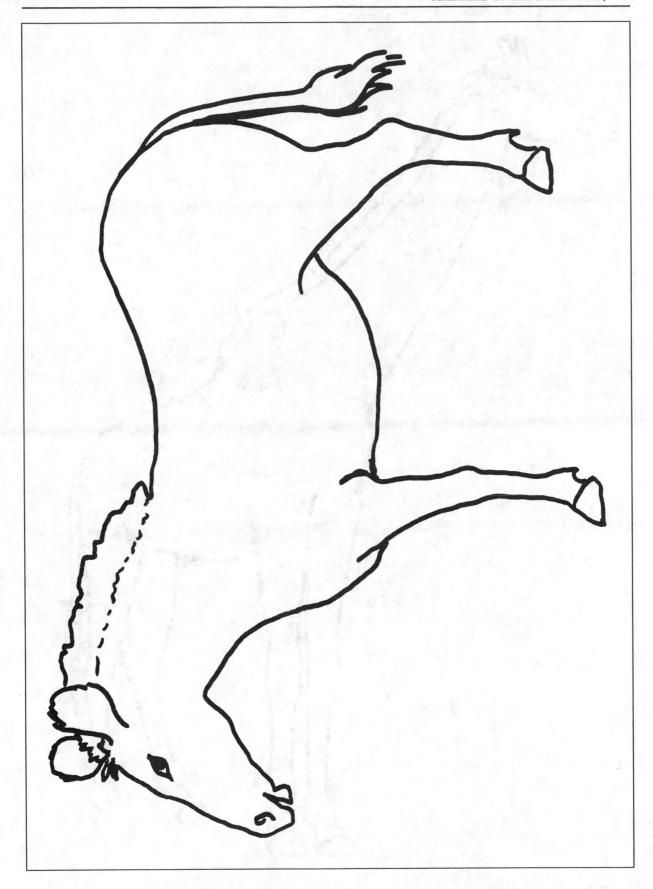

Fig. 5.3.

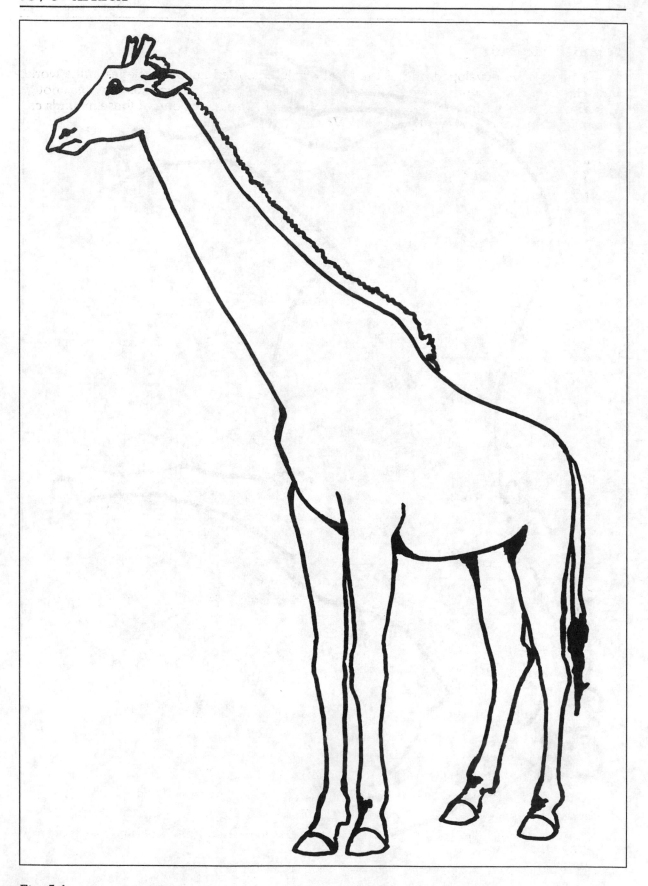

Fig. 5.4.

Termite Mounds

Termites have developed one of the most highly organized animal societies in the world. Their cities, termite mounds, are easily recognizable (see fig. 5.5). The mounds are large enough that in some areas of the continent, people live in them. A picture of one of these mounds can be found in *Ants and Termites* by Gwynne Vevers.

Termite Mound Cutout

Materials:

- Brown sandpaper
- Construction paper
- Scissors
- Glue

Cut the steep towers and base of the termite mound from sandpaper and glue onto construction paper.

Termite Mound Picture

Materials:

- Brown butcher paper
- Sponges, cut into small squares
- Brown tempera
- Scissors

Cut tall mounds from butcher paper. Use a sponge to press brown paint over surface of the picture. When the termite mound picture is dry, display it on the wall.

REFERENCES

The Arts of Mankind: Painting, Architecture and Music. Englewood Cliffs, NJ: International Geographic Society, 1962.

Bare, Colleen Stanley. *Who Comes to the Water Hole?* New York: Cobblehill Books, 1991.

English, Peter. *South Africa in Pictures*, Visual Geography series. New York: Sterling, 1970.

Glubok, Shirley. *The Art of Africa*. New York: Harper & Row, 1965.

Grifalconi, Ann. *The Village of Round and Square Houses*. Boston: Little, Brown, 1968.

Mattison, Christopher. *Snakes of the World*. New York: Facts on File, 1992.

McGavin, George. *Bugs of the World*. New York: Facts on File, 1993.

Mehrtens, John M. *Living Snakes of the World in Color*. New York: Sterling, 1987.

Pollack, Peter. *Understanding Primitive Art*. New York: Lion Press, 1972.

Redmond, Ian. *The Elephant in the Bush*. Milwaukee, WI: Gareth Stevens, 1990.

Samachson, Dorothy, and Joseph Samachson. *The First Artists*. Garden City, NY: Doubleday, 1970.

Sattler, Helen Roney. *Giraffes: The Sentinels of the Savannahs*. New York: Lothrop, Lee & Shepard, 1989.

Vevers, Gwynne. *Ants and Termites*. New York: McGraw-Hill, 1966.

Fig. 5.5.

FURTHER READING

Atmore, Anthony, and Gillian Stacey. *Black Kingdoms, Black Peoples: The West African Heritage.* London: Orbis, 1979.

Bram, Leon L., ed. *Funk & Wagnalls New Encyclopedia*, vol. 1. New York: Funk & Wagnalls, 1986.

Burns, William A. *A World Full of Homes.* New York: McGraw-Hill, 1953.

East Africa. Amsterdam: Time-Life, 1986.

McHenry, Robert, ed. *The New Encyclopaedia Britannica*, vols. 1, 4–5, 11–12. Chicago: Encyclopaedia Britannica, 1992.

Mordecai, Carolyn. *Gourd Craft: Growing, Designing and Decorating Ornamental and Hardshelled Gourds.* New York: Crown, 1978.

Palmer, Laurence. *Fieldbook of Natural History*, 2d ed. New York: McGraw-Hill, 1975.

Scheffel, Richard L., ed. *ABC's of Nature.* Pleasantville, NY: Reader's Digest Association, 1984.

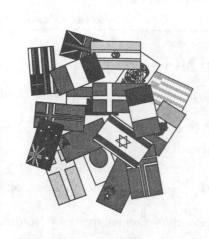

6
ISRAEL

Capital: **Jerusalem**
Government: **Republic (Parliamentary democracy with unicameral legislature, the Knesset)**
Population: **4,614,000**
Area: **7,992 square miles**

Israel is a small country, but its influence in the world has been enormous. Israel has special significance for three of the world's major religions: Judaism, Christianity, and Islam. To the followers of Judaism, one of the world's oldest religions, Israel is more than a country, it is the land promised to them by their god, Yahweh. To Christians, Israel is the Holy Land, the place where Jesus was born, preached, and died upon the cross. To Muslims, Israel is the place from which Mohammed ascended to heaven on a white horse, a place he, himself, declared holy. Israel is where the concept of one God over all the earth, an important concept of Judaism, Christianity, and Islam, arose from polytheistic roots.

Many different cultures coexist in Israel, though not always peacefully. Here, history, religion, and art are irrevocably intertwined for the peoples. The past is still present in ancient buildings that share the streets with modern architecture and in ancient traditions that are still practiced today in what is now a Jewish state after centuries of Muslim rule.

A unit on Israel will introduce students not only to the roots of Christianity, Judaism, and Islam, but will expose them to unique architectural styles and the natural wonders of Israel.

ART IN ISRAEL

Israeli art extends far back into ancient times and combines elements not only of the three major religions, but of the many peoples who have conquered Israel throughout the ages.

Assyrian Stone Carvings

The Assyrians came from Mesopotamia to conquer the lands of Israel in the eighth century B.C. They left detailed stone carvings telling of events taking place under their rule. Assyrian kings recorded their deeds in monumental reliefs that bring biblical narratives to life. Figures in these reliefs are curved and rounded, with natural body positions, unlike the stiff unnaturalness of Egyptian figures. Although the bodies are in profile, as in Egyptian art, the faces of Assyrian figures face forward. Pictures of Assyrian figures can be found in *The Art of Lands in the Bible* by Shirley Glubok.

Assyrian Picture

Materials:

- Construction paper
- Crayons
- Tempera paint (black) mixed thinly
- Paintbrushes

Study Assyrian stone carvings and see how they tell stories. Then pick out a story to illustrate. Color the scene with crayons, pressing hard. When you are finished coloring your scene, paint over the picture with black tempera. The effect will be similar to that of the Assyrian stone carvings.

Ottoman Mosaics

Israel was conquered by the Ottomans, Muslim Turks, in the fifteenth century and remained under Ottoman rule until the early twentieth century. Turkish influences are clearly seen in the many beautiful tile mosaics on architecture throughout Jerusalem and other Israeli cities. Pictures of these mosaics can be found in *Jerusalem: Rock of Ages* by Fosco Maraini.

Mosaic Picture

Materials:

- Colored construction paper
- White paper
- Scissors
- Glue

Cut the colored paper into small (½ inch) rectangles and arrange them onto the paper to make a mosaic design. When your pattern is complete, glue the pieces to the paper.

Hebrew Seals

Hebrew seals were clay disks carved with Hebrew symbols used to seal important documents. Many examples of these disks survive today.

Clay Disks

Materials:

- Modeling clay
- Toothpicks
- Paint
- Paper

Shape your clay into an oval disk and use a toothpick to carve the letters of your name into the clay. After the disk hardens, use the seal and paint to stamp your name on paper.

Silver Filigree

Artisans in Israel today still produce lovely silver filigree just as they have done for thousands of years.

Pie Plate Jewelry

Materials:

- Aluminum pie plates
- Sharp, pointed object such as a thin nail
- Yarn
- Heavy-duty scissors

Cut an interesting shape from the bottom of a pie plate. With a nail, scratch a design on one side of the metal, being careful not to poke the nail all the way through. This will create a raised design on the other side of the metal. Poke a hole through the top of the piece and string it onto a length of yarn.

Arabesque Medallions

Because Muslims are commanded not to make graven images, Muslim art seldom depicts the human form. Instead, intricate arabesques are found throughout Muslim art. These geometric and floral motifs adorn many Israeli city walls. Pictures of arabesque art can be found in *Jerusalem* by Colin Thubron and *The Glory of Jerusalem: An Explorer's Guide* by Shlomo S. Gafni.

Arabesque Picture

Materials:

- Construction paper
- Scissors
- Glue
- Colored felt-tip markers or colored pencils (optional)

Study samples of arabesque art. Cut your paper into rectangles for mosaics and lay out a design on an oval piece of paper. Combine geometric and floral shapes and make your designs as intricate as possible. You might prefer to draw the designs with markers or colored pencils.

ARCHITECTURE IN ISRAEL

The history of architecture in Israel is varied, reflecting the various rulers and conquerors of the country. Israeli archaeology reveals the country in its wealth of styles and history. Obtain as many pictures as possible of buildings in Israel and allow students to choose one to study in depth. There are several books listed at the end of this chapter that contain pictures of Israeli buildings. The following are some of the possible buildings the students might study, and suggestions for making models of the buildings.

The Dome of the Rock

This gold-capped building, the oldest extant Islamic monument, marks the stony outcropping from which, in Muslim tradition, Mohammed leapt to Heaven astride his miraculous horse. The rock is also sacred in Judeo-Christian tradition as the site where Abraham nearly sacrificed Isaac. The dome was built on the site of the Temple of Solomon between 685 and 691 by the caliph (king) of Damascus as a shrine for pilgrims. Christians and Muslims during the Middle Ages believed the Dome to be the actual Temple of Solomon. During the Crusades, the Knights Templar were headquartered at the Dome, and Templar churches in Europe were built to the same plan.

Dome of the Rock Picture
Materials:

- Gold metallic paint
- Paintbrushes
- Blue and white construction paper, cut into small rectangles
- Construction paper
- Scissors and glue

Choose a color for the background. Paint a white octagonal base. Use small blue and white rectangles to create a tile mosaic on the base. Then paint a dome at the top with the gold metallic paint. Tall, narrow arches run all the way around the base of the building.

The Fortress of Masada

This fortress is situated on a rock above the Dead Sea. In the year 74, Jewish resistance fighters—960 men, women, and children—chose to commit mass suicide on this spot rather than yield to besieging Romans. It took a Roman army of 15,000 men nearly two years to overcome the fortress, which fell when the Romans set fire to the wooden walls. Only seven women and children, who hid in a water conduit, survived. The fortress is also known as the site of Herod's palace and is noted for its tiered construction. A three-dimensional representation of this fortress, depicting the ruins and passages of the buildings, might be made with clay or mud.

The Lion's Gate

This gate is also known as the Damascus Gate. This is one of the finest examples of Muslim architecture and is considered to be the most beautiful of the gates of old Jerusalem. It was the royal entrance to the city. A picture of this gate could be drawn on butcher paper and hung at the entrance to the classroom.

The Wailing Wall

Also known as the Western Wall, this is the most sacred Jewish site. It is a relic of the Second Jewish Temple, which was destroyed by the Romans in the year 70. Jews make pilgrimages to pray in front of the walls and even slip prayer requests in the cracks between the stones. Read *The Wailing Wall* by Leonard Everett Fisher.

Wailing Wall Mural
Materials:

- White butcher paper
- Gray or black paint and paintbrushes
- Dried grass
- Glue

Cover a large section of the classroom wall with white butcher paper. As a class, paint lines showing the individual stones and the cracks. Glue dried grass in between the stones, then write a wish on a piece of paper and glue it to the wall.

The Pillar of Absalom

This was popularly believed to be the tomb of Absalom, the son of David. Because Absalom rebelled against his father, devout Jews, Christians, and Muslims, in an unusual blending of religions, would throw stones at this monument whenever they passed. As a result, it was completely covered with stones.

Clay Pillar

Materials:

- Clay
- Small rocks

Shape a model of this conical monument out of clay and cover it with small pebbles.

Minaret Towers

A minaret is a tower which is next to a Muslim mosque, or temple. Five times a day the muezzin, or official who proclaims the call to prayer, climbs to a balcony atop the minaret and sings a chant calling Muslims to prayer. He sings the chant four times, facing each compass direction in turn. Today, many mosques have installed electronic recordings of the call to prayer, replacing the traditional muezzin.

Miniature Minaret

Materials:

- Found items—lids, small boxes, paper towel tubes, oatmeal boxes, and so on
- Wood glue
- Paint
- Paintbrushes

Study pictures of Moslem minarets, then use assorted items to build a minaret tower. Glue the items together with wood glue and paint the model with a neutral color.

LANGUAGE IN ISRAEL

Hebrew was spoken in the Middle East until the third century B.C., after which it faded out of popular use, being used only by rabbis and scholars. In 1880, a Lithuanian Zionist, Eleizer Ben-Yehuda, revived the language, creating a complete vocabulary of more than 30,000 words so that the Jewish people would have a spoken language of their own. Modern Hebrew is the only known colloquial speech based on a written language. *A Child's Picture Hebrew Dictionary* by Ita Meshi and *Alphabet Art* by Leonard Everett Fisher contain the symbols of the Hebrew alphabet.

Hebrew Alphabet Picture

Materials:

- White paper
- Colored felt-tip markers, pens, or watercolors
- Copy of Hebrew alphabet

Copy characters from the Hebrew alphabet from library books onto your paper. At first, simply copy the characters. Then, if you want, try to write your name or a simple proverb in Hebrew.

MUSICAL INSTRUMENTS IN ISRAEL

Israel has a rich musical heritage. Musical instruments feature heavily in art and literature, including many mentions in the Bible and the Koran.

Tambourine

In the Judeo-Christian tradition, Aaron's sister Miriam is mentioned playing the tambourine during the Hebrews' Exodus after the crossing of the Red Sea.

Paper Plate Tambourine

Materials:

- Paper plates
- Yarn
- Small rocks

- Jingle bells or shells
- Hole punch

Punch holes all the around the edges of the plates. Place several small pebbles inside and lace the plates together with the yarn, weaving the bells or shells onto the yarn.

Shofar

The shofar is one of the most ancient instruments in the world. It is made from a ram's horn and is mentioned in the Bible. The musician blows into the small end of the horn, which is capable of blowing only two different notes. It is still used for New Year's and Yom Kippur celebrations in Jewish temples.

Paper Shofar

Materials:

- Construction paper
- Tape

- Crayons

Draw a ripple design on the paper, simulating the rings of a ram's horn. Then roll the paper into a cone and tape it to represent a shofar.

Lyre

The lyre is a stringed instrument, prominent in religious tradition and mythology. It is represented frequently in Israeli artwork.

Cardboard Lyre

Materials:

- Cardboard or tagboard
- Crayons or paint and paintbrushes

- Scissors
- String

Cut a rectangular frame (cut a rectangle and then cut a smaller rectangle from the middle) from the tagboard, curving the corners. Then cut slits along the top and the bottom of the frame and tightly wrap string around it, securing the string in the slits. The lyre can then be colored or painted brown.

JEWISH SYMBOLS

As with most religions, Judaism is full of symbolism. In fact, in many ways, even the Orthodox way of life is a symbol of the Jew's devotion to God. Judaism has many different divisions ranging from the very conservative Hasidic Jews, to the more liberal Reform Jews. There are also Jews who are nonbelievers, and they also often participate in the symbolic activities of Judaism to maintain their ties to their people. A good book about Jewish symbols is *Menorahs, Mezuzas and Other Jewish Symbols* by Miriam Chaikin.

Havdallah Candle

Havdallah is the ceremony for the separation from the Sabbath, the Jewish day of rest. For Havdallah, a special braided candle with two wicks is lit. One wick stands for the regular days of the week, the other for the holiness and joy of the Sabbath. *Shabbat: A Peaceful Island* by Malka Drucker details the importance of the Sabbath.

___

Havdallah Candle Picture

Materials:

- Construction paper
- Drawing materials

Study pictures of Jewish Havdallah candles. Then design and draw your own on paper.

Spice Box

The spice box is another part of the Havdallah ceremony. It can be a simple box or a more elaborate creation designed like a tower or even a flower that opens. Inside, the box contains cloves or other fragrant spices. According to Jewish tradition, people receive an additional soul on the eve of the Sabbath. This extra, or Sabbath, soul departs at the end of Sabbath. At the end of Havdallah, the box is passed around for everyone to sniff for the sake of the Sabbath soul, hoping it will remember the pleasantness of the Sabbath and return again.

___

Cardboard Spice Box

Materials:

- Any small box
- Paint
- Paintbrushes
- Cloves and other fragrant spices
- Scissors
- Tape

Paint your boxes, either with a pretty design or with some symbolism in mind, and let it dry. Then fill the box with spices and tape it closed. With the sharp point of the scissors, poke holes so you can smell the fragrance.

Menorah

When Moses commanded the Israelites to build the Holy Ark for the Ten Commandments, he also commanded them to make an eternal lamp as a symbol of God's eternal presence. Under the guidance of an artist named Bezalel, the people built a large seven-branched candlestick, called a menorah, of beaten gold. They kindled the eternal light in one of its seven cups. Now the menorah is one of the major symbols of the Jewish faith and has come to symbolize the "tree of life."

Menorah Picture

Materials:

- Black construction paper
- Yellow paper
- Scissors
- Glue

Cut a menorah from the black paper, making the design as ornate or simple as you choose. Although most menorahs are shaped like nesting U's, you can experiment and create a new shape for your menorah, keeping in mind that it must have seven candleholders. For example, some menorahs are shaped like the six-pointed star of David. Cut flames from the yellow paper and attach them to the candles.

Mezuzah

These prayer cylinders are attached to the doors of Jewish homes so that as a person enters they may touch the mezuzah, sending a prayer to God. The design can be very simple or intricate.

Cardboard Tube Mezuzah

Materials:

- Toilet paper tubes and cardboard
- Construction paper or paints
- Paintbrushes
- Glue

Glue your paper tubes to the cardboard to form your mezuzah, then decorate it with paper or paints. If you want, write a motto on a piece of paper and slip it inside.

THE HISTORY OF ISRAEL

Most of Israel's culture is rooted in history. During the past 3,000 years, the land has been conquered by various people, including the Israelites, the Babylonians, the Greeks, the Romans, the Arabs, the Turks, and the Crusaders. Because of the influence of the Bible and the Koran, names such as Jordan, Jerusalem, Jericho, and Bethlehem are universally familiar. These names belong to real places in Israel, where one can walk on the same ground as Abraham, Moses, Mohammed, and Jesus.

The Dead Sea Scrolls

In 1947, a nomad shepherd boy made one of the most famous archaeological finds of the twentieth century, discovering the Dead Sea Scrolls in a desert cave. These texts were written more than 2,000 years ago by a small Jewish sect called the Essene. Some of the scrolls contain parts of the Old Testament, while others are special books about the Essene community.

Paper Scrolls

Materials:

- Toilet paper or paper towel tubes
- Paper (12 by 18 inches)
- Scissors
- Glue

Cut the paper so that it is as tall as the cardboard tubes and glue each end of the paper to one of the tubes. Copy characters from the Hebrew alphabet onto the scrolls or try writing a story on the scroll.

Sukkot

Sukkot, the Jewish Festival of the Tabernacles, takes place in October. Then Jewish people build little shelters of branches to recall the living conditions of the ancient Israelites during their years of exile in the desert. A good book about this holiday is *Sukkot: A Time to Rejoice* by Malka Drucker.

___

Toothpick Shelters

Materials:

- Toothpicks or craft sticks
- Glue
- Leaves

Study pictures of Sukkot shelters then build small replicas with your craft sticks. Add small leaves to the sticks to help simulate branches.

THE GEOGRAPHY OF ISRAEL

The geography of Israel is varied and unique. Although mostly desert, the landscape is anything but barren. Israel is full of unusual geological features and oddities.

The Dead Sea

At 1,312 feet below sea level, the Dead Sea is the lowest point on earth. The sea is called "dead" because the ratio of salt to water is 1:3; The water is so salty that only bacteria can live there. Fish that are carried in by the Jordan River die instantly. This high salinity also makes the water so dense bathers do not sink but instead float on the surface. Salt formations crop out of the water like stalagmites. The Dead Sea has historical significance in that the biblical cities of Sodom and Gomorrah are possibly submerged in the southern part of the sea. It also served as a place of refuge for David and King Herod I. A picture of the Dead Sea can be found in *Israel* by Nora Benjamin Kubie.

___

Dead Sea Picture

Materials:

- Blue construction paper
- Salt
- Glue mixed 1:1 (with water)
- Brushes for glue
- Crayons

Brush glue mixture over the bottom of the paper and sprinkle with salt. Create salt pillars like those found in the Dead Sea and then add pictures of bathers floating on the surface with crayons.

Limestone Caves

Israel is home to many beautiful limestone caves, including the Soreq Cave, which many experts say is one of the most beautiful in the world. The stalactites and stalagmites form a wealth of shapes—macaroni, cave corals, and others, surpassing all imagination. For pictures and more information, read *Caves* by Roma Gans.

3-D Cave Picture

Materials:

- Puff paint (equal parts flour, water, and salt)
- Macaroni and other collage items
- Heavy black paper
- Glue
- Watercolors
- Paintbrushes

Make a model of the limestone caves on the black paper, using the puff paint and collage materials to form the stalactites and stalagmites. When the model is dry, paint with thin watercolor wash. Here is a chance for you to let your imagination run wild.

Red Sea Coral Reefs

This reef is considered to be one of the most varied and colorful reefs in the world. Divers come from all over to view the many varieties of life that live in this reef. Pictures of the reef can be found in *The Red Sea and Persian Gulf,* edited by Pat Hargreaves.

Red Sea Reef Picture

Materials:

- Paint, mixed thinly
- Straws
- Glue
- Patterned tissue paper
- Scissors

Choose a pink or red shade of paint and, with a straw, blow the paint over a piece of paper, crossing and interconnecting lines until the paper is covered with curvy lines. This is the reef background. Cut fish from the tissue paper and glue them on top of the reef painting to show the colorful tropical fish darting along the reef.

REFERENCES

Chaikin, Miriam. *Menorahs, Mezuzas and Other Jewish Symbols.* New York: Clarion Books, 1990.

Drucker, Malka. *Shabbat: A Peaceful Island.* New York: Holiday House, 1983.

———. *Sukkot: A Time to Rejoice* New York: Holiday House, 1986.

Fisher, Leonard Everett. *Alphabet Art: Thirteen ABC's from Around the World.* New York: Four Winds Press, 1978.

———. *The Wailing Wall.* New York: Macmillan, 1989.

Gafni, Shlomo S. *The Glory of Jerusalem: An Explorer's Guide.* Jerusalem: Jerusalem Publishing House, 1978.

Gans, Roma. *Caves.* New York: Thomas Y. Crowell, 1976.

Glubok, Shirley. *The Art of Lands in the Bible.* New York: Atheneum, 1966.

Hargreaves, Pat, ed. *The Red Sea and Persian Gulf.* Morristown, NJ: Silver Burdett, 1981.

Kubie, Nora Benjamin. *Israel.* New York: Franklin Watts, 1978.

Maraini, Fosco. *Jerusalem: Rock of Ages.* New York: Harcourt, Brace & World, 1969.

Meshi, Ita. *A Child's Picture Hebrew Dictionary.* New York: Adama Books, 1985.

FURTHER READING

Alpert, Carl. *Israel*. New York: Crescent Books, 1979.

Asimov, Isaac. *Asimov's Guide to the Bible: The Old Testament*. New York: Avon Books, 1968.

Bram, Leon L., ed. *Funk & Wagnalls New Encyclopedia*, vols. 13, 18. New York: Funk & Wagnalls, 1986.

Cone, Molly. *Purim*. New York: Thomas Y. Crowell, 1967.

Domnitz, Myer. *Judaism*, Religions of the World series. New York: Bookwright, 1986.

Goldstein, David. *Jewish Legends*, Library of World Myths and Legends series. New York: Peter Bedrick Books, 1980.

Israel. Amsterdam: Time-Life, 1986.

Johnson, Paul. *Civilizations of the Holy Land*. New York: Atheneum, 1979.

Kertzer, Rabbi Morris N. *What Is a Jew?* New York: Macmillan, 1978.

Lippman, Thomas. *Understanding Islam: An Introduction to the Moslem World*. New York: Harcourt, Brace & World, 1982.

McHenry, Robert, ed. *The New Encyclopaedia Britannica*, vols. 3–8, 10–11. Chicago: Encyclopaedia Britannica, 1992.

Ringgren, Helmer, and Åke V. Ström. *Religions of Mankind: Yesterday and Today*. Philadelphia: Fortress Press, 1967.

Tames, Richard. *The Muslim World*. Morristown, NJ: Silver Burdett, 1982.

Thubron, Colin. *Jerusalem*. Amsterdam: Time-Life Books, 1976.

Zohar, Daniel. *Israel*, The Land and Its People series. London: MacDonald Educational, 1977.

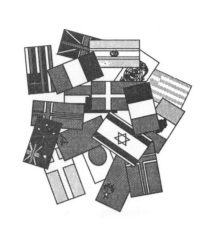

7
EGYPT

Capital: **Cairo**
Government: **Republic (Socialist state)**
Population: **53,170,000**
Area: **385,229 square miles**

Egypt is called the "Land of the Sun," or as Herodotus called it in the fifth century B.C., the "Gift of the Nile." Sixty thousand years ago the Nile River began its yearly cycle of flooding the Egyptian desert, leaving rich soil in the river basin when it receded. This fertile land was very attractive to wandering tribes. By the seventh millennium B.C., people had built settlements, and by 3200 B.C., the country had settled into a system of dynastic rule by pharaohs who held absolute power over a strongly unified government. The government was theocratic; not only was the pharaoh's power absolute, but he was considered to be a god on earth.

This system continued until the Roman conquest in 30 B.C. Until that time, Egypt had the longest unified history of any civilization in the ancient Mediterranean. The people of the country were united by their dependence upon the Nile, and were isolated from outside influences, producing a culture that changed very little over a 3,000-year span.

In ancient Egypt, art in all forms had only one purpose, to serve the king, the state, and the gods. Because the pharaoh was the state as well as the god, all art was dedicated to him.

The Egyptians observed the regular patterns of nature in the annual floods of the Nile and in the cycle of day and night. These patterns were considered to be gifts to the people of Egypt from their gods, and led to the deep respect for order that permeated their culture. Change was not considered important. In Egyptian art, the idea was not to create something that had never been created before, but to create an object that would serve the pharaoh and preserve his essence throughout eternity.

In no other country has there been such a blend of art, history, customs, and beliefs. A unit on Egypt will stimulate the students' imagination and creativity, as well as introduce them to the beauty of art from this ancient land.

HOMES IN ANCIENT EGYPT

The ancient Egyptians' homes were square or oblong, and built of mud or bricks. The homes of the wealthy were often several stories high, with railings on the roof where the family slept when it was hot. The homes opened onto courtyards with carefully tended gardens. Pictures of an ancient Egyptian home can be found in *Life of the Ancient Egyptians* by Eugene Strouhel.

Shoebox House

Materials:

- Shoeboxes
- Brown butcher paper
- Construction paper scraps
- Gray construction paper
- Brown paint
- Paintbrushes
- Scissors
- Glue

Create a model of an ancient village in your classroom by spreading the brown butcher paper on the floor or table. Paint the shoeboxes brown, cut holes for doors and windows. Place them on top of the paper. Cut a railing from brown paper and glue it to the top of the boxes. Create a courtyard with trees, flowers, and a small pond from construction paper scraps and lay it out next to each home. Each home should be surrounded by a wall, which can be made from stiff gray construction paper, folded in half lengthwise. Fold the two open edges back about ¼ inch from the edge and glue those edges to the butcher paper.

Bricks

The ancient Egyptians formed bricks from the mud on the banks of the Nile River. They mixed the mud with straw and then let them dry in the sun.

Mud Bricks

Materials:

- Half-pint milk cartons
- Sand
- Potting soil
- Dried grass
- Water
- Pail for mixing

Mix sand and potting soil in equal amounts in the pail. Add water until mixture is stiff. Throw in some handfuls of dried grass. Scoop mixture into milk cartons. Compress the mud mixture to press the excess water out. Leave the bricks in the sun to dry, checking frequently to pour off the excess water that will gather on top. When the brick is dry, peel off the milk carton.

ANCIENT EGYPTIAN MEASURES OF TIME

The time of day was calculated mainly by Egyptian priests for the observance of divine worship. Common people just looked at the sun in the sky and used that to judge the relative time of day.

Water Clock

The water clock, one of the ways ancient Egyptians devised to measure time, was a conical vessel, about 18 inches tall. It was pierced with a hole near the bottom, and its capacity and size were calculated so that when it was filled with water, it took exactly 12 hours for the water to drain out. Twelve horizontal bands measured the passing hours. The outside of the water clock was ornamented, often with astronomical figures. A picture of a water clock can be found in *Everyday Life in Egypt in the Days of Ramesses the Great* by Pierre Montet.

Flowerpot Water Clock

Materials:

- Large plastic or ceramic flowerpot (for class project) or Styrofoam drinking cups (for individual projects)
- Poster paints or black felt-tip markers

The outside and inside of the pot or cup can be decorated with hieroglyphics. The outside ornamentation should be done in rows all around the pot. Older students might enjoy actually making a working model by plugging up the hole in the bottom of the pot, leaving a much smaller hole for the water to drain out and calculating how much water the pot should have for it to measure 12 hours accurately.

Sundials

As the sun in Egypt is rarely obscured by clouds, sundials were a reliable method for telling time during the day. There were two types of sundials used. In one, the length of the shadow was measured to determine time of day, in the other, the angle at which the shadow fell was measured.

Cardboard Sundial

Materials:

- Cardboard
- Sharpened pencils
- Scissors
- Crayons or colored felt-tip markers

Cut a circle from cardboard. Lay the circle on the ground outside. Stick a pencil through the center of the circle into the ground in the sunlight. Mark where the shadow of the pencil falls every hour. If you want, draw Egyptian hieroglyphics on the sundial.

ANCIENT EGYPTIAN ART

Sculpting and Pottery

Many of the sculptures and pottery of the ancient Egyptians have survived till today. The pyramids of Egypt have brought forth many examples of Egyptian pottery—vases, bowls, cups; as well as samples of statuary. Pictures of Egyptian pottery can be found in *The Art of Ancient Egypt* by Shirley Glubok.

Clay pottery

Materials:

- Self-hardening clay
- Acrylic paints
- Paintbrushes

Using the clay, make a sculpture based on your study of ancient Egyptian pottery. You may wish to form the head of one of the pharaohs or make a vase or a bowl. Let the items dry and then paint them with acrylic paints.

Weaving

Egyptian linens, made from flax, were famous throughout the ancient world. Some linens discovered in tombs were made thousands of years ago but were still as strong as if they had been made in the twentieth century. Today, cloth woven from cotton is one of Egypt's most important manufactured products.

Paper Weaving

Materials:

- Construction paper, various colors
- Tape
- Scissors

Cut several differently colored sheets of paper into strips 9½ inches long. Take a sheet of uncut paper, 9½ by 18 inches. Fold the paper widthwise and cut slits from the folded edge to within 1 inch of the open end. Weave the paper strips through these slits, taping them at the ends to keep the strips in place.

Burlap and Yarn Weaving

Materials:

- Loose-weave burlap
- Yarn and yarn needles

Thread the yarn onto the needle and weave it through the burlap. Pieces of nylon net or mesh such at that used for latch hook designs can be substituted for the burlap.

Shoebox Loom

Materials:

- Shoebox lid
- Yarn
- Yarn needles
- Scissors

Turn shoebox lid open end up. Cut slits on the ridge, about ½ inch apart on the ends of the lid. Wrap yarn around the slits, crossing over the top of the box lid. Tie off the loom yarn. Using a yarn needle, weave yarn through the yarn on the shoebox loom.

Embroidery

The Egyptians today are known for their fine embroidery, often with gold or silver thread on silk. The art of embroidery extends back to ancient Egypt. Tomb pictures show embroidered cloths, hangings, and tents.

Muslin Embroidery

Materials:

- Embroidery thread and needles
- Pencils
- Bleached muslin

Draw a simple design on a piece of muslin with pencil. Then sew over your design with a needle and thread. Make your stitches as small as possible. Ask your teacher to demonstrate a simple cross stitch. (Imagine an X on the fabric; the top two points on the X are labeled A and B, the bottom two are labeled C and D. The needle comes up at A, down at D, up at B, down at C.)

Wigs

Both men and women in ancient Egypt wore wigs made from artificial hair. Men's wigs were short, just covering the ears or possibly dropping to the shoulders, while women's wigs were long. Wigs were often ornamented with braids, jewels, and flowers.

Paper Bag Wigs

Materials:

- Paper grocery bags
- Black yarn, thick and thin
- Ribbons, foil, and other found materials
- Black construction paper
- Scissors
- Glue

Cut off the top half of the grocery bag. Cut a rectangle to frame the face from the front of the bottom half of the bag. Cover this frame with strips of black paper and braided yarn and decorate with other found materials.

EGYPTIAN RECORD KEEPING

The ancient Egyptians were consummate record keepers, a skill facilitated by the invention of paper made from papyrus reeds. What began mostly as a way for priests to keep track of events was soon adopted by the general populace, who kept intricate records detailing every facet of their lives.

Paper Making

It is not certain whether the ancient Egyptians were the first to discover the art of paper making, but they certainly put it to the greatest use. Their paper was made from papyrus, a reed that grows in the swamps surrounding the Nile.

Homemade Paper

Materials:

- Newspaper
- Water and pail
- Screen in a wooden or metal frame (cooling racks for cakes will work in a pinch)
- Rolling pins
- Lint from clothes dryer

Fill the bucket about halfway with water. Tear the newspaper into small shreds and drop them into the water. Throw in several handfuls of lint from the clothes dryer. Stir until the mixture is a pulpy mess and let it soak overnight.

The next day pour off as much of the water as possible and add new water. Stir and let soak. Repeat this for two days.

After two days, spread thick layers of newspaper on a table and put the screen on top. Pour the excess water from the bucket and put the pulp on top of the screen. Cover with more layers of newspaper and then press the rolling pin on top, rolling firmly and evenly. Peel off the top layer of newspaper, and let the screen dry in the sun. When dry, the homemade paper can be peeled off the screen and used for artwork.

Hieroglyphics

Hieroglyphics are the pictorial characters that made up the ancient Egyptian system of writing. Hieroglyphs were first used by the priests to show the acts of various gods and to express religious beliefs. It took archaeologists a long time to decipher the hieroglyphics, but with the discovery and translation of the famous Rosetta Stone, thousands of writings from temple walls, papyrus scrolls, and elsewhere have been translated. There are many samples of Egyptian hieroglyphics available for students to study. Obtain as many examples as possible from the library. A good reference book is *Hieroglyphs: The Writing of Ancient Egypt* by Norma Jean Katan.

Hieroglyphics Picture

Materials:

- Paper
- Pencils or crayons
- Samples of Egyptian hieroglyphics, obtainable from library

After studying samples of Egyptian hieroglyphics, copy some onto your paper. Then, if you want, write a history of your life or a favorite story using hieroglyphics.

Stelae

Stelae are stone columns that were erected and inscribed to tell stories, often detailing the lives of pharaohs or significant events in their lives. The stelae in front of the famous Sphinx recount the dream of Pharaoh Tuthmosis IV in which he was promised the throne of Egypt by the god Harmarchis (identified by some ancient Egyptians with the Sphinx) if he would free Harmarchis' statue's body from the sand that covered it. Pictures of stelae can be found in *Everyday Life in Egypt in the Days of Ramesses the Great* by Pierre Montet.

Cardboard Tube Stele

Materials:

- Crayons
- Toilet paper or paper towel tubes or manila paper rolled and glued into a tube

Study pictures of stelae and hieroglyphics and then tell a story on your stele using hieroglyphs or your own symbols.

EGYPTIAN RITES OF BURIAL

The ancient Egyptians are probably more famous for their rites of burial than anything else. In preparing the bodies of their kings and queens for the afterlife, they left lasting monuments that stand today as testament to their civilization and way of life.

Pyramids

Of the seven wonders of the ancient world, the Great Pyramids and the Sphinx of ancient Egypt are the only ones that have survived. The first pyramid, the Step Pyramid, was built around 2700 B.C. It was designed by Imhotep under the reign of Zoser, who wanted a structure so solid and so enormous that it would survive forever as evidence that the Egyptians were the greatest kingdom in the world. The Great Pyramid of Cheops was built in 2650 B.C. and is made from 2.5 million blocks of stone, some weighing as much as 15 tons. There are many books with pictures of the pyramids, among them *Egypt*, from the Monuments of Civilization series by Claudio Barocas, *The Pyramids* by John Weeks, *The Man-Made Wonders of the World* by Dorothy Turner, and *Pyramid* by David Macauley.

Paper Bag Pyramid

Materials:

- Paper grocery bags
- Newspaper
- Masking tape

Fill paper grocery bags with crumpled newspaper. Fold the tops down and tape them securely to form blocks. Working with other students, form a step pyramid with the blocks. Put about eight blocks together on the floor, put four blocks on top, then two, with one single block on the very top.

Cube Pyramid

Materials:

- Any small block-like material: wooden cubes, toy blocks. (Sugar or Styrofoam cubes can be used with glue if a permanent structure is desired.)

Use the blocks to create a pyramid. If you wish, glue the cubes together.

Pyramid Picture

Materials:

- Brown and gray construction paper
- Crayons or colored felt-tip markers
- Scissors
- Glue

Cut the gray paper into small rectangles to represent bricks and glue them onto brown paper in a pyramid shape. Use crayons or markers to add details to your pyramid scenes. For example, you might choose to depict the making of the pyramids, with slaves dragging the heavy stone blocks into place.

Mazes

Not all tombs were in pyramids. Many were carved into the walls of the Valley of Kings, which was riddled with the tombs of the pharaohs. The inner passages of these tombs and of the pyramids twisted and turned, often leading into blind alleys and dead ends in an effort to confuse grave robbers.

Maze Picture

Materials:

- Gray and brown construction paper
- Glue
- Scissors

Cut the gray paper into rectangles. Lay these rectangles out in a maze on the brown paper. Be sure to have plenty of blind alleys as well as a proper route.

Cube Maze

Materials:

- Tagboard or cardboard
- Small building materials such as blocks (you can use sugar cubes and Styrofoam cubes with glue if you want)

Lay out the interior of a pyramid or a tomb with your cubes, designing mazes, false tunnels, and secret entrances. For added interest, make a map for your pyramid.

Mummies

Mummies represented the cycle of life as well as death in ancient Egypt. The rich and powerful were mummified and buried with treasures so that they would enter the next life with power and status. The preservation techniques of the ancient Egyptians, combined with the hot, dry air, have resulted in countless mummified bodies for us to study today. Two books about mummies are *Mummies and Their Mysteries* by Charlotte Wilcox and *Mummies Made in Egypt* by Aliki Brandenberg.

Toilet Paper Mummies

Materials:

- White toilet paper
- Dolls

Wrap a doll or a fellow student (with his or her permission) in toilet paper to make mummies. Read about mummies to see how your technique differs from that of the ancients.

Paper Doll Mummies

Materials:

- Paper dolls or full-sized figures cut from catalogues
- White construction paper cut into thin strips
- Glue

Glue the strips of paper across the doll figures to make mummies.

Tomb Painting

The wall of burial tombs were painted with elaborate hieroglyphics telling of the life and death of the person buried in the tomb. These paintings often showed scenes of daily life, and birds and other animals were commonplace. One of the most noticeable features today is that the subjects are depicted in profile and in a straight line in relation to each other. The bodies look stiff and unyielding. Pictures of these paintings can be found in *Egypt*, from the Monuments of Civilization series by Claudio Barocas, *The Pyramids* by John Weeks, and *The Arts of Mankind: Painting, Architecture and Music* from the International Geographic Society.

Silhouette Pictures

Materials:

- Bright light source
- Light brown sheet of butcher paper
- Pencils
- Paintbrushes
- Paints

One at a time, have each student assume a position in profile in front of the brown paper. Shine the light on that person and trace around their shadow on the paper. Use paints to add Egyptian-style clothing and hair to the silhouettes.

THE GEOGRAPHY OF EGYPT

Ninety percent of Egypt is made up of desert consisting of rocks, coarse gravel, barren hills, and mountains. There are never any clouds or mists, and all the colors are sharp and well defined. Day after day, the colors never change.

Desert Picture

Materials:

- Blue construction paper
- Sandpaper
- Scissors
- Glue

Construct a desert scene by cutting pyramids, hills, and rocks from the sandpaper and gluing to the blue paper.

Mirages

When traveling mile after mile in the hot desert and suffering from dehydration and heat, the imagination runs wild, creating visions of lush oases and huge bodies of water.

Mirage Picture

Materials:

- Brown construction paper
- Paints, crayons or colored felt-tip markers
- Plastic wrap
- Glue

Imagine that you've been traveling in the desert for hours. Imagine the heat, the thirst. Then draw a mirage on the brown paper. Cover the paper with plastic wrap to produce the shimmering quality of a mirage.

The Nile River

Herodotus said that Egypt was "The Gift of the Nile" for good reason. The river dominates the country. The ancient Egyptians ordered their lives around its seasonal floods, and as it is Egypt's only source of fresh water, its course determined the placement of towns and villages. Three good books about this river are *The Nile: The Story of Pharaohs, Farmers and Explorers* by Ruth Warren, *The Nile*, from the Rivers of the World series by E. Barton Worthington, and *The Nile: Lifeline of Egypt* by Violet Weingarten.

Nile Mural

Materials:

- Blue and brown butcher paper
- Construction paper scraps
- Scissors and glue
- Pencils

Refer to an atlas or other reference sources to make a Nile River mural. Hang the brown butcher paper on the wall and glue a curving blue strip across the middle of the paper to represent the river. Use construction paper to make pyramids, trees, and houses on the sides of the Nile. Be sure to include dahabiehs (described in "Transportation in Egypt," and crocodiles and hippopotamuses (described in "The Animals of Egypt," p. 105).

TRANSPORTATION IN EGYPT

Camel

The camel, with its ability to go for several days without drinking water, was and still is an invaluable animal for desert travel.

Camel Picture

Materials:

- Blue construction paper
- Sandpaper
- Construction paper scraps
- Camel pattern (see fig. 7.1)
- Pencils and crayons
- Scissors and glue

Trace the camel pattern onto sandpaper and cut it out. Glue the shape onto blue paper. With scraps, add bundles and boxes on top of the camel, or draw riders in place. Put all the pictures on the wall and make a caravan traveling across the desert.

Dahabieh

These boats were designed to make the long voyage up and down the Nile. They are actually floating houses, with two eyes painted on the rudder blade at the stern to keep the boat from trouble. They are crescent shaped, with a single mast and an enormous sail for going downstream and rowers for upstream passage (see fig. 7.2). Pictures of dahabiehs can be found in *The Pyramids* by John Weeks and *The Arts of Mankind: Painting, Architecture and Music* from the International Geographic Society.

Dahabieh Picture

Materials:

- Brown and white construction paper
- Drinking straws
- Scissors, stapler, and glue
- Pencils

Cut a shallow crescent shape from the brown paper. Cut a long rectangle, shorter than the crescent, and glue it in the center of the crescent for the house. Glue a drinking straw on top of the house, and cut a large triangular sail from white paper and glue it to the straw. Put two smaller rectangles, with a square window cut out of the top of each, at the front and back of the boat. Draw eyes on the back of the boat on either side. Place your boat on the blue portion of the Nile River mural.

(Text continues on page 105.)

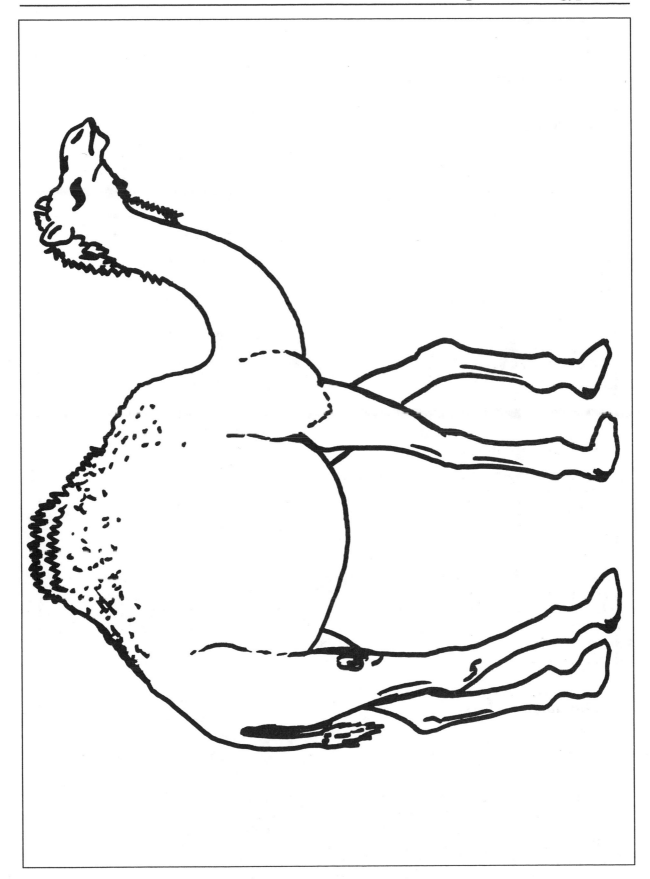

Fig. 7.1.

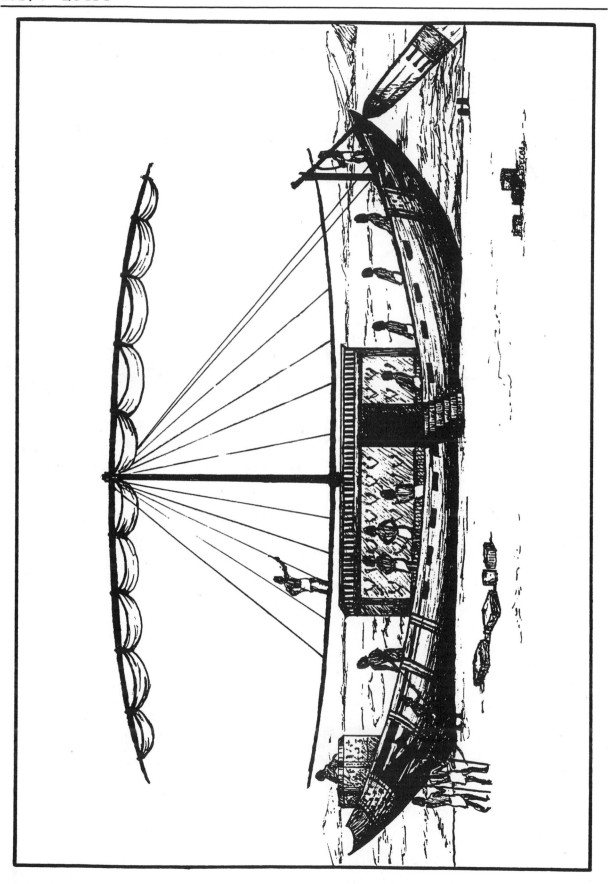

Fig. 7.2.

THE ANIMALS OF EGYPT

Crocodiles

In some parts of Egypt crocodiles were feared, and killed on sight. In other parts they were worshipped and kept as pampered pets, decorated with necklaces and jeweled earrings.

Crocodile Picture

Materials:

- Green construction paper
- Dried green peas
- Pencils
- Scissors
- Glue
- Crocodile patterns (see figs. 7.3 and 7.4)

Choose a crocodile pattern and trace it onto green paper. Cut the shape out and glue green peas onto it to represent bumpy skin. Place your crocodile figure along the sides of the Nile on the mural.

Hippopotamuses

The Egyptians often encounter these animals in the swamps of the Nile River. They have long been hunted for their meat, fat, and ivory teeth. The Egyptians prize fat and one hippo can yield up to 200 pounds of fat.

Hippo Picture

Materials:

- White construction paper
- Scissors
- Glue
- Pencils
- Blue and green watercolor paint
- Paintbrushes
- Black or gray crayons
- Hippopotamus pattern (see fig. 7.5)

Cut out the hippopotamus pattern and trace it onto white paper. Color your hippo black or gray. Use blue and green watercolors to paint water and reeds around and over the hippo. When your picture is dry, cut the hippo out and place it on the sides of the Nile River on the mural.

(Text continues on page 109.)

Fig. 7.3.

Fig. 7.4.

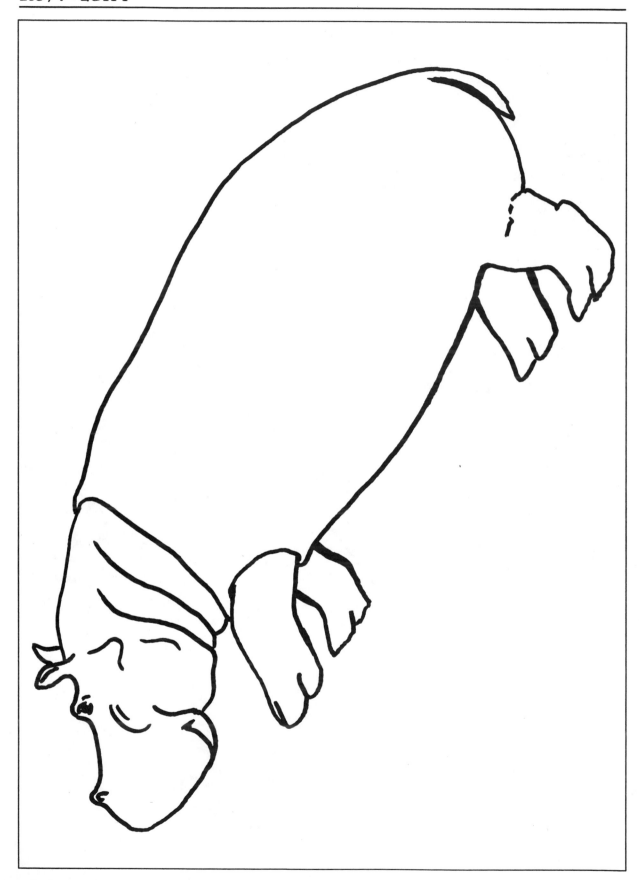

Fig. 7.5.

REFERENCES

The Arts of Mankind: Painting, Architecture and Music. Englewood Cliffs, NJ: International Geographic Society, 1962.

Barocas, Claudio. *Egypt*, Monuments of Civilization series. New York: Grossett & Dunlop, 1972.

Brandenberg, Aliki. *Mummies Made in Egypt.* New York: Thomas Y. Crowell, 1979.

Glubok, Shirley. *The Art of Ancient Egypt.* New York: Atheneum, 1966.

Katan, Norma Jean. *Hieroglyphs: The Writing of Ancient Egypt.* New York: Atheneum, 1981.

Macauley, David. *Pyramid.* Boston: Houghton Mifflin, 1975.

Montet, Pierre. *Everyday Life in Egypt in the Days of Ramesses the Great.* Philadelphia: University of Pennsylvania Press, 1981.

Strouhel, Eugene. *Life of the Ancient Egyptians.* London: Opus, 1992.

Turner, Dorothy. *The Man-Made Wonders of the World.* Minneapolis, MN: Dillon, 1986.

Warren, Ruth. *The Nile: The Story of Pharaohs, Farmers and Explorers.* New York: McGraw-Hill, 1968.

Weeks, John. *The Pyramids.* Cambridge, England: Cambridge University Press, 1971.

Weingarten, Violet. *The Nile: Lifeline of Egypt.* Champaign, IL: Garrard, 1964.

Wilcox, Charlotte. *Mummies and Their Mysteries.* Minneapolis, MN: Carolrhoda Books, 1993.

Worthington, E. Barton. *The Nile*, Rivers of the World series. Morristown, NJ: Silver Burdett, 1978.

FURTHER READING

Bram, Leon L., ed. *Funk & Wagnalls New Encyclopedia*, vol. 9. New York: Funk & Wagnalls, 1986.

Brander, Bruce. *The River Nile.* Washington, DC: National Geographic Society, 1966.

Brier, Bob. *Egyptian Mummies: Unraveling the Secrets of an Ancient Art.* New York: W. Morrow, 1994.

Koenig, Vivian E. *The Ancient Egyptians: Life in the Nile Valley.* Brookfield, CT: Millbrook Press, 1992.

Malek, Jaromir, ed. *Egypt*, Cradles of Civilization series. Norman: University of Oklahoma Press, 1993.

McHenry, Robert, ed. *The New Encyclopaedia Britannica*, vols. 3–4, 8. Chicago: Encyclopaedia Britannica, 1992.

Oliphant, Margaret. *The Egyptian World.* New York: Warwick Press, 1989.

Patrick, Richard. *All Color Book of Egyptian Mythology.* Seacus, NJ: Chartwell Books, 1989.

Stead, Miriam. *Egyptian Life.* Cambridge, MA: Harvard University Press, 1986.

8

RUSSIA

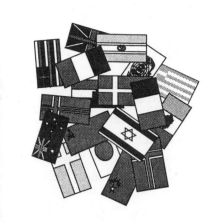

Capital: Moscow
Government: Federal Republic
Population: 148,041,000
Area: 6,592,800 square miles

The Russian culture is imaginative and beautiful, combining elements from many different ethnic groups, reflecting the Russian history of frequent invasions by other cultures. Russian geography is composed mainly of level lowlands, making it easy to invade. The land was first inhabited by Asians, who were conquered by the Goths, who were conquered by the Huns, and so on, until Peter the Great began a series of territorial acquisitions resulting in the establishment of the Russian Empire in 1721. This empire lasted until the Russian Revolution of 1917 and the subsequent formation of the Soviet Union (USSR).

The successive invasions by so many different groups resulted in the frequent addition of new cultural elements. In addition to many types of unique folk art, the most important artforms in Russian and Soviet cultural life have historically been literature, music, and dance. Famous Russian writers include Aleksandr Pushkin, Leo Tolstoy, Fyodor Dostoyevsky, Anton Chekhov, Aleksandr Solzhenitsyn, and Boris Pasternak. Famous composers include Peter Ilich Tchaikovsky, Sergey Rachmaninoff, Igor Stravinsky, and Sergey Prokofief. The Bolshoi Theater was organized in the mid-1770s and Western dance has been highly influenced by Russian ballet.

Under the Soviet Union, which was a communist regime, artists were severely restricted. State approval was required for publication of writings or display of artwork. For example, Nobel-prize winner Boris Pasternak published *Dr. Zhivago* in Italy in 1957 but it was not published in the Soviet Union until 1987.

However, the increased emphasis of the Soviet government on education resulted in a people so starved for quality art and literature that a black market in arts and ideas developed. Books that were refused license by the Soviet government spread through illicit, typewritten copies. The poet-actor-balladeer Vladimir Vysotsky, who sang of pain and political disillusionment, developed a nationwide following through word of mouth and black-market tape recordings of his concerts in bars.

With the collapse of the Soviet Union, of which the country of Russia was only a single part, there are signs that the Russian government is easing its restrictions on the arts and literature. It is a tribute to Soviet artists that, by drawing on the wealth of cultural traditions within the widely diverse Soviet Union, they were able to keep innovation alive while deprived of contact with the outside world and while they were so strictly censored.

110

THE RUSSIAN HOME AND FAMILY

Since the days of the Russian Empire, the home has been the traditional center of Russian life. Family life is very important and great effort is put into making the home comfortable and attractive.

Wooden Houses

Russia is often called a nation of woodcutters. Entire towns were constructed of wood, and carpenters spoke of "cutting" rather than "building" a town. Both rich and poor lived in wooden houses. The construction style was very simple: logs were piled one on top of another until the house was the desired size, often three stories tall. The walls and roofs were finished, and openings were cut for windows and doorways that were then set off with carved trim or balconies. A picture of a traditional Russian home can be found in *Take a Trip to Russia* by Keith Lye.

Refrigerator Box House

Materials:

- Refrigerator box
- Brown and black paint and paintbrushes
- Brown butcher paper
- Glue or tape

Turn the refrigerator box on its side. Cut out windows and a door and paint the sides of the box brown. When the paint is dry, add black lines to simulate logs. Attach brown butcher paper to the top of the box for the roof.

Milk Carton House

Materials:

- Cardboard milk cartons, any size
- Cardboard
- Construction paper, various colors, especially brown
- Scissors
- Glue

Cut a door and window out of the milk carton. Cut brown paper into small strips and glue them to the sides of the carton to form log walls. Glue large brown rectangles to tops of cartons to form the roof. Glue the bottom of the milk carton to the cardboard base.

Log House Picture

Materials:

- Scissors
- Construction paper: white, brown, and other colors
- Glue

Cut brown paper into strips. With the strips, create a log cabin on the white paper, using other colors to add details such as windows, doors, trees, flowers, and so on.

Carved Motifs

Beautifully carved motifs hundreds of years old are still seen on the window shutters of houses along the Volga River. Many of the designs echo those made for the bows of wooden river boats, which are no longer seen. Flowers, fruit, birds, and animals are common motifs used to decorate household shutters. Pictures of these motifs can be found in *Russia: Then and Now*, edited by Mary M. Rodgers, Tom Streissguth, and Colleen Sexton.

Cardboard Motif

Materials:

- Brown construction paper
- Cardboard
- Poster paints
- Pencils
- Scissors
- Glue
- Paintbrushes

Draw a simple design onto cardboard and cut it out. Trace around cardboard shape onto brown paper and cut out. Glue brown paper cutout onto the cardboard cutout. Paint your motif design.

Domovoy

Every peasant home had its own house spirit, called a *domovoy*, who was an old dwarf living either under the threshold or in the stove of the house. The domovoy did not like to be seen and punished people for curiosity or neglect. Families took care of their domovoy, setting out food for it and treating it with respect. They even took their domovoy with them if they moved, gathering some of the ashes from the stove to take to their new home for the domovoy.

Domovoy Picture

Materials:

- Paper
- Colored pencils, crayons, colored felt-tip markers, or paints

Design your own personal domovoy for your house.

Double Windows

To help keep out the chill of the cold Russian winters, double windows were installed in Russian homes in October and not removed till May. Salt or sand was put between the panes and arranged in fanciful designs, or artificial flowers were planted inside. Each home arranged their windows differently and tours were made through the towns to see how the windows were decorated.

Double Window Picture

Materials:

- Waxed paper
- Salt or sand
- Flowers cut from construction paper
- Steam iron

Arrange salt or sand in a design on a piece of waxed paper. Add flowers cut from construction paper. Place another sheet of waxed paper over design. Have your teacher press the waxed paper sheets carefully with a hot iron until the wax melts, sealing the sheets together.

RUSSIAN CLOTHING

Like everything else Russian, the traditional clothing is rich in design. Russian women were famous the world over for their embroidery, using finely colored threads, gold, silver, pearls, jewels, and other items.

Chirinka

This elaborately embroidered handkerchief was made for a Russian woman's wedding. It was decorated with pearls and colored threads. The bride held it in her hand when she went to church.

Embroidered Handkerchief

Materials:

- White handkerchiefs
- Embroidery needles
- Embroidery thread in many colors
- Small beads

Create an embroidered handkerchief by attaching small beads and using different colors of thread to create a design. You may embroider freestyle or create a specific design. Red was a common color used in chirinkas, and common designs were of the sun, birds, flowers, and trees.

Lace

In the 1800s Russian lace was sold in Paris as *guipure russe*. The lace was made from gold and silver thread and was famous throughout Europe.

Paper Lace

Materials:

- Gold or silver foil wrapping paper
- Scissors

Fold and cut the wrapping paper into intricate designs as you would if you were making paper snowflakes.

Kokoshniki

The *kokoshniki* was a headdress worn by Russian women. The kokoshniki varied from region to region and came in many shapes and sizes. One could tell where a woman came from by looking at the style of her headdress. The headdresses were heavily embroidered with gold and silver threads, pearls, and jewels; some women attached feathers and flowers, while others even attached mirrors or veils to their headdresses.

Paper Headdress

Materials:

- Construction paper
- Glue
- Collage materials (feathers, aluminum foil, tissue paper, painted pasta, yarn, and so on)

- Stapler
- Scissors

Measure construction paper to fit around crown of your head, stapling two pieces together if necessary. Cut and staple the edges together to form the base of your headdress. Cut a second piece of paper in a design and staple it to the top of the headband to form the top of the headdress. Decorate with collage materials.

RUSSIAN ARCHITECTURE

The Russian love of beauty and enchantment is never seen more clearly than in their architecture. Their cathedrals and palaces look like fairy castles. The Russians are masterful users of color and motif throughout their architecture.

Byzantine Domes

Byzantine domes are a favorite motif in Russian buildings. St. Basil's Cathedral in Moscow has eight domes, all different and interconnected inside. Pictures of Byzantine domes can be found in *Russia: Then and Now*, edited by Mary M. Rodgers, et al.; *Take a Trip to Russia* by Keith Lye; and *Land of the Firebird: The Beauty of Old Russia* by Suzanne Massie.

Dome Picture

Materials:

- Construction paper
- Tissue paper
- Metallic gold paint
- Scissors
- Glue
- Paintbrushes

Look at pictures of Byzantine domes. Cut a building from construction paper and glue it onto a white or blue background. Design domes to top your building, using colored construction paper, colored tissue paper, and metallic gold paint to create beautiful dome designs.

Potemkin Villages

Shortly after Catherine the Great's Field Marshall, Grigory Potemkin, masterminded the annexation of the Crimea in 1783, he took the empress on an inspection trip down the Dnieper River to show her the richness of the newly acquired land. On display for her to see were newly built, prosperous towns. In actuality, the towns were only facades, built to fool the empress, although this was not as deceptive as people first thought because the towns were built later, after Catherine's tour.

3-D Village Mural

Materials:

- Large sheet of butcher paper
- Crayons or colored felt-tip markers
- Paints
- Paintbrushes
- Empty cereal boxes
- Construction paper
- Scissors
- Glue

Cover the cereal boxes with paper and paint a cottage on each. Decorate and glue each box onto the butcher paper mural. Add the details of a village with crayons, colored felt-tip markers, paints, and construction paper.

CYRILLIC ALPHABET

The Russian alphabet was named after Saint Cyril, the Greek missionary who helped convert ancient Russia to Christianity in the ninth century. The alphabet was originally derived from the Greek alphabet by Saint Cyril and his brother Saint Methodius. A copy of the Cyrillic alphabet can be found in *Alphabet Art* by Leonard Everett Fisher.

Cyrillic Alphabet Picture

Materials:

- Paper
- Copy of Cyrillic alphabet
- Pens or pencils

Practice copying the letters of the Cyrillic alphabet. If you want, try writing a simple story or letter using the Cyrillic alphabet.

RUSSIAN FAIRY TALES AND SYMBOLS

The Russian culture has an extensive background of folk tales. Symbols from their folk and fairy tales can be seen frequently in their artwork, clothing, and architecture. Several Russian folk tales can be found in *Stories from Old Russia* by Edward W. and Marguerite P. Dolch, *Favorite Fairy Tales Told in Russia* by Virginia Haviland, *The Falcon Under the Hat* by Guy Daniels, and *How the Moolah Was Taught a Lesson and Other Tales from Russia* by Estelle Titiev and Lila Pargment.

Matrioshka

The *matrioshka* is the Russian wooden nesting doll. The wooden doll opens to reveal a smaller doll. That doll also contains a smaller replica, and so on. All of the dolls in a set have the same theme, although colors and decorations may be different. The first matrioshka was made in the late nineteenth century; the most famous ones today come from Polkhov-Maideon in Gorky.

There are many legends about the origin of the doll. In one legend, the matrioshka comes from a goddess named Jumala in the foothills of Ural. The Vikings tried unsuccessfully to find this goddess, who was reputed to be made from pure gold. According to the chronicles, Jumala was a statue with a hollow interior containing three figures, one inside the other. She hid in an ancient sacred forest allowing no one to see her. As people passed the forest, they would leave offerings for her. The offerings were collected, and when there was enough gold, it was melted down to create another new shell for the goddess. Today matrioshka dolls come in many designs and sizes.

Matrioshka Picture

Materials:

- Construction paper
- Colored felt-tip markers
- Scissors

Choose a theme for your matrioshka, for example, a peasant girl, a young boy, an animal, and so on. Cut the paper into eight rectangles of decreasing size and color a variation of your matrioshka on each rectangle.

Fairy Tale Characters

Characters from Russian folk tales are frequently depicted in Russian folk art. Students will enjoy hearing Russian folk tales and drawing the characters on paper. Popular characters include:

Baba Yaga

Baba Yaga is a wicked witch. She lives in a house built on rooster's feet that runs after her victims. Baba Yaga flies through the air in a mortar, rowing with a pestle.

Kaschei the Immortal

This is an evil sorcerer who hides a needle that is the secret to his power inside an egg.

The Firebird

This beautiful bird has feathers of scarlet and gold, and crystal eyes.

Grandfather Frost

Grandfather Frost brings the winter every year. His breath makes the icicles and his hair is a blizzard.

RUSSIAN ART

Russian art is colorful, richly bedecked with jewels, and often gilded. Much of the artwork is religious, and Russians incorporate art into their everyday lives.

Icons

These religious paintings of saints and religious figures were often embellished with jewels, gold, and silver. Frames were encrusted with jewels, often commanding more attention than the painting itself. Pictures of icons can be found in *Land of the Firebird: The Beauty of Old Russia* by Suzanne Massie.

Icon Picture

Materials:

- White paper
- Paint
- Metallic gold paint
- Colored paper
- Paintbrushes
- Glue
- Pearl pasta that has been spray painted bright colors, including gold

Choose a subject for your icon and paint a portrait of that person. When the paint is dry, glue painted pearl pasta where appropriate in your painting and add trim with gold metallic paint. Mount your painting on colored paper, leaving a 1- to 2-inch border around the edges. Embellish the border with metallic gold paint and colored pearl pasta.

Lubki

These wood block prints date from the sixteenth century and were popular throughout Russia. They often poked fun at people or events, and were hand colored in three or four bright colors. These printing techniques disappeared during the Russian revolution and have not been seen since.

Lubki Picture

See the techniques for printing in chapter 1 (see "Block Printing," pp. 9-10) for printing activities. Once the printed picture has dried, paint between the lines with bright colors.

Painted Tiles

Russians used painted tiles to decorate their stoves, fireplaces, roofs, and the walls of churches. The tiles were bright and cheerful. Floral and herbal motifs were common.

Painted Tiles

Materials:

- Brightly colored paint
- Ceramic tiles (often obtainable from builder's or floor stores)
- Paintbrushes

Paint bright designs on a tile.

DECORATED EGGS

In Russia, eggs symbolize life and hope. Early Christians used the egg as a symbol of the Resurrection and life beyond the grave. Nowhere were eggs used in celebration more than Russia. Millions of eggs were sold at Easter. They were given as gifts, used in games, and eaten. Eggs of all sizes were used, from the tiny wren egg to the giant ostrich egg.

Red-Dyed Eggs

Eggs dyed red were given to the parish priest on Easter in recognition of the Resurrection. Commoners carried red-dyed eggs in their hands wherever they went for several days after Easter.

Colored Eggs

Materials:

- Red food coloring
- Water and vinegar
- Hollowed-out eggshells (made by poking a hole in each end of a raw egg and blowing out the contents)

Pour water in bowl or cup. Add a spoonful of vinegar and a few drops of red food coloring. Then dip the eggshells into the solution.

Decorated Eggs

Decorated eggs were given as gifts to friends, loved ones, and acquaintances.

Decorated eggs

Materials:

- Wax crayons
- Food colors
- Vinegar
- Water
- Hollowed-out eggshells (made by poking a hole in each end of a raw egg and blowing out the contents)

Carefully color a design on surface of your eggshell with a wax crayon. Pour water into a bowl or cup. Add a spoonful of vinegar and several drops of food coloring. Dip the colored egg into the mixture. The crayon shines through the dye, creating a beautiful effect.

Fabergé Eggs

These beautiful Imperial Easter Eggs were made for the last two tsars of Russia, Alexander III and Nicholas II, under the supervision of master jeweler Peter Carl Fabergé. Probably 55 eggs were created, of which 43 are still known to exist today. The design was always a careful secret. When the Bolsheviks "nationalized" the House of Fabergé (made it the property of the government), the jeweler retired, taking the secret of how he created his magnificent eggs with him to the grave. Pictures of these eggs can be found in *Fabergé Imperial Eggs and Other Fantasies* by Hermione Waterfield.

Replica Fabergé Egg

Materials:

- Narrow ribbon, lace, gold or metallic braid
- Sequins, beads
- Small Styrofoam ball (that will fit inside egg)
- Pencils
- Tiny artificial flowers
- Nail scissors
- Paper towel or toilet paper tube
- Glitter
- Cotton
- Glue
- Hollowed-out eggshells (made by poking a hole in each end of a raw egg and blowing out the contents)

Draw an oval window on the side of the egg with a pencil. Trace over the pencil line with glue and allow it to dry. Carefully insert the point of a pair of nail scissors into the glue line and cut along the glue line. Remove the window created in the eggshell.

Decorate the outside of the egg with sequins, glitter, ribbon, and other trim. Cut the Styrofoam ball in half. Stick artificial flowers into the flat part of the Styrofoam ball. Apply glue to the rounded end and stick cotton to the glue. Put a thick layer of glue in bottom of decorated egg and put the Styrofoam ball on top. The cotton helps make the ball stick inside the egg.

Make an egg stand from a cardboard ring cut from the paper towel tube. Decorate the tube with sequins and other materials.

SCIENCE AND TECHNOLOGY IN RUSSIA

The Russians (later as Soviets) were leaders in the fields of science and technology, and at least two of their achievements have had a direct influence on technology in the United States.

Roller Coasters

Fun-loving Russians made the most of their cold, snowy winters. Not having hills to sled on in their lowland country, they created ice hills at Christmas and festival times and people from all walks of life enjoyed sledding down them. The slides were so popular that in the summer, the hills were converted to polished wood and people slid down them on scraps of carpet. In the late nineteenth century, mechanized carts were developed. For some reason, in Russia these rides were called "American hills," while in the United States, we know them as "roller coasters."

Roller Coaster Mural

Materials:

- Roll of butcher or shelf paper
- Construction paper
- Craft sticks
- Crayons
- Glue
- Scissors

Hang a length of butcher paper on the wall. Using craft sticks, create the frame of a wooden roller coaster. Add cars cut from construction paper. People and other details may be added with paper or crayons.

Sputnik I

The first artificial satellite of earth was launched by the Soviets in October 1957, setting off a fast and furious era of scientific study in the United States. The Soviets also had several other firsts in space history, including Luna 2 in September 1959, which was the first lunar probe to hit the moon.

Model Satellite

Materials:

- Boxes
- Aluminum foil
- Toothpicks
- Other collage materials
- Scissors
- Glue

Create models of satellites by covering boxes with aluminum foil and gluing toothpicks and other collage materials over surface.

Soviet Cosmonauts

The Soviet space program was full of firsts. The first manned orbital flight, Vostok 1, took place in April 1961. Yuri Gagarin was the cosmonaut on that flight. In June 1963, Valentina Tereshkova flew on the Vostok 6 mission and became the first woman in space. Alexei A. Leonov, in March 1965, became the first human to walk in space.

Paper Bag Space Helmet

Materials:

- Paper grocery bags
- Paper plates
- Collage items
- Stapler
- Scissors
- Glue

Staple a paper plate to the front of a grocery bag, near the top. Cutting through both layers, cut a rectangle for eyes. Glue collage materials onto sack to make it look like a cosmonaut helmet.

REFERENCES

Daniels, Guy. *The Falcon Under the Hat.* New York: Funk & Wagnalls, 1969.

Dolch, Edward W., and Marguerite P. Dolch. *Stories from Old Russia.* Champaign, IL: Garrard, 1964.

Fisher, Leonard Everett. *Alphabet Art: Thirteen ABC's from Around the World.* New York: Four Winds Press, 1978.

Haviland, Virginia. *Favorite Fairy Tales Told in Russia.* Boston: Little, Brown, 1961.

Lye, Keith. *Take a Trip to Russia.* London: Franklin Watts, 1982.

Massie, Suzanne. *Land of the Firebird: The Beauty of Old Russia.* New York: Simon & Schuster, 1980.

Rodgers, Mary M., Tom Streissguth, and Colleen Sexton, eds. *Russia: Then and Now.* Minneapolis, MN: Lerner, 1992.

Titiev, Estelle, and Lila Pargment. *How the Moolah Was Taught a Lesson and Other Tales from Russia.* New York: Dial Press, 1976.

Waterfield, Hermione. *Fabergé Imperial Eggs and Other Fantasies.* New York: Bramhall House, 1980.

FURTHER READING

Bram, Leon L., ed. *Funk & Wagnalls New Encyclopedia,* vol. 23. New York: Funk & Wagnalls, 1986.

McHenry, Robert, ed. *The New Encyclopaedia Britannica,* vols. 3–4, 9–10, 12. Chicago: Encyclopaedia Britannica, 1992.

Morey, George. *Soviet Union,* The Land and Its People series. Morristown, NJ: Silver Burdett, 1975.

Sinclair, Marianne. *Russia.* London: Marshall Cavendish, 1970.

Walker, Martin. *The Waking Giant: Gorbachev's Russia.* New York: Pantheon Books, 1986.

Wallace, Robert. *Rise of Russia.* New York: Time-Life, 1967.

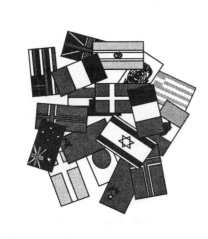

9 FRANCE

Capital: **Paris**
Government: **Republic**
Population: **56,411,000**
Area: **210,206 square miles**

The French people take great pride in their uniqueness and their traditions, and so they should. They are fiercely individualistic as a people and have great pride in their nation and in their cultural achievements.

This individualism extends to the art world, for the French are masters in all fields of art. Artists and fashion designers alike dream of studying in Paris, as do writers and poets. The French are trendsetters, eagerly embracing new ideas. Art to them is a means of expressing their individuality, of setting themselves apart from the rest of the world. It extends into all areas of life; the homes they live in, the food they eat, even the buildings for their animals are works of art.

Culture is so important to the French that in 1959 they established a Ministry of Culture to preserve their cultural heritage. In recent years, this ministry has made several controversial attempts to protect French culture from outside influences by resisting the addition of non-French words to the French language and other methods.

France is a land of beauty in its landscapes and buildings, and a land of charm and romance. A unit on France will introduce students to some of the world's most influential art styles and artists, to innovations in science, and to a courageous, fun-loving, and creative people.

PARIS

France wouldn't be France without Paris, city of artists, poets, and lovers. In 2,000 years Paris has grown from a tiny fishing village on the Seine River to become one of the world's most beloved cities.

The Eiffel Tower

The tower was built by Gustave Eiffel for the Great Exhibition of 1889. At 984 feet, it is the tallest building in Paris. People come from all over the world to climb the 2,710 steps to the top. Besides being a tourist attraction, the tower is also a major telecommunications center. Pictures of the Eiffel Tower can be found in *France: The Crossroads of Europe* by Susan Balerdi and *France*, from The Land and Its People series by Danielle Lifshitz.

Eiffel Tower Picture

Materials:

- Toothpicks or craft sticks
- Picture of the Eiffel Tower
- Paper
- Glue

Using toothpicks or craft sticks, create a picture of the Eiffel Tower on a piece of paper. If you feel really ambitious, try building a three-dimensional model of the tower with craft sticks or toothpicks.

Arc de Triomph

The *Arc de Triomph* is second only to the Eiffel Tower as Paris's leading tourist attraction. The giant carved arch was ordered by French emperor Napoleon Bonaparte in 1806 as a giant altar to the nation, but it was not completed until 30 years later! Pictures of the arch can be found in *All Paris* by Giovanni Magi.

Appliance Box Arc de Triomph

Materials:

- Large box
- Paint
- Construction paper or butcher paper
- Paintbrush
- Knife
- Glue

Cut two large arches from the front and back of the box. Cover the box with construction paper or butcher paper and paint it with the markings of the Arc de Triomph.

Notre Dame Cathedral

This cathedral, built more than 700 years ago, is considered to be one of the most beautiful in the world. It is said that when Louis VIII halted construction on the cathedral during the crusades, the stonecutters continued their work secretly by night. The two towers on the front of the cathedral flank a great stained glass wheel, while eerie stone gargoyles keep watch from the towers. Pictures of the cathedral can be found in *The Seine* by C. A. R. Hills and *Passport to France* by Dominique Norbrook.

3-D Picture of Notre Dame

Materials:

- Salt dough (equal parts flour, salt, and water mixed together)
- Photocopies of front of cathedral
- Cookie sheets
- Paint
- Paintbrushes

Lay the salt dough on top of a picture of the cathedral and mold it into the shape of the cathedral. Let the dough dry. When hard and dry, paint your model.

THE RIVER SEINE

Although most people associate the Seine River with Paris, that is only an 8 mile section of the river's 485 miles. A journey from its source in Burgundy to the English Channel is one of charm and beauty. Read *The Seine* by C. A. R. Hills for more information and for pictures.

Create a mural of a trip down the Seine on the walls of the classroom. Cut out a river from blue butcher paper, tape it to the walls, and decorate it with scenes including many of the following elements.

Vineyards

France produces the most famous wines in the world; some of the finest French wines are made from grapes grown in vineyards near the mouth of the Seine.

Vineyard Picture

Materials:

- Green construction paper
- Purple paint
- Scissors

Cut the construction paper into strips 4 inches wide. Press your thumb into purple paint and then on the strips. Hang the strips together on the wall to create a vineyard.

Outdoor Laundries

Away from the cities in rural parts of France there are still women who prefer to wash their clothes in the pure waters of the Seine. Along the upper part of the river are several outdoor laundries, built so that the water flows through the building. A good picture of one of these laundries can be found in *The Seine* by C. A. R. Hills.

Laundry Mural

Materials:

- Butcher paper
- Red construction paper
- Black paint and paintbrushes
- Crayons
- Scissors
- Glue

Cut a long, low building from the butcher paper. Paint stone markings on the side of the building with black paint. Use red construction paper rectangles for the tile roof. Add drawings of women kneeling to wash their clothes at the stream.

Barges

At Troyes, the Seine is deep enough for freight-bearing barges. These have traveled up and down the river for centuries. Years ago, they were propelled by sails and oars, now they have gasoline or diesel engines or are pulled by tugboats.

Shoebox Barge

Materials:

- Shoebox lids
- Construction paper
- Magazines
- Scissors and glue

Turn your shoebox lid into a flat barge. Add details with construction paper cutouts or magazine pictures to represent the cargo.

Eels

The Seine passes through the village of Nogent, which is famous for the eels that are trapped in the river there.

Eel Picture

Materials:

- Black or gray construction paper
- Scissors

Cut squiggly eels from the construction paper and display them on the wall.

Bookstalls

Along the quays on the Left Bank of the Seine in Paris are long wooden boxes clamped to the wall above the embankment filled with old books and prints. During bad weather, the stalls are closed, but when it is pleasant, they are open-air bookstores. The bookstalls have been on the quays for hundreds of years and many people stop to browse and buy.

Picture of Bookstalls

Materials:

- Construction paper
- Crayons

Using one sheet of construction paper for each stall, design a bookstall, using crayons to draw the covers of books in the stall. Put your bookstall on the wall as part of the growing Seine River mural.

Bridges

There have been bridges over the Seine for many centuries. They have been made from stone, wood, cast iron, and steel. Until 1800, the bridges had shops and houses on them. Collapses were frequent, though, some caused by fire, some by flood, some by the tall sails of boats passing underneath. Now it is against the law to build a building on a bridge. Pictures of the bridges can be found in *The Seine* by C. A. R. Hills and *Terence Conran's France* by Terence Conran.

Posterboard Bridges

Materials:

- Posterboard
- Colored felt-tip markers or paints and paintbrushes
- Scissors

Cut a bridge from posterboard and decorate it with markers or paints, keeping in mind the beauty of the Parisian bridges.

The Pantheon

Sainte-Genevieve is one of the patron saints of Paris and is considered to be its guardian angel. Genevieve lived in the time of Attila the Hun. A devout Christian, she prayed that the Huns would bypass Paris as they advanced across France. When the Huns did not invade Paris, the people believed that Genevieve's prayers had saved them.

Later, Paris did come under siege. The Seine was controlled by enemy tribes both above and below Paris, and the people were in danger of starving. Genevieve chose several men to attempt to get past the opposing forces. They muffled their oars and rowed up the river one night as a heavy mist hid them. They reached the city of Troyes, loaded their boat with wheat, and returned to feed the hungry people of Paris.

A hill on the left bank of the Seine is named for Genevieve and the people of Paris planned a church, the Pantheon, in her honor. Instead, the Pantheon became a tomb for many famous Frenchmen (Rousseau, Voltaire, and Victor Hugo, among others). The wall paintings of the Pantheon, however, tell the story of Sainte-Genevieve and it is these that people come to see. Pictures of the Pantheon can be found in *France*, from the Life World Library series by D. W. Brogan and *All Paris* by Giovanni Magi.

Picture of the Pantheon

Materials:

- Butcher paper
- Paints and paintbrushes

Paint the Pantheon on the paper and beside it paint a mural with scenes from Genevieve's life.

Chalk Country

Near where the Seine flows into the English Channel is chalk country. All this part of France has a chalk foundation, and hills rising from the river show patches of white chalk. There are caves in some of the chalk cliffs with people living in them, and there is even an underground church. Only the steeple is visible! The chalk caves have provided people with shelter during wartime.

Chalk Hills Picture

Materials:

- Blue butcher paper or construction paper
- White chalk
- Colored paper
- Scissors
- Glue
- Liquid starch (optional)

Using the blue paper for background, draw the chalk hills with white chalk. Add trees and other details cut from construction paper. Coating the paper with liquid starch before using the chalk will help keep it from rubbing off or smudging, but is not necessary.

FASHION

Designer Clothing

Paris has been the center for elegant fashion ever since the time of Louis XIV (1638–1715). Every spring and fall, the Parisian designers host shows of their fashion designs for the season. Although mass production has made the fashion designers' clothes available to a much wider public, the influence of the *haute couture* designers has not faded. French fashion designs can be found in *The 1940s*, from the Fashions of a Decade series by Patricia Baker, *The 1960s*, from the Fashions of a Decade series by Yvonne Connike, and *Terence Conran's France* by Terence Conran.

Fashion Picture
Materials:

- Fabric scraps
- Paper
- Colored pencils
- Glue
- Scissors

Study the fashions of famous designers and attempt to create your own fashions in their style by drawing with colored pencils or gluing fabric scraps on paper.

POIRET

In the early 1900s this designer did away with the corset and introduced soft, flowing, empire waist gowns.

CHRISTIAN DIOR

In the mid-1900s Dior emphasized femininity with cinched waists above flowing A-line skirts.

COCO CHANEL

In the 1960s, Coco Chanel designed for the career woman with short, straight skirts and suits.

COURREGES

In the 1960s, this designer gave the world the miniskirt.

Perfume

France is also home to many designer perfumes! Most French perfumes are made in the city of Grasse in Provence. Each perfume has a secret formula that is a mixture of many ingredients.

Homemade Perfume

Materials:

- Flower petals
- Small jar
- Grapeseed oil (from health food store)
- Coffee filter
- Tincture of benzoin (from health food store)

Bruise flower petals by crushing slightly. Put them in the jar, filling it to the top. Cover the petals with grapeseed oil. Put the lid on the jar and store in a warm, dark place for four days. Shake the jar each day. On the fourth day, strain the oil through a coffee filter. Fill the jar with fresh, bruised petals, and pour the same oil back into the jar, adding more oil if necessary. Repeat until the fragrance of the oil is the desired strength. Strain it through a coffee filter. Add three drops of tincture of benzoin as a preservative and store the perfume in a dark place.

Wigs

Before the French Revolution in the late eighteenth century, French nobles wore intricately detailed white powdered wigs, a fashion that probably started because it was hard to keep one's own hair looking as nice as a wig.

Paper Bag Wig

Materials:

- Paper grocery bags
- Cotton balls
- Polyester fiberfill
- Scissors
- Glue

Cut the top half off the grocery bag. Cut out one side from the remaining bottom half. Cover the rest of the bag with cotton balls and fiberfill arranged in the style you have chosen. When the wig is dry, wear your creation.

FRENCH ART

France is probably known best for its art. Artists dream of studying in Paris, street artists sell their wares along the Seine, and France has been the birthplace of many major artistic styles.

Cave Paintings

The paintings in the caves at Lascaux were created more than 20,000 years ago by Cro-Magnon settlers and are said to be the most beautiful prehistoric drawings ever discovered. For pictures, see *France*, from The Land and Its People series by Danielle Lifshitz and *The First Artists* by Dorothy and Joseph Samachson.

Cave Drawing Mural

Materials:

- Brown butcher paper
- Paints
- Paintbrushes

Crumple the paper to replicate the rough surface of a cave wall. Hang the butcher paper on the wall and paint pictures on the surface using your hands or a paintbrush.

Artistic Styles

IMPRESSIONISM

This nineteenth-century realistic style originated with Edoard Manet and was further developed by Claude Monet. Impressionist painters used blobs of color to convey feelings and neglected form for visual impression. They especially explored the representation of light. View the great Impressionist works in books and then attempt to create your own paintings in an impressionistic style. See *Impressionism* by Pierre Courthian or *Famous Paintings: An Introduction to Art for Young Readers* by Alice Elizabeth Chase for examples of this type of painting.

FAUVISM

This style of painting appeared in Paris in 1905 and enjoyed a brief, five-year life span. In fauvism, the colors were bright, even violent. The artists resisted mixing the colors, preferring to have the color itself become the subject of the picture. Famous fauvist painters were Henri Matisse and Andre Derain. Study prints of works by some of these artists then attempt to create a painting in the fauvist style. See *Matisse* by Frederick Brill for examples of fauvist art.

CUBISM

Cubism was developed in the early 1900s. Its most famous practitioner was Pablo Picasso who, although of Spanish birth, spent his adult life in France and was influenced by French artists. Cubists attempted to show on the flat area of the canvas how much space an object actually filled. When painting a table, the cubist would not only show the surface, but would show all the sides of the table top as well as all sides of the legs. Painting in the cubist style will provide an interesting exercise in perspective as well as in art. See *Introducing Picasso* by Juliet Heslewood for examples of cubist art.

Art Museum

Mount your paintings on construction paper and display them with those of your classmates along the walls and hung from the ceiling to create a classroom art gallery.

Poster Art

Posters have been designed to advertise everything from books to concerts to shoes. However, the French have elevated posters to an artform. Poster art reached its peak in the 1930s. Some of the most distinguished poster artists were Kiffer, Cassandre, and Fix-Masseau. *Terence Conran's France* by Terence Conran contains samples of French poster art.

Posters

Materials:

- Posterboard
- Paints and paintbrushes or colored felt-tip markers

Study examples of poster art, then create your own poster advertising a product or event.

FRENCH ARCHITECTURE

Architecture is an artform in France; the inhabitants have drawn upon locally available materials to produce the most aesthetically pleasing buildings possible. In some areas, homes are built from stone, in others they are built from clay or wood. The walls of your classroom can be turned into a Parisian village that is in itself a work of art.

Pigeon Cotes

The countryside of France is dotted with small towers rising among the fields. These are pigeon cotes and many of them are architectural masterpieces, topped with spires, arches, or weathervanes. Examples of French pigeon cotes can be found in *Terence Conran's France* by Terence Conran.

Cardboard Box Pigeon Cote

Materials:

- Small boxes
- Paper
- Scissors
- Glue
- Colored felt-tip markers or paints and paintbrushes
- Found materials such as straws, pebbles, toothpicks, toilet paper tubes, and film containers

Cover the boxes with paper and decorate with markers or paints, adding turrets or other details with the found materials in the following architectural styles:

Stone walls decorated with patterns of small pebbles
Mosaic frieze made from stone
Layers with stone and brick alternated
Cross-timbered with wooden frames filled with brick or clay
Herringbone, or tiles arranged in a herringbone pattern

Doors

Doors on French homes range from brightly painted arched entrances, to geometric patterns carved in wood, to doors formally painted in shiny, deep colors. Pictures of doors can be found in *Terence Conran's France* by Terence Conran.

Door Picture

Materials:

- Posterboard
- Paints and paintbrushes

Use your imagination to design a door on posterboard. There seem to be as many styles of door in France as there are individuals, so be creative.

Shop Fronts

The villages of France are full of traditional shops. Carefully designed storefronts beckon to customers, inviting them to come in, browse, and hopefully buy. From the intricately painted panels beside the windows to the elaborately carved signs, the shop front becomes an advertisement for the store within. Pictures of shop fronts can be found in *Terence Conran's France* by Terence Conran.

Shop Front Picture

Materials:

- Posterboard
- Paints and colored felt-tip markers
- Paintbrushes

Design a storefront on the posterboard. Attach a sign to indicate the type of business, such as a shoe for a shoe store or a bouquet of paper carnations for a florist.

REFERENCES

Baker, Patricia. *The 1940s*, Fashions of a Decade series. New York: Facts on File, 1992.

Brill, Frederick. *Matisse*. London: Paul Hamlyn, 1967.

Brogan, D. W. *France*, Life World Library series. New York: Time-Life, 1960.

Chase, Alice Elizabeth. *Famous Paintings: An Introduction to Art for Young Readers*. New York: Platt & Munk, 1962.

Connike, Yvonne. *The 1960s*, Fashions of a Decade series. New York: Facts on File, 1960.

Conran, Terence. *Terence Conran's France*. Boston: Little, Brown, 1987.

Courthion, Pierre. *Impressionism*. Translated by John Shepley. London: H. N. Abrams, 1972.

Heslewood, Juliet. *Introducing Picasso*. Boston: Little, Brown, 1993.

Hills, C. A. R. *The Seine*. Morristown, NJ: Silver Burdett, 1981.

Lifshitz, Danielle. *France*, The Land and Its People series. Morristown, NY: Silver Burdett, 1973.

Magi, Giovanni. *All Paris*. New York: Charles Scribner's Sons, 1975.

Norbrook, Dominique. *Passport to France*. London: Franklin Watts, 1986.

Samachson, Dorothy, and Joseph Samachson. *The First Artists*. Garden City, NY: Doubleday, 1970.

FURTHER READING

Balerdi, Susan. *France: The Crossroads of Europe*. Minneapolis, MN: Dillon, 1984.

France. Amsterdam: Time-Life Books, 1984.

McHenry, Robert, ed. *The New Encyclopaedia Britannica*, vols. 3, 4, 9, 10. Chicago: Encyclopaedia Britannica, 1992.

Regoli, Gigetta Dalli, et al. *Louvre Paris*. New York: Newsweek, 1967.

Ruspoli, Mario. *The Cave of Lascaux: The Final Photographs*. New York: Doubleday, 1986.

10
THE NETHERLANDS

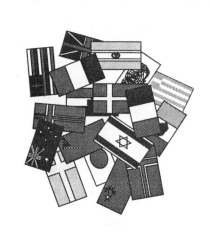

Capital: Amsterdam; The Hague
Government: Constitutional monarchy
  (parliamentary system of government)
Population: 14,934,000
Area: 16,164 square miles

The Netherlands is a small country about the size of the state of Maryland, but it is a land of indomitable spirit. With more than one half of its surface below sea level, the Dutch have fought a centuries-long battle with the sea, slowly winning their country inch by inch from the water. It is a flat land which has been ravaged countless times by floods, but the people have never given up. Through windmills, pumps, and dikes, they have succeeded in adding farmland and living space to their tiny country.

Dutch art is practical in nature with an emphasis on handicrafts and portraiture, which is one of the most practical types of painting, because it provided a means of capturing likenesses before the advent of photography. Some of the world's greatest portrait artists have been Dutch.

The Netherlands is a land of charm and beauty. A unit on Holland will introduce students to a people of incredible courage and determination, and to a unique way of life.

MADURODAM

Madurodam is a Lilliputian town on the outskirts of Hague, known as "the smallest town in the world." Everything is built on a scale of 1:25. The town was built in 1952 complete with models of shops, farms, and factories. At night, when illuminated by over 40,000 lights, it is a breathtaking sight. Pictures of Madurodam can be found in *We Live in the Netherlands* by Preben Kristensen and Fiona Cameron and *The Netherlands*, from the Enchantment of the World series by Dennis B. Fradin.

What better way to immerse students in Dutch culture than by having them create their own version of Madurodam in the classroom?

Homes in the Netherlands

Dutch homes tend to be small because the country is crowded. In the cities, homes are narrow but at least two stories high. The Dutch love of beauty is expressed by the flowers they grow in window boxes, which are considered as important as the paint on the wall. Pictures of Dutch homes can be found in *The Netherlands*, from the Enchantment of the World series by Dennis B. Fradin or *Take a Trip to Holland* by Chris Fairclough.

Model Dutch Village

Materials:

- Shoeboxes and other small containers
- Construction paper
- Glue
- Paints and paintbrushes
- Plastic ice cream parlor bowls with clear lids
- Small paper parasols (found in craft stores)
- Found materials
- Cardboard
- Crayons
- Scissors

Decorate shoeboxes as Dutch homes, turning them on end and cutting construction paper flowers to decorate the windows. Dutch homes often have a tall, narrow second story door in the center of the house. This was used to raise and lower goods from street vendors. Begin to create your classroom's village by arranging the shoebox houses side by side along a street made from brown or gray paper. Add other buildings made from different-sized boxes for shops and offices.

Dikes

A Dutch proverb states, "He who cannot master the sea is not worthy of the land." The Dutch have certainly worked hard at mastering the sea. Thousands of miles of dikes stretch across the land, separating it from the relentless incursions of the ocean. The process of building a dike involves dredging sand and clay, building a firm foundation from nylon and plastic, and overlaying the dike with roads or grassland. Pictures of dikes can be found in *The Netherlands*, Enchantment of the World series by Dennis B. Fradin.

Model Dikes

Cover small boxes (gelatin or pudding boxes would be ideal) with green paper and lay them atop blue construction paper to show the dike cutting through the ocean. Paint a road along the dike with gray paint or cut one from construction paper. For added detail, place small toy cars along the road.

Canals

The network of canals and waterways that winds through many Dutch cities is called the *grachten*. Boats glide through these canals, serving as transportation and vehicles for sightseers. Pictures of the canals can be found in *Take a Trip to Holland* by Chris Fairclough, *We Live in the Netherlands* by Preben Kristensen and Fiona Cameron, and *The Netherlands*, from the Enchantment of the World series by Dennis B. Fradin.

Model Boats

The plastic bowls with clear domes lids that ice cream parlors use for banana splits are ideal to use for the glass-topped boats on the canals. Lay blue strips of paper through the model city to represent these waterways and place the boats on the canals. Line the sides of the canals with vendor's carts made from small boxes, or umbrella-topped tables. (Cut tables from cardboard, top with small parasols found in craft stores or cut from construction paper.) Use an upside-down shoebox, with the long sides cut out, to create a bridge going over the canal.

Polders

The Dutch long ago discovered that tidelands drained of water, called polders, make good farmland. Since the tenth century, the Dutch have added more than 2,000 square miles of arable land with lush meadows for grazing and cultivation. Pictures of polders can be found in *The Netherlands*, from the Enchantment of the World series by Dennis B. Fradin.

Model Polder

In your model town, use green sheets of paper to lay out the farmland on the town side of your dike. Cut cows (see fig. 10.1) from heavy construction paper, using small cardboard strips to help them stand. Color the cows if you want. Add trees cut from paper, and a farmhouse made from a box. Fold a piece of red construction paper over the top to create the steeply gabled roof.

Windmills

Holland would not be Holland without its windmills. Although they are no longer used to drain water from the land, they still dot the landscape, a cheerful reminder of the past. Pictures of windmills can be found in *Take a Trip to Holland* by Chris Fairclough and *The Netherlands*, from the Enchantment of the World series by Dennis B. Fradin. Use a tall, narrow box for the windmill and cut sails from construction paper. The sails can be attached with a metal brass fastener to allow movement.

Windmill Picture

Materials:

- Colored construction paper
- Brass metal fasteners
- Scissors

Cut a tall, narrow trapezoid from the construction paper. Attach two narrow strips of paper, crisscrossed at the top of the trapezoid, with brass metal fasteners.

DUTCH PRODUCTS

Diamond Cutting

Amsterdam ranks with Antwerp, Belgium, as a world-famous center for the diamond industry. Diamond cutters exercise exquisite craftsmanship as they saw, cut, and polish the stones.

Fig. 10.1.

Diamond Picture

Materials:

- Glitter
- Glue (mixed 1:1 with water)
- Paper
- Brush for glue
- Scissors

Cut a diamond shape from the paper. Brush a thin layer of the glue mixture over the entire surface and sprinkle it with glitter.

Dutch Chocolate

The Dutch are famous for their rich chocolate, which is used in candies and baking.

Chocolate Picture

Materials:

- Chocolate pudding, instant, prepared according to package directions
- Finger-paint paper
- Manila paper

Finger-paint on a piece of paper with the pudding. When you are finished, lay a sheet of manila paper on top of the wet pudding and press to make a print of the design. Mount on colored paper.

Tulips

The Netherlands is famous for its several thousand varieties of tulips, which are raised mainly for their bulbs. These flowers were originally introduced from Turkey in the sixteenth century.

Tulip Mural

Materials:

- Blue butcher paper
- Green paper
- Colored construction paper and tissue paper
- Glue
- Scissors

Make a tulip garden mural. Cut stems from green paper and cut U-shaped blossoms with scalloped tops from colored construction paper. Cut some from tissue paper to vary the colors and textures. Glue all the tulips across the sheet of butcher paper and hang the mural on the wall.

Klompen

The Dutch seldom wear these traditional wooden shoes anymore, preferring to wear more modern footgear to keep their feet dry; however, artisans still handcraft wooden klompen for the tourists.

Paper Bag Klompen

Materials:

- Paper lunch bags
- Paints or colored felt-tip markers
- Paintbrushes
- Scissors and stapler

Paint a design on two paper sacks. Staple the sacks closed, then cut a hole in one side for your foot to slip through. Wear your klompen and pretend you are walking through the polders.

North Sea Fishing Industry

The Netherlands owes its prosperity in part to the fishing industry. Herring is one of the main catches, but fishermen also bring back mussels, haddock, cod, shrimp, oysters, and eels.

Underwater Picture

Materials:

- Colored tissue paper, blue, purple, green, and white
- Glue (mixed 1:1 with water)
- Brushes for glue
- Scissors
- Construction paper

Tear the tissue paper into strips and pieces. Paint construction paper with diluted glue. Lay pieces of tissue paper on top of glue, overlapping edges to make a tissue paper collage covering the whole paper, resembling water. Cut fish from construction paper and glue them over the tissue paper to create an underwater scene.

Fishnet Picture

Materials:

- White construction paper
- Colored construction paper scraps
- Scissors
- Glue

Fold the white paper several times and cut out rows of tiny triangles. When unfolded, the paper will have a fishnet effect. Glue tiny construction paper fish to the net.

Shipbuilding

Shipbuilding has been one of the Netherlands's most important industries for hundreds of years. The Dutch are master shipbuilders and can build anything from tiny sailboats to huge supertankers. Read *The Shipbuilders* by Leonard Everett Fisher.

Ship Picture

Materials:

- Paper
- Pencils

Study pictures of ship designs and models of ships. Choose a design to copy on paper. You may enjoy putting an actual model of a ship together.

ART IN THE NETHERLANDS

The Netherlands is world famous for its artists. The government strongly supports the arts, even purchasing works from artists who can't sell their work elsewhere.

The Dutch Masters

The Netherlands is home to many artistic geniuses. In the seventeenth century, the Dutch Masters dominated the art world. Rembrandt, Hals, and Vermeer were especially known for their portraits. Portraits by these artists can be found in *Louvre Paris* by Gigetta Dalli Regoli, et al., and *Famous Paintings: An Introduction to Art for Young Readers* by Alice Elizabeth Chase.

Self Portraits

Materials:

- Paper
- Crayons
- Mirrors

Create a self portrait with crayons. Mount it on colored paper to display in the classroom.

M. C. Escher

M. C. Escher's woodcuts are masterpieces of illusion based on higher mathematics. See *The World of M. C. Escher* by M. C. Escher and J. L. Locher.

Mathematical Pictures

Materials:

- Pencils
- Paper

Study the works of M. C. Escher and then try to draw an Escher-style picture.

Delftware

Delftware, the world-famous, handmade porcelain, gets its unique brilliance from an enamel made of tin. Pictures of delftware can be found in *Take a Trip to Holland* by Chris Fairclough, *We Live in the Netherlands* by Preben Kristensen and Fiona Cameron, *The Netherlands*, from the Enchantment of the World series by Dennis B. Fradin, and *From Gold to Porcelain: The Art of Porcelain and Faïence* by Ruth Berges.

Decorated Paper Plate

Materials:

- White paper plates
- Blue felt-tip markers

Use blue markers to draw designs on white paper plates.

REFERENCES

Berges, Ruth. *From Gold to Porcelain: The Art of Porcelain and Faïence*. New York: Thomas Yoseloff, 1963.

Chase, Alice Elizabeth. *Famous Paintings: An Introduction to Art for Young Readers*. New York: Platt & Munk, 1962.

Escher, M. C. and Locher, J. L. *The World of M. C. Escher*. New York: H. N. Abrams, 1971.

Fairclough, Chris. *Take a Trip to Holland*. London: Franklin Watts, 1982.

Fisher, Leonard Everett. *The Shipbuilders*. New York: Franklin Watts, 1971.

Fradin, Dennis B. *The Netherlands*, Enchantment of the World series. Chicago: Childrens Press, 1983.

Kristensen, Preben, and Fiona Cameron. *We Live in the Netherlands*. New York: Bookwright, 1985.

Regoli, Gigetta Dalli, et al. *Louvre Paris*. New York: Newsweek, 1967.

FURTHER READING

Huggett, Frank E. *The Netherlands*. Morristown, NJ: Silver Burdett, 1976.

McHenry, Robert, ed. *The New Encyclopaedia Britannica*, vols. 3, 4, 8. Chicago: Encyclopaedia Britannica, 1992.

Ripley, Elizabeth. *Vincent Van Gogh*. Oxford: Oxford University Press, 1954.

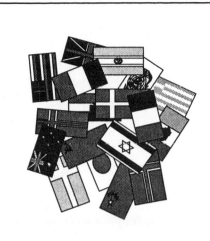

11
ITALY

Capital: **Rome**
Government: **Democratic Republic**
Population: **57,512,000**
Area: **116,324 square miles**

The nation of Italy was first politically unified only about a century ago, yet the Italian people have been bound together for centuries by a much stronger tie than nationality, that of being descendants of the ancient Romans, who built one of the greatest empires the world has seen.

The Italians have always been explorers and adventurers. An Italian sailor, Christopher Columbus, re-discovered America for the Western world. An Italian explorer, Marco Polo, wrote about his experiences in the Orient, paving the way for increased trade between the Eastern and Western worlds.

Italians have been adventurous in art as well. Italy is the birthplace of the Renaissance. Italian musicians invented opera. The traditional language of opera is Italian. For Italians, art has been the tie that has held their people together through wars and political turmoil. A unit on Italy will help students come to an understanding of the fine arts of Italy, as well as an appreciation of the adventurous spirit of the Italian people.

CITIES IN ITALY

Pisa

This central Italian city is home to the University of Pisa and the famous Leaning Tower of Pisa, where Galileo is said to have performed his famous experiment demonstrating that two items of different weights dropped off the tower will land at the same time, although there is no evidence that he actually did so. The Tower is cylindrical in shape with eight stories and serves as a bell tower. It was begun in 1174 but not completed until the second half of the fourteenth century. It leans because of the soft soil and shallow foundation. Pictures of this tower can be found in *Italy*, from the Enchantment of the World series by R. Conrad Stein and *Take a Trip to Italy* by Chris Fairclough.

Leaning Tower of Cans

Materials:

- Small food cans (tuna or pet food cans are ideal)
- Construction paper
- Packaging tape
- Colored felt-tip markers
- Glue

Stack eight cans slightly off-center so they lean. Tape the cans securely. Cover your tower with white or gray construction paper and draw lines separating the eight stories with black markers. Add further embellishments with the markers.

Venice

Venice was built on an archipelago of islets, mud flats, and sand banks more than 1,500 years ago by refugees after the fall of the Roman Empire. The settlers drove logs into the cluster of mud banks to make foundations for their homes and churches. To get about in Venice, people must walk or take boats. The Grand Canal flows through the city in a gentle double curve, and water buses transport people on the Canal. There are approximately 400 little bridges crossing these canals. Pictures of Venice can be found in *The Man-Made Wonders of the World* by Dorothy Turner, *Venice: Birth of a City* by Piero Ventura, *Italy*, from the Enchantment of the World series by R. Conrad Stein, and *Take a Trip to Italy* by Chris Fairclough.

Venice Mural

Materials:

- White construction paper
- Paints
- Pictures of people cut from magazines
- Black construction paper
- Light brown butcher paper
- Paintbrushes
- Scissors
- Glue

After studying pictures of Venice, paint a building or a row of buildings on your white paper. Display them on the brown butcher paper with the buildings painted by your classmates. Leave plenty of space between each picture to represent the Venetian canals. Cut arched bridges from white paper and use them to connect one painting of a building with the next. Add wide, flat-bottomed boats cut from black paper for gondolas and put the pictures of people in the gondolas.

Pompeii

On August 24, 79, the volcanic Mt. Vesuvius above the cities of Pompeii and Herculaneum erupted. Fire and ash rained down upon the people, who tried to flee, terrified that the gods were taking a fiery vengeance upon them. But there was no escape, and the citizens of Pompeii and Herculaneum were buried in lava and hot ash, caught in the business of everyday life.

Today, we can walk through the excavated ruins of Pompeii, viewing the rich lifestyle of these ancient Romans, so amazingly preserved by the ash. Two good books about Pompeii are *Pompeii: Exploring a Roman Ghost Town* by Ron Goor and *The Secrets of Vesuvius* by Sara Louise Clark Bisel.

Mt. Vesuvius Picture

Materials:

- Brown construction paper
- Red plastic wrap
- Scissors and glue
- White tissue paper or cotton batting

Cut a volcano shape from the brown paper. Glue strips of plastic wrap along the sides of the mountain to represent rivers of lava. Then add puffs of smoke made from torn tissue paper and cotton batting.

Clay Pompeii

Materials:

- Modeling clay

Shape the ruins of Pompeii from modeling clay, forming people, buildings, animals, serving dishes, or whatever you wish.

Pompeii Picture

Materials:

- Gray and white construction paper
- Glue
- Scissors

Cut out details of Pompeii from gray paper and glue them onto white paper.

THE GEOGRAPHY OF ITALY

The geography of Italy is mountainous and highly elevated. Although the Po River Valley contains some of the most productive farmland in Italy, 80 percent of the land in Italy is made up of steep mountains and hills. The hot sun in the summer dries the crops and the cold winters freeze them. Springtime floods have eroded most of the arable soil and the autumn droughts leave crops gasping for water. Despite these hardships, up until World War II, Italy was largely an agricultural country. Today it is one of the leading nations in the production of grapes and olives.

Topographical Map of Italy

Materials:

- Relief map of Italy
- Tracing paper and carbon paper
- Heavy butcher paper
- Pencils
- Dry cereals
- Corn meal
- Dried coffee grounds
- Pasta
- Green peas
- Glue

Refer to an atlas or other reference materials for this project. Use tracing paper to trace the different geographical areas of the topographical map. Lay the tracing paper over a sheet of carbon paper over the heavy white butcher paper. Then trace over drawing again. Glue various collage materials onto the white butcher paper to represent the different geographical areas, for example, using coffee grounds for desert areas, dried peas for farmland, and so on.

ITALIAN ART

One of Italy's greatest contributions to the world has been its many artists. Nearly every city can point to some artist or another as a native son. Italy is where the Renaissance was born, which ended the Middle Ages. Italy is also the home of baroque style architecture. Italy has produced great artists for more than 1,000 years and continues to do so today.

Baroque

The baroque style is heavily ornate, with great attention to detail. Extravagant realism marks baroque paintings, most of which were religious in nature. One of the greatest baroque architects was Gianlorenzo Bernini, a seventeenth century architect and sculptor. Some of his most famous work can be seen at St. Peter's Cathedral in Rome. Examples of baroque art can be found in *The Arts of Mankind: Painting, Architecture and Music* from the International Geographic Society and *Baroque and Rococo* by Ian Barras Hill.

Baroque Picture

Materials:

- Paints and paintbrushes
- Paper

Study several baroque-style paintings and attempt to copy the style in your own painting. Pay careful attention to the use of light and shadows and use bright, flamboyant colors.

The Italian Renaissance

Renaissance artists were rebelling against the stale, formulaic art of the medieval years. They studied the human form, as well as perspective, and used their knowledge to create works of realism and expressiveness. It was not enough to faithfully reproduce the form, they wanted to show what was going on in the mind behind the form. Three of the most famous Renaissance artists were Leonardo da Vinci, Michelangelo, and Raphael. There are several books containing examples of Renaissance art, including *The Renaissance* by Tim Wood, *Famous Paintings: An Introduction to Art for Young Readers* by Alice Elizabeth Chase, and *The Golden Book of the Renaissance* by Irwin Shapira.

Renaissance Picture

Materials:

- Paints and paintbrushes
- Paper

Study the works of several Renaissance artists before attempting to copy their style. Remember that the expression is just as important as the form.

Michelangelo

Michelangelo Buonarroti is known as one of the world's greatest artists. He was a painter, poet, sculptor, and architect, and two of his most famous works are the statue of David and the frescos on the west wall and ceiling of the Sistine Chapel in the Vatican. The paintings on the ceiling depict events and persons from the Old Testament, while the painting on the west wall is of the Last Judgment. For more information about this artist, read *Introducing Michelangelo* by Robin Richmond.

Group Picture

Materials:

- Paper
- Newspaper
- Paints
- Paintbrushes
- Tape

As a class, choose a subject for everyone to work on. For example, you may decide to paint a story the whole class enjoys. Tape the pieces of paper to the undersides of the desks or tables in the classroom. Spread newspapers underneath to protect the floor and lie on your backs underneath the desks to paint your part of the picture on the paper. When the pictures are dry, display them together on the wall or ceiling of the room.

DRAMATIC ARTS

Opera

Opera, which combines the arts of acting, music, painting, costuming, and set design to express the gamut of human emotions, was invented in Florence in about 1600. Opera is as popular in Italy as soccer, and Italians still flock to the opera houses to hear the works of the great composers such as Verdi, Puccini, and Rossini. For an example of an opera, read *The Story of Aida, Based on the Opera by Giuseppe Verdi* by Florence Stevenson.

Opera Mural

Materials:

- White butcher paper
- Paints
- Construction paper
- Crayons
- Paintbrushes
- Glue
- Scissors

Choose an existing opera or make up an opera of your own from a favorite story. Paint a lavish backdrop on the butcher paper, and design elaborately costumed characters on construction paper with crayons. Either place the characters on the set for display or glue them to craft sticks for a performance of your opera.

Puppet Theater

The puppet theater of Sicily is a thriving tradition that has remained essentially unchanged for centuries. The puppets are brilliantly painted marionettes that stand nearly 3 feet tall. They are maneuvered by strings and iron rods. The characters are usually knights fighting classic battles of chivalry. The most famous puppet of all is Pinocchio, from the book written by Carlo Collodi in the 1880s.

Cloth Puppet

Materials:

- Fabric
- Needles and thread
- Craft sticks
- Paper
- Sewing scissors
- Glue

Cut the shape of a person from two pieces of cloth and sew around the outside edges. Stuff the head with paper and draw a face on it. Tie a piece of thread around the head, hands, and feet. Attach these strings to craft sticks so that you can manipulate the puppet.

Harlequinade

This form of theater combines acting, singing, dancing, and fencing as well as juggling, conjuring, and acrobatics. Today's circus acts and slapstick comedy borrow heavily from the genre, and such famous comics as Charlie Chaplin, the Marx Brothers, and the Monty Python troupe have their roots in the Harlequinade. The main character of this theater is the Harlequin, who wears a patchwork coat of many colors.

Harlequin Picture

Materials:

- Construction paper
- Patterned wallpaper samples (squares, stripes, or plaid patterns)
- Scissors and glue

Cut a human figure from the patterned wallpaper sample. Add head, props, and a background cut from colored construction paper. Remember that the Harlequinade was an acrobatic form of drama, so cut the figure to express movement. Glue the figure onto white or colored paper.

FAMOUS ITALIANS

Christopher Columbus

Columbus was born in Genoa. In 1492, while working for Spain, he re-discovered the continent of America for the Western world in an attempt to find a westward sea passage to the Orient. The story of his three ships, the *Nina*, the *Pinta*, and the *Santa Maria* is well known, as is the story of his voyage. Ironically, Columbus died without ever realizing that he had discovered a new world. He believed till his death that the lands he had found were part of the Orient, hence the name he gave to the islands he found was the "West Indies."

Columbus's Ships

Materials:

- Blue watercolors
- White construction paper
- Paintbrushes
- Crayons

With the crayons, draw a picture of one of Columbus's ships. Paint over and around the drawing with blue watercolor paint.

Amerigo Vespucci

Amerigo Vespucci was an Italian traveler and navigator who participated in two early voyages to the New World between 1499 and 1502. During the 1502 voyage, Vespucci became convinced that the newly discovered lands were not part of Asia as Columbus had claimed, but were, in actuality, a "new world." Vespucci's letters about his voyage were published in 1507 by Martin Waldseemüller, who in an introduction to the letters, suggested that the new land be called America. This name also appeared for the first time on a large planisphere of Waldseemüller.

Early Map
Materials:

- Manila drawing paper
- Colored felt-tip markers

Study old maps from the era of the discovery of the "New World." Draw a map on the drawing paper, perhaps of Italy, of Columbus's ocean voyage, or of the Americas.

Galileo Galilei

Galileo was born in Pisa in 1564. He is best known for his trial by the Roman Catholic Church for heresy when he publicly confirmed Copernicus's theory that the earth was not the center of the universe. Under the threat of torture, Galileo recanted his statement. The legend that he told the court afterwards, "It does move, though" is probably just a story.

Galileo perfected the telescope to a power of 32. With it he discovered the mountains of the moon, sunspots, Jupiter's satellites, and the phases of Venus. He did not stop exploring the sky after his trial, but continued his explorations until he went blind. Galileo also conducted experiments about the nature of gravity, vacuums, and many other subjects. For more information on this great thinker and scientist, read *Galileo* by Leonard Everett Fisher.

Cardboard Tube Telescope
Materials:

- Toilet paper tubes
- Black construction paper
- Needles
- Rubber band
- Scissors

Cut 4-inch squares from the construction paper. Poke holes in the paper, in the shape of a constellation, with the needle. Secure the paper over one end of the toilet paper tube with a rubber band. When you look through the tube at a source of light it will look like stars seen through a telescope.

Model of the Solar System
Materials:

- Black construction paper
- Colored paper
- Scissors
- Glue

Cut out and glue a model of the solar system onto the black paper.

Marco Polo

Marco Polo lived in the thirteenth century. He was the son of a Venetian merchant. In 1271 he, his uncle, and his father started an overland journey to China. The journey lasted four years as they traveled through lands torn apart by war, barren deserts, and frigid mountains. Two good books about this explorer are *Marco Polo: Voyage to the Orient* by Carol Greene and *Marco Polo and the Medieval Explorers* by Rebecca Stefoff.

Marco Polo's Sights

Materials:

- Paper
- Crayons

Discuss what Marco Polo might have seen on his journey that would have seemed fantastic to him. Then draw a picture of one of the sights with crayons.

Leonardo da Vinci

Da Vinci was born in Tuscany in 1452. Not only was he a famous painter, but he was also a great inventor. His many designs included armored cars, diving helmets, gliders, and a helicopter. For more information, read *Da Vinci* by Mike Venizia.

Invention Designs

Materials:

- Colored pencils
- Paper

Use paper and pencil to design a new machine. Draw a diagram showing how your invention will work.

ITALIAN FOOD

Pasta

Pasta is one of Italy's finest contributions to the world of food. It comes in many shapes and sizes and is served with dozens of different sauces.

Pasta Picture

Materials:

- Many different sizes and shapes of pasta
- Colored paper
- Glue

Make a pasta collage using different types of pasta.

Pizza

Pizza started in Naples as a flattened dish of bread dough topped with olive oil, tomatoes, and mozzarella cheese. As it spread throughout Italy, different regions developed their own toppings. Pizza made in Rome, for instance, used onions and olives for toppings instead of tomatoes. The dish spread to the United States through the Italian community and is now one of the most popular foods in the United States with toppings ranging from pepperoni sausages, to mushrooms, to fruit.

Picture

Materials:

- Scissors
- Glue
- Colored paper: red, yellow, and other colors as desired

Cut a circle from manila paper. Cut a slightly smaller circle from red paper and glue on top. Cut another smaller circle from yellow paper and glue on top of the red paper. Now cut toppings of choice from colored paper and glue on the yellow paper.

Olives

Italy is one of the largest producers of olives. Olives are picked either unripe or ripe. Unripe olives are green, and ripe olives are dark blue when picked and turn black during pickling. The regions of Tuscany and Umbria are especially known for their olive oils, some of which are still pressed by hand-drawn or mule-driven presses. Olive oils are displayed in ornate bottles with fancy lettering and a variety of pictures. Some olive oils are precious enough to be given as gifts.

Olive Tree Picture

Materials:

- White construction paper
- Green and dark blue tempera
- Rubber spatula
- Paint made by mixing 4 parts powdered detergent to 1 part liquid starch with a dash of brown tempera

Paint a picture of a tree trunk and branches on the paper, using the brown detergent paint and applying it with a spatula. Let the paint dry, then dip your finger in green tempera and press over and around the branches of your tree to make leaves. Let the paint dry and then dip your finger in the blue paint and press it among the leaves to make olives.

Olive Oil Bottle Picture

Materials:

- Construction paper (white or manila)
- Crayons, colored pencils, or colored felt-tip markers

Imagine that you are designing a bottle for your family's olive oil. The olive oil company has been in your family for generations, and it is very expensive oil of the highest quality. What kind of image will you use to represent your olive oil? Draw a label for your oil and design a shape for your bottle. Think about what you want your label to say and how you want to say it.

ROMAN EMPIRE

The Roman Empire lasted from 27 B.C. to A.D. 476 and extended from Italy through Greece, North Africa, Spain, the Middle East, and into parts of Britain. The English alphabet, much of our language, our laws, and even the engineering of our buildings came from the Roman Empire. Some good books about the Roman Empire are *Life in Ancient Rome* by Pierre Miquel; *Classical Rome,* edited by John D. Clare; and *City: A Story of Roman Planning and Construction* by David Macauley.

Soldiers' Armor

The Roman army was large and well trained. Most of the soldiers were volunteers, attracted by the good food and pay. A soldier served in the army for 25 years. See figure 11.1 for an example of Roman armor.

Roman Soldier Costume

See chapter 2, "Samurai Warriors," on pp. 27-29 for directions for making a Roman soldier's costume: armor, helmet, sword, and shield. Study pictures of Roman armor and change the decorations of your armor accordingly.

Ancient Roman Architecture

Roman buildings were made of concrete, which the Romans invented. They were faced with brick and covered with painted stucco. The Romans also used the arch very heavily in their architecture, allowing them to create huge domed buildings.

Building Pictures
Materials:
- Butcher paper
- Crayons
- Pencils
- Construction paper
- Paints
- Paintbrushes

Study pictures of ancient Roman architecture, then draw models of Roman buildings on butcher paper and hang them on the walls of the classroom.

COLOSSEUM

The Colosseum was the largest arena in the Roman Empire and still inspires awe. This was the site of gladiator games, chariot races, and sometimes it was even flooded for gladiatorial sea battles. Pictures of the Colosseum can be found in *Italy,* from the Enchantment of the World series by R. Conrad Stein and *Take a Trip to Italy* by Chris Fairclough.

On butcher paper draw or paint a model of the Colosseum. Surround it with colored pictures of a Colosseum event of your choice.

Fig. 11.1.

PANTHEON

This magnificent domed building was built in 27 B.C. to celebrate all the gods and goddesses of Roman mythology. Over the years it became a Christian church and a burial place and memorial to famous artists and politicians. A picture of the Pantheon can be found in *The Art of Ancient Rome* by Shirley Glubok.

Surround a model of the Pantheon with colored pictures of gods and goddesses from Roman mythology.

TENEMENT

Poor people in ancient Rome lived in tall, narrow, block apartment buildings. Quarters were cramped and smelly, with no indoor plumbing, and fire was a constant threat.

Surround butcher paper pictures of Roman tenements with drawings of Roman street life: people gathering water from the public fountains, children playing in the street, and women cooking in the streets or buying food at roadside stalls.

ROMAN ART

Mosaics

Wealthy Romans adorned the floors and walls of their homes and buildings with tile mosaics.

Paper Mosaic

Materials:

- Paper
- Colored construction paper
- Pencils
- Scissors
- Glue

Draw a simple design on paper. Cut the colored paper into small, rectangular pieces and use the pieces to fill in the lines of the drawing.

Frescoes

Romans also adorned their buildings with painted frescoes, murals painted on plaster while the plaster was still wet. Pictures of frescos can be found in *Italy*, from the Enchantment of the World series by R. Conrad Stein.

Plaster-of-Paris Fresco

Materials:

- Plaster of paris
- Cookie sheets or Styrofoam meat trays
- Paints
- Paintbrushes

Mix the plaster of paris and pour it into the cookie sheet. Paint a scene on the plaster while it is still wet. When the plaster is dry, remove your fresco from the cookie sheet.

REFERENCES

The Arts of Mankind: Painting, Architecture and Music. Englewood Cliffs, NJ: International Geographic Society, 1962.

Bisel, Sara Louise Clark. *The Secrets of Vesuvius.* New York: Scholastic, 1990.

Chase, Alice Elizabeth. *Famous Paintings: An Introduction to Art for Young Readers.* New York: Platt & Munk, 1962.

Clare, John D., ed. *Classical Rome.* San Diego, CA: Harcourt Brace Jovanovich, 1993.

Fairclough, Chris. *Take a Trip to Italy.* London: Franklin Watts, 1981.

Fisher, Leonard Everett. *Galileo.* New York: Maxwell Macmillan International, 1992.

Glubok, Shirley. *The Art of Ancient Rome.* New York: Harper & Row, 1965.

Goor, Ron. *Pompeii: Exploring a Roman Ghost Town.* New York: Thomas Y. Crowell, 1986.

Greene, Carol. *Marco Polo: Voyage to the Orient.* Chicago: Childrens Press, 1987.

Hill, Ian Barras. *Baroque and Rococo.* New York: Galley Press, 1980.

Macauley, David. *City: A Story of Roman Planning and Construction.* Boston: Houghton Mifflin, 1974

Miquel, Pierre. *Life in Ancient Rome.* New York: Hamlyn, 1980.

Richmond, Robin. *Introducing Michelangelo.* Boston: Little, Brown, 1991.

Shapira, Irwin. *The Golden Book of the Renaissance.* New York: Golden Press, 1961.

Stefoff, Rebecca. *Marco Polo and the Medieval Explorers.* New York: Chelsea House, 1992.

Stein, R. Conrad. *Italy,* Enchantment of the World series. Chicago: Childrens Press, 1984.

Stevenson, Florence. *The Story of Aida, Based on the Opera by Giuseppe Verdi.* New York: Putnam, 1966.

Turner, Dorothy. *The Man-Made Wonders of the World.* Minneapolis, MN: Dillon Press, 1986.

Venezia, Mike. *Da Vinci.* Chicago: Childrens Press, 1989.

Ventura, Piero. *Venice: Birth of a City.* New York: G. P. Putnam's Sons, 1987.

Wood, Tim. *The Renaissance.* New York: Penguin Books, 1993.

FURTHER READING

Burke, Peter. *The Italian Renaissance: Culture and Society in Italy.* Princeton, Princeton University Press, 1972.

Chamberlin, E. R. *Rome.* Amsterdam: Time-Life, 1976.

Cornell, Tim, and John Matthes. *Atlas of the Roman World.* New York: Facts on File, 1982.

Dyson, John. *Columbus—For Gold, God, and Glory.* New York: Simon & Schuster, 1991.

Hibbert, Christopher. *Venice: The Biography of a City.* New York: W. W. Norton, 1989.

Italy. Amsterdam: Time-Life, 1985.

Leprohon, Pierre. *Venice.* Geneva: Minerva, 1979.

Mansione, E. *Rome and the Vatican.* London: F. Muller, 1983.

McHenry, Robert, ed. *The New Encyclopaedia Britannica,* vols. 3, 5–10, 12, 13, 29. Chicago: Encyclopaedia Britannica, 1992.

Regoli, Gigetta Dalli, et al. *Louvre Paris.* New York: Newsweek, 1967.

Ward-Perkins, John, and Amanda Claridge. *Pompeii A.D. 79.* New York: Alfred A. Knopf, 1978.

12
GREECE

Capital: Athens
Government: Democratic Republic
Population: 10,053,000
Area: 50,949 square miles

Greece is a rocky country on the northern shore of the Mediterranean. Sixty percent of its surface is highlands and islands bare of anything but scrub and heath. Yet here we find an ancient civilization that has had a profound influence on our own. From Greece we received our system of government; the study of mathematics, and many other branches of science; as well as our most influential ancient literature. The gods and goddesses of ancient Greek mythology have inspired many tales of heroism and have heavily influenced Western artists, poets, and authors. The patterns of our plays and theater—comedy and tragedy—were initiated in Greece and came to the Western world by way of Italy.

The Greeks are a questioning people. They developed the science of philosophy out of a love of wisdom and knowledge, and also created the first schools in logic. They applied their questioning minds to politics, the question of human origins, the study of human behavior, predictions of the future, and the universe itself.

Out of their studies, the Greeks developed a fierce respect for human dignity, and for the value of each and every person. Greek art was characterized by the representation of the human figure. Artists strove for an accurate portrayal of the human form, with proportion and the dynamics of action and emotion. Depictions of monsters, plants, and animals were secondary, the most important subject was the human figure, which was also considered to be the divine figure. The purpose of art was to produce religious objects and to commemorate important events. Decorative art was only for private use. A unit on Greece will introduce students to classic art and literature, as well as the study of philosophy and logic.

GRECIAN ART

Sculpture

The ancient Greeks were consummate sculptors, and devoted students of the human form. Show students examples of Greek art, noticing in particular the attention to detail. From statues to reliefs on columns and buildings, the ancient Greek masters created fine works of art. Pictures of sculpture can be found in *Let's Travel in Greece*, edited by Darlene Geis, and *The Art of Ancient Greece* by Shirley Glubok.

Sculpture Picture

Materials:

- Large sheets of white butcher paper
- Crayons and scissors

Study books to choose an example of Greek sculpture to copy. Sketch a copy of your subject on the white paper, then cut it out to display on the wall.

Plaster-of-Paris Statuette

Materials:

- Wooden block for base
- Wire cutters and pliers
- Plaster of paris, bucket
- Paints and paintbrushes
- Spatulas
- Files and sandpaper
- Hammer and nails
- Rags
- Sturdy, pliable wire (electrical or spool wire is good, but a coat hanger works fine for simple projects)

Nail one end of the wire to the center of the block. Fashion the rest into a framework for the figure, attaching smaller pieces of wire to the shoulder areas to make the arms. Mix the plaster of paris as directed on the package, making a thick mixture. Cut rags into strips, dip them into the plaster, and wind them around the wire, forming the basic shape of the sculpture. Once the basic shape is formed, build details with plaster, using a spatula. Let the plaster harden and smooth it with a file and sandpaper. Define the statuette's features with the file. When the statuette is finished, you can paint it as it was done in ancient Greece.

Pottery

The Greeks also made beautiful pottery, using many different styles and techniques.

AMPHORAE

The beautiful two-handled amphora was used for storing fine wines and oils. It was decorated around the base with scenes from Greek life or from mythology. Pictures of amphorae can be found in *The Art of Ancient Greece* by Shirley Glubok.

Clay Amphora

Materials:

- Modeling clay
- Paints and paintbrushes

Form a pottery container from the clay. When the clay has dried, paint pictures on the surface as the ancient Greeks did.

Amphora Picture

Materials:

- White paper and scissors
- Paints and paintbrushes

Cut the shape of a two-handled vase from the paper. Paint figures around the base of the vase. Popular Grecian scenes were chariot races and dancers.

TERRA COTTA

Some Greek potters used red, terra-cotta clay for their pottery, decorating their work in intricate detail. Greek pottery was exported throughout the ancient world. Pictures of Greek pottery can be found in *Ceramica Greca* by Paolino Mingazzini and *The Greeks, Their Legacy* by Janet Van Duyn.

Terra-Cotta Picture

Materials:

- Oaktag or posterboard with shiny surface
- Terra-cotta colored crayons
- Black paint and paintbrushes
- Toothpicks

Cover the paper with the crayon, making a solid area of color in the shape of a piece of pottery. Apply two layers of black paint over the crayon layer. When the paint is completely dry, scratch a design through the black paint with a toothpick, exposing the red layer underneath.

GREEK ARCHITECTURE

Columns

Columns are one of the most distinctive features of Greek architecture. There are three main styles of columns used by the Greeks. The Doric column is simple, with a grooved length, a plain, rectangular top, and no base. The Ionic column is more decorative. It is taller and slimmer than the Doric column. The length is fluted, with a flattened ridge between each flute, and a scroll shape at the top and a ridged base. The Corinthian style was fluted like the Ionic column but the top was carved ornately with curled leaves. Pictures of columns can be found in *Let's Visit Greece* by Garry Lyle and John C. Caldwell; *Let's Travel in Greece*, edited by Darlene Geis; *The Arts of Mankind: Painting, Architecture and Music* from the International Geographic Society; and *A Greek Temple* by Fiona MacDonald.

Clay Columns

Materials:

- Self-hardening clay
- Toothpicks
- Stiff cardboard
- White or gray paint
- Paintbrushes
- Glue

Roll the clay into two columns thick and sturdy enough to stand upright. Form several flat tiles of clay as bases for the columns to rest upon. Add wider round discs at the top and bottom. Use toothpicks to scoop out the fluting and decorate the tops. Form clay leaves from small balls of clay and attach them to the top of the column with a drop of water. Set the columns on their bases, and secure all with a drop of water. If you want, make a rectangular crossbeam to lay across the top of the columns. Let all pieces harden thoroughly. Glue the floor tiles to the cardboard base. Glue the columns to the tiles. Paint your columns white or light gray.

Cardboard Tube Columns

Materials:

- Cardboard tubes
- White or gray paint
- Paintbrushes
- Flat cardboard
- Glue
- Tape

Cut out a square of cardboard for the base of the columns. Tape the cardboard tube to the base in an upright position. Cut leaves and other ornaments from cardboard and glue them around the top of the column. Paint the column gray or white.

GREEK MYTHOLOGY

The exciting legends of the Greek gods and goddesses, with their human frailties, form the basis for much of Western literature and art. Students will enjoy reading the stories and comparing them to fairy tales or stories of modern-day heroes. See *Myths and Enchantment Tales* by Margaret Evans Price or *The Olympians: Great Gods and Goddesses of Ancient Greece* by Leonard Everett Fisher for stories from Greek mythology.

The Golden Fleece

After a long, dangerous voyage, Jason and the Argonauts, with the help of Medea, recovered the fleece of the golden ram from the sacred grove in Colchis. Read *Jason and the Golden Fleece* by Leonard Everett Fisher.

Cotton Ball Fleece

Materials:

- Cotton balls
- Cardboard
- Metallic gold spray paint
- Glue

Cover the surface of the cardboard with cotton balls. Then spray with metallic gold paint. (Be sure to use adequate ventilation when using spray paint.)

The Trojan Horse

Everyone knows the tale of the great wooden horse built by the Greeks during the Trojan War. The Greek soldiers hid inside and when the Trojans pulled it inside the gates of their walled city, the Greek soldiers jumped out and attacked them. For more information about the Trojan War, read *The Iliad by Homer*, adapted by Diana Stewart.

Trojan Horse Picture

Materials:

- Brown butcher paper
- Crayons

Draw a large wooden horse on wheels. Then add figures of Greek soldiers leaping out from the inside to attack the surprised Trojans.

The Minotaur's Labyrinth

Theseus was one of the great kings of Athens. Among the many legends about his life is the story of how he entered the labyrinth on the island of Crete, and with the help of Ariadne, slew the Minotaur. Read *Theseus and the Minotaur* by Leonard Everett Fisher.

Maze Picture

Materials:

- Yarn
- Paper
- Glue
- Crayons
- Scissors

Draw a maze on the paper and then lay out a trail with the yarn, gluing it onto the paper.

Hermes

Hermes was the messenger to the gods and the patron of athletes. He was the deity of trade, wealth, oratory, and thieves. With his winged feet and hat, he hastened messengers throughout the land.

Winged Hat

Materials:

- Stiff cardboard
- Paper
- Feathers or white crepe paper
- Scissors
- Glue

Cut a large circle from the paper and cut a slit from one edge to the center. Overlap the cut edges and staple or glue them together to make a hat. Cut two wings from stiff cardboard and attach them to the sides of the hat. Glue white feathers to the wings. Make feathers from crepe paper if real ones are not available.

Daedalus and Icarus

Daedalus was a great inventor who designed the Minotaur's maze for the king of Crete. The king imprisoned Daedalus and his son, Icarus. In an effort to escape, Daedalus formed wings for himself and Icarus, and they tried to fly off the island. Icarus flew too near the sun and melted the wax on his wings, so he fell to the earth and was killed. Read *Wings* by Jane Yolen or *Daedalus and Icarus* by Penelope Farmer.

Posterboard Wings

Materials:

- Posterboard or white paper
- White crepe paper
- Strips of elastic
- Scissors and glue

Cut two large triangles from the white posterboard. Attach elastic strips to underside at the top and the bottom as straps. Cut small strips of white paper and glue them onto the posterboard for feathers. Wear the wings and act out the story of Daedalus and Icarus.

Pandora's Box

Prometheus was one of the Titans. He befriended humans and stole the gods' fire to give to people. In retaliation, the gods created a beautiful woman, Pandora, and gave her to Prometheus. Prometheus, however, sensed a trick and refused Pandora, so his brother, Epimetheus, married her instead. She brought with her a big, beautiful box that she was forbidden to open. Curiosity overcame her and she opened the box, letting loose a host of plagues upon humans, but also releasing hope into the world. For a version of the story of Pandora, read *Pandora's Box* by Lisl Weil.

Pandora's Box Picture
Materials:

- Brown construction paper
- White drawing paper
- Scissors
- Colors

Cut a treasure chest shape from brown paper. Draw pictures of the evils that escaped the box and place them around the chest. Finally, draw a picture of hope, and display it above the other drawings.

Arachne

Arachne was so skillful in weaving that she challenged the goddess Athena to a weaving contest. When it seemed that Arachne might win the contest, Athena ripped Arachne's cloth. In despair, Arachne hanged herself and was changed into a spider.

Yarn Webs
Materials:

- Styrofoam meat trays
- Scissors
- Yarn

Cut slits all the way around the edges of the meat tray. Wrap yarn around the edges and cross and tie them to create a spider web.

Midas

Greedy King Midas of Phrygia asked the gods to grant him the golden touch, so that everything he touched turned to gold. At first he was happy, but then he discovered that he couldn't eat or drink, and he even turned his daughter to gold. The golden touch was really a curse. For the whole story, read *The King Has Horse's Ears* by Peggy Thomson, *King Midas and the Golden Touch* by Al Perkins, or *King Midas and His Gold* by Patricia and Fredrick McKissack.

The Golden Touch Picture
Materials:

- Metallic gold paint
- Paper
- Paintbrushes

Use gold paint to depict everyday items that King Midas might have turned to gold.

Constellations

Greek mythology is full of stories of heroes and heroines who were turned into stars after they died, such as Andromeda; the Twins, Castor and Pollux; and Cassiopeia, to name just a few. A wonderful book on constellations, with lots of pictures, is *The Glow in the Dark Night Sky Book* by Clint Hatchett.

Star Picture

Materials:

- Black paper
- Foil gummed stars

Arrange the gummed stars on the paper in the shape of your favorite constellation.

REFERENCES

The Arts of Mankind: Painting, Architecture and Music. Englewood Cliffs, NJ: International Geographic Society, 1962.

Farmer, Penelope. *Daedalus and Icarus.* New York: Harcourt Brace Jovanovich, 1971.

Geis, Darlene, ed. *Let's Travel in Greece.* Chicago: Childrens Press, 1964.

Glubok, Shirley. *The Art of Ancient Greece.* New York: Atheneum, 1969.

Fisher, Leonard Everett. *Jason and the Golden Fleece.* New York: Holiday House, 1990.

———. *The Olympians: Great Gods and Goddesses of Ancient Greece.* New York: Holiday House, 1984.

———. *Theseus and the Minotaur.* New York: Holiday House, 1988.

Hatchett, Clint. *The Glow in the Dark Night Sky Book.* New York: Random House, 1988.

Lyle, Garry, and John C. Caldwell. *Let's Visit Greece.* New York: John Day, 1969.

MacDonald, Fiona. *A Greek Temple.* New York: Peter Bedrick Books, 1992.

McKissack, Patricia, and Fredrick McKissack. *King Midas and His Gold.* Chicago: Childrens Press, 1986.

Perkins, Al. *King Midas and the Golden Touch.* London: Collins and Harvill, 1968.

Price, Margaret Evans. *Myths and Enchantment Tales.* Eu Claire, WI: E. M. Hale, 1960.

Stewart, Diana. *The Iliad by Homer.* Milwaukee, WI: Raintree, 1981.

Thomson, Peggy. *The King Has Horse's Ears.* New York: Simon & Schuster, 1988.

Weil, Lisl. *Pandora's Box.* New York: Atheneum, 1986.

Yolen, Jane. *Wings.* San Diego: Harcourt Brace Jovanovich, 1991.

FURTHER READING

Bowra, C. M. *Classical Greece.* New York: Time-Life, 1965.

Hamilton, Edith. *Mythology: Timeless Tales of Gods and Heroes.* Boston: Little, Brown, 1940.

McHenry, Robert, ed. *The New Encyclopaedia Britannica*, vol. 5. Chicago: Encyclopaedia Britannica, 1992.

Mingazzini, Paolino. *Ceramica Greca.* New York: Hamlyn, 1969.

Spelios, Thomas. *Pictorial History of Greece.* New York: Crown, 1967.

Van Duyn, Janet. *The Greeks, Their Legacy.* London: Cassell, 1974.

Williams, Susan. *The Greeks.* New York: Thomson Learning, 1993.

Zimmerman, J. E. *Dictionary of Classical Mythology.* New York: Bantam Books, 1964.

13
THE BRITISH ISLES

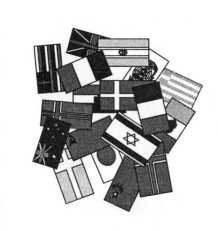

(Great Britain and Ireland)

At one time it was said that the sun never set on the British Empire. During the eighteenth and nineteenth centuries, this statement was true. Great Britain had colonies on every continent, and it was literally daytime somewhere in the world over lands claimed by the British. Today, although no longer the most powerful nation in the world, England is still a major influence on the world today and on our society. Most of the former colonies of the British Empire, and America is one, are independent now. The countries that make up the United Kingdom today are England, Scotland, Wales, and Northern Ireland. The other major country of the British Isles is the Republic of Ireland, which became independent of English rule in 1949.

After the British Isles were taken over by the Anglo-Saxons, visual arts became predominantly Christian beginning in the Middle Ages with religious ornamentation. Painting first appeared at this time in illuminated manuscripts, usually of the Bible, while some of the finest products of British art in the Middle Ages were the great Gothic cathedrals.

In the eighteenth century, a distinctive British style of painting began to develop with the work of portrait painters William Hogarth, Sir Joshua Reynolds, Thomas Gainsborough, and George Romney. These artists combined informal poses and elegance for a new style in portraiture. British artists slowly began to shake off their dependence on the influences of foreign artists and started to emerge on their own as a force in the artistic world.

ENGLAND

Capital: **London**
Government: **Constitutional Monarchy**
Population: **47,900,000**
Area: **50,363 square miles**

England is a land steeped in history. Nowhere, it seems, can one go without being reminded of some aspects of England's historical background, some of it extending back to prehistoric times. The English countryside is dotted with ruins of ancient buildings and barrows, while in the towns and cities of England one finds monuments and places familiar to us from history amidst the modern buildings. Much of Western culture has its foundation in England, and English

159

writers, artists, and scientists have made countless contributions to the world, particularly in the fields of architecture, literature, and drama. A unit on England will introduce students to one of the cultural bedrocks of American society.

ENGLAND'S ANCIENT HISTORY

Humans first came to the British Isles 6,500 years ago. The oldest remnants we have found of prehistoric civilizations are long barrows dating from 4300 B.C. We can learn quite a lot about these early inhabitants from their remains, but about some of their most lasting monuments we can only speculate.

Stonehenge

Stonehenge means "the hanging stones." Huge stone blocks, weighing between 40 and 50 tons each, were dragged to a spot on top of a hill in southern England over a distance of at least 24 miles by people who didn't have horses, carts, or wheels. How they completed such a monumental undertaking is only now beginning to be understood.

Stonehenge was built in three phases, spanning the years between 3100 B.C. and 1100 B.C. The stones of the outer circle are each 7 feet wide and 13½ feet tall. Some people have speculated that the stones served as a sort of calendar, indicating the starting date of certain seasons, but no one really knows for sure why the stones were put in place. Although some have speculated that Druids built Stonehenge, there were no Druids in the area until long after Stonehenge was constructed. Pictures of Stonehenge can be found in *The Man-Made Wonders of the World* by Dorothy Turner, *The Mystery of Stonehenge* by Harriette Abels, *The Mystery of Stonehenge* by Nancy Lyon, and *The Mystery of Stonehenge* by Franklyn M. Branley.

Cardboard Box Stonehenge

Materials:

- Appliance boxes or large sheets of heavy cardboard
- White paint and paintbrushes

Flatten the appliance boxes and have your teacher cut the ends off. Curve the box or cardboard into a circle. On both the inside and outside of the circled box, paint large, white, rectangular stones to form the outer circle of the monument.

3-D Stonehenge Picture

Materials:

- Heavy paper such as cardboard, posterboard, etc. (green would be ideal)
- White and light blue construction paper
- Scissors and glue

Use the heavy paper for the base. Cut rectangles from the white and blue paper. Fold the bottom ¼ inch of the paper rectangle and glue it to the base.

With your paper rectangles, re-create the layout of Stonehenge. The outside circle consists of 30 white stones; the inner circle consists of 20 blue stones. The 30 pillars in the outer circle are joined into pairs by lintel stones laid across the top. Inside the blue circle is a series of stones in a horseshoe pattern. These stones are larger than those on the outer circle and are also joined by lintel stones. Inside the large horseshoe is a smaller horseshoe consisting of 19 stones. These stones are just a few feet high. The altar stone is a single, towering stone at the very center of Stonehenge.

Beaker Folk

This group of people came to England 6,000 years ago from the Rhine and Danube River areas in eastern Europe. They are called the Beaker Folk because of the shape of the drinking vessels that have been found buried with their dead. They knew about metalworking and made bows, arrows, and other weapons from bronze. Some have speculated that the Beaker Folk were the creators of Stonehenge.

Clay Beakers

Materials:

- Self-hardening modeling clay
- Cord, yarn, or string
- Dark red paint
- Paintbrushes

Shape your modeling clay into a bell-shaped vessel. When the clay is dry, paint your pot red and cover it with twisted cord, yarn, or string arranged in horizontal lines.

MEDIEVAL ENGLAND

This is probably one of the most heavily romanticized periods in English history. The legend of Robin Hood stems from medieval times, as well as the stories of King Arthur and the Crusades. In reality this was a time of great bloodshed and jockeying for power among the nobility. For the lower classes, or serfs, this was a time of little or no education, disease, and a great dependence on religion. This period of English history holds much interest for historians.

Knights

Strong, brave, honest, and true to their king. This was the ideal of the knight in shining armor. Under the system of feudalism, lords were given lands and peasants in return for their pledge to protect the king. These lords and their vassals became knights. These knights engaged in tournaments to hone their battle skills and jostle for power. For more information about medieval knights, read *The Days of Knights and Castles* by Pierre Miquel.

Paper Bag Armor

See chapter 2, "Samurai Warriors," on pp. 27-29 for directions for making a knight's armor and helmet. Study pictures of medieval knights and change the decorations of your costume accordingly.

Coat of Arms

Because few people could read in medieval England, it was important for knights to identify themselves so people could tell at a glance who was a friend and who was an enemy on the battlefield. The coat of arms, usually decorated with symbols and animals from mythology, served as a sort of ID card.

Cardboard Coat of Arms
Materials:

- Cardboard
- Aluminum foil
- Colored construction paper
- Scissors
- Glue

Study pictures of heraldry, or coats of arms. Then cut a 12-by-18 inch shield from your cardboard. The bottom of your shield should be either rounded or pointed. Design a coat of arms for yourself. Use construction paper and aluminum foil to add details. A small rectangular strip can be cut out of cardboard and glued or taped on the back of your shield for a handhold.

Sword

What was a knight without his sword? Of course, the most famous sword of legend has to be Excalibur, the sword that King Arthur pulled from the stone, which ended up in the hands of the Lady of the Lake.

Cardboard Sword
Materials:

- Cardboard
- Construction paper
- Sequins, glitter, pearl pasta, and so on
- Aluminum foil
- Scissors
- Glue

Cut a sword shape from cardboard. Cover the blade with aluminum foil and decorate the handle with sequins, glitter, and pearl pasta. Cut a rectangle from construction paper twice the size of the blade of the sword. Fold the rectangle over and glue it around the edges, leaving top edge open, to create a sheath.

Lady's Hat

In medieval times, women of the nobility always kept their heads covered.

Paper hat
Materials:

- Construction paper
- Tissue paper
- Scissors
- Glue

Cut your paper into a triangle with a wide base and roll it into a cone. Glue the overlapping edges to make a tall, pointed hat. Glue a wide streamer of tissue paper to the top.

Mummers

Villagers often wore animal masks and performed plays to entertain at street fairs. On Christmas, these mummers visited the lord's castle and performed skits in return for Christmas food and money.

Paper Bag Mummer's Mask

Materials:

- Paper grocery bags
- Construction paper
- Scissors
- Glue

Cut the top 6 inches off the paper bag, so that when the bag is put over your head, it will fit better. Cut a wide rectangle out of the front of the sack for your eyes. Finally, add animal features cut from construction paper—brown fringes for a lion's mane, a conical horn for a unicorn's head, red ears and pointed nose for a fox, and so on.

Robin Hood

The legend of Robin Hood is gaining renewed popularity thanks to several recent films. The idea of robbing from the rich to give to the poor has always had a certain attraction to it, which may be one reason why this legend has endured. Read *Robin Hood* adapted by J. Walker McSpadden.

Robin Hood's Hat

Materials:

- Green construction paper (12 by 18 inches)
- Glue
- Feathers (or cut them from construction paper)

Fold a sheet of green paper in half hamburger style. With the folded side at the top, fold the top two corners inward to meet in the middle. Glue these flaps securely. Fold the bottom edge of the paper up in the front and the back to make a brim. Glue a feather in the corner of the front of the hat.

ENGLISH ARCHITECTURE

English architectural styles drew heavily on the material available to the builders—lots of wood and stone.

Castles

Castles were built primarily for defensive capabilities and not for comfort. Built mostly from stone, these buildings were cold and drafty, but nevertheless protected many a noble family from their enemies. Some good books about castles are *See Inside a Castle* by R. J. Unstead, *The Days of Knights and Castles* by Pierre Miquel, and *Castle* by David Macauley.

Appliance Box Castle

Materials:

- Large appliance box
- Gray paint and paintbrushes
- Straw or grass
- Yarn or string
- Sharp knife
- Tape

Have your teacher cut the flaps off an appliance box and stand it upright with the open end up, then cut notches in the top of the box like a tower. Cut a three-sided rectangle near the bottom of one side of the box, leaving it attached at the bottom edge. Attach this rectangle to the sides of the box with yarn or string and tape; now you have a drawbridge that can be raised or lowered. Paint the outside of the box gray. Scatter straw or grass on the floor of the box. Narrow windows may be cut near the top of the box, if you want.

Cardboard Box Castle

Materials:

- Small boxes, shoeboxes, cartons, empty film containers, and so on
- Gray paint
- Posterboard for base (ideally green)
- Construction paper
- Heavy wood glue
- Scissors
- Paintbrushes

Use your imagination to create a castle from the boxes, using wood glue to attach the pieces together. Use posterboard for the base of the castle, and add details with construction paper. When the glue has dried, paint the castle gray.

Castle Picture

Materials:

- Construction paper, especially gray
- Crayons
- Glue
- Scissors

Cut the gray paper into small rectangles. Arrange these on blue or white paper to form a castle. Add details with crayons.

Tapestries

These huge wall hangings provided warmth against the cold stone walls of castles by blocking drafts. When a nobleman traveled from one castle to another, his tapestries traveled with him. They were usually of hunting scenes or pictures of romantic subjects. Pictures of tapestries can be found in *Inside Great Britain* by Ian James and *The Arts of Mankind: Painting, Architecture and Music* from the International Geographic Society.

Tapestry Mural

Materials:

- Large sheet of butcher paper
- Paints
- Paintbrushes
- Pencils

This is a good group project. Choose a scene for your class tapestry. Decide whether you want to sketch in the details of your tapestry before painting or if you just want to get in and paint. Study pictures of tapestries and notice the importance of intricate detail and the fact that tapestries usually told stories.

Cathedrals

The cathedral is considered by many to be the greatest and most lasting achievement of medieval society. The great cathedrals of England were created by hand, made of stone, and designed not by architects, but by master masons. The tall, gothic spires are characteristic of the era. Pictures of cathedrals can be found in *Inside Great Britain* by Ian James and *Cathedral* by David Macauley.

Small Box Cathedral

Materials:

- Paper towel tubes, shoeboxes, and other small boxes
- Gray paint
- Wood glue
- Posterboard
- Construction paper
- Printed tissue paper
- Scissors
- Paintbrushes

Construct your cathedral as you did the Cardboard Box Castle on p. 164. The paper towel tubes can serve as the spires; shoeboxes and other small boxes form the base of the building. Glue the pieces together with wood glue and place the cathedral on a posterboard base. Paint the cathedral gray. Add construction paper details. Cut holes in the boxes for windows, and glue printed tissue paper over the windows for a stained glass effect.

Cathedral Picture

Materials:

- Construction paper, especially gray
- Printed tissue paper
- Glue
- Scissors

Cut gray paper into rectangles and glue them onto white or blue construction paper in the shape of a cathedral. Make sure your spires are tall and thin. Add rectangles of printed tissue paper for stained glass windows.

Stained Glass Windows

The cost of the stained glass windows (see fig. 13.1) decorating medieval cathedrals was immense. Even ordinary glass was so expensive during this time that when the rich moved from house to house, they took their window glass with them. Pictures of stained glass windows can be found in *The Arts of Mankind: Painting, Architecture and Music* from the International Geographic Society.

Fig. 13.1.

Stained Glass Picture

Materials:

- Black construction paper
- Colored tissue paper
- Pencils
- Scissors and glue

Using the fold-and-cut technique, cut freeform shapes from black paper, leaving only thin black lines of paper between the spaces. Trace each cutout onto different colors of tissue paper and cut around these lines, but outside the lines so that the tissue paper cutout is slightly larger than the corresponding hole in the black paper. Put a thin line of glue on the edge of tissue paper cutouts and glue them to black frame. Put completed picture in classroom window for a very pretty stained glass effect.

Herringbone Cottages

This style of architecture was very popular in English villages and many examples can be seen today. A combination of stone and wood, called half-timbered, often appeared in a herringbone design but is also seen in a straight rectangular pattern. Pictures of herringbone cottages can be found in *The Arts of Mankind: Painting, Architecture and Music* from the International Geographic Society and *Let's Travel in England*, edited by Darlene Geis.

Cottage Picture

Materials:

- Black and white construction paper
- Crayons
- Scissors
- Glue

Draw a house on white paper. Cut long, thin rectangles from black paper and glue them onto the house in the desired design. Add doors, windows, and a black roof to your picture. Other details can be added with crayons.

The Tower of London

The Tower of London is actually several interconnected towers. Kings traditionally stayed in the Tower while awaiting their coronation. The Tower also housed many famous royal prisoners, among them Anne Boleyn, one of Henry VIII's wives; Elizabeth I, before she became queen; Mary, Queen of Scots; and the young King Edward V and his brother Richard, the Duke of York, who were allegedly killed by their uncle. The question of whether or not Richard III actually killed his two young nephews is one of the most fascinating murder mysteries of all time and is still hotly debated by historians.

The crown jewels of England are kept in an underground room in the Tower of London, guarded by the famous Beefeaters. Pictures of the crown jewels can be found in *The Arts of Mankind: Painting, Architecture and Music* from the International Geographic Society. For more information on the Tower, read *The Tower of London* by Leonard Everett Fisher.

Paper Crown

Materials:

- Construction paper
- Sequins, glitter, pearl pasta, aluminum foil
- Scissors
- Glue

Cut and glue a crown from construction paper, measuring it to fit your head. Decorate with sequins, glitter, pearl pasta, and aluminum foil.

THE ARTWORK OF ENGLAND

England has given the world many great artists. Most cities or large towns have art galleries. The English appreciate their art treasures and work hard to preserve them.

Landscapes

Landscape paintings became very popular in the nineteenth century in response to the pride the gentry felt in their farmland, which had become newly productive as a result of better farming practices. One of the most famous British landscape artists was John Constable, who painted many of his landscapes in Stour Valley in Suffolk. Samples of Constable's painting can be found in *The Great Century of British Painting: Hogarth to Turner* by William Gaunt.

Landscape Picture

Materials:

- Paint
- Paper
- Paintbrushes
- Pencils

Take your paper outside and draw a landscape. You can draw an outline with pencil, or paint straight onto the paper if you want.

Wedgwood China

English bone china is one of England's finest exports today. All the china comes from a district in Midlands known as the Potteries. There are kilns smoking everywhere and the houses are covered with soot, but the people who live there produce some of the most beautiful china in the world. Josiah Wedgwood began making his blue jasperware in the 1700s. Pictures of Wedgwood china can be found in *The Collector's Book of Wedgwood* by Marian Klamkin and *Let's Travel in England,* edited by Darlene Geis.

China Picture

Materials:

- Blue and white construction paper
- Glue
- Scissors

Cut plates and platters from the blue paper and decorate them with white cutouts.

ENGLISH GARDENS

The English are great gardeners. From the largest palace to the tiniest cottage, it seems that every home has a garden, even if it is only a window box.

Flower Gardens

Stately manors and large estates in England go to a great deal of effort designing and maintaining their large and beautiful gardens. Tours are organized just to view the gardens of the country. In the days of servants, a good gardener was prized over all with the exception, perhaps, of the cook. Pictures of English gardens can be found in *Let's Travel in England,* edited by Darlene Geis.

Garden Picture

Materials:

- Seed catalogs
- Paper
- Scissors
- Glue

Go through the seed catalogs and cut out flower pictures. Lay your pictures out on paper and design your own garden.

CELEBRATIONS

Many English holidays center around patriotic or historical events.

Guy Fawkes Day

Guy Fawkes Day is celebrated on November 5. In 1605, Guy Fawkes tried unsuccessfully to blow up King James I and the Houses of Parliament. As part of the festival, children make stuffed dummies called "guys." They go from house to house asking for pennies for the guy, collecting as much money as they can. Then they build a huge bonfire and burn the dummy on top of the bonfire while setting off fireworks.

Stuffed Guy

Materials:

- Old clothes
- Newspaper
- Paper grocery bag
- Sticks
- Orange paper
- Crayons
- Scissors

Stuff old clothes with crumpled newspaper. Draw facial features on a grocery bag and stuff it with paper to form the head. Sit the guy on top of a pile of sticks and arrange orange construction paper flames around figure.

Trooping the Colour

This festival occurs in June when the Queen reviews her troops. The Royal Guardsmen march in a parade with their bright red jackets and tall black hats.

Paper Guardsman Hat

Materials:

- Construction paper
- Glue
- Black pompoms or crumpled pieces of black tissue paper

Glue two pieces of construction paper together at the short end and measure it to fit around your head, cutting and gluing accordingly. Cover the hat with black pom poms. If you have a red shirt, wear it with your hats and have your own Royal Parade.

THE LONDON FOG

A study of England would not be complete without mention of the fog that has figured so prominently in English poetry and literature.

Fog Picture

Materials:

- Blue construction paper
- White tissue paper (facial tissue works well)
- Crayons
- Glue

Draw a city scene on the blue paper. Glue a layer of tissue over the picture to create a fog effect.

WALES

Capital: **Cardiff**
Population: **2,825,000**
Area: **8,019 square miles**

Lying to the west of England, Wales has a character very distinct from England and a people proud to be Welsh. Wales is a country of poets; even the language, with its Gaelic roots, is lyrical.

Traditionally, culture, history, and knowledge were passed orally. A great deal of emphasis has always been placed on poetry and in vocal music, especially choral singing. In recent years, the Welsh have shown a renewed interest in preserving their culture, and they believe that preservation of their language is an important part of that goal. Famous people from Wales include Lewis Carroll, Dylan Thomas, Bertrand Russell, and Richard Burton. Students studying Wales will gain an appreciation of the beauty of the language and the Welsh legends.

RED DRAGONS

The red dragon is the national symbol of Wales and comes from a story about the magician, Merlin. When Merlin was a boy, he was brought to King Vortigren, who wished to sacrifice him to break an evil spell that kept the foundations of a great fortress from being built. Merlin told the king that the real reason the foundations were disappearing was that two dragons lay beneath the fortress. At night, the dragons awoke to fight, shaking the earth and destroying the foundations. Workmen dug down and found two sleeping dragons, one red and one white. Merlin told Vortigren that the red dragon represented the Celts and the white one the Saxons, and that they would continue to fight as long as the two peoples fought each other.

Dragon Picture

Materials:

- Red, yellow, and white construction paper
- Dragon pattern (see fig. 13.2)
- Scissors
- Glue

Cut one dragon from red paper and one from white paper and glue them together onto the yellow paper.

Fig. 13.2.

SCOTLAND

Capital: Edinburgh
Population: 5,090,000
Area: 30,418 square miles

Scotland, home of clans and plaids, kilts and bagpipes, glens and lochs. The Scottish people hold fast to the old traditions. Folk art is very popular in Scotland, especially folk music. Mary Stuart was Scottish, as was Sir Walter Scott, MacBeth, Robert Burns, Robert Louis Stevenson, and James Barrie. A good book about the country is *Scotland* by Ian Digby.

PLAIDS

Kilts have been worn for centuries in the Scottish highlands and probably evolved from the dress of the early Celts. The designs of the plaids are unique to each clan. There are several good books with pictures of tartan plaids, including *Tartans, Their Art and History* by Ann Sutton, Richard Carr, and David Cripps; *The Clans and Tartans of Scotland* by Robert Bain; and *Tartans of the Clans of Scotland* by James Grant.

Tartan Picture

Materials:

- Crayons
- Paper

Study the tartans of different clans and practice drawing their plaid pattern on paper. Do you have a Scottish name? Can you find your family's tartan? If not, make up a plaid pattern of your own.

LOCH NESS MONSTER

Loch Ness is probably the best known loch in the world because of the reported sightings of Nessie, the Loch Ness monster, which some say is a leftover dinosaur or a sea monster. Although the existence of Nessie has never been proven, sightings extend back over several hundred years and thousands of people visit Loch Ness each year hoping for a glimpse. One of the most famous photos of the monster was recently revealed to have been a hoax.

Nessie Picture

Materials:

- White construction paper
- Crayons, especially black
- Blue tempera, mixed thinly
- Paintbrushes

Draw a picture of the Loch Ness monster with a black crayon. Use blue tempera to paint the loch around Nessie, leaving only the monster's head sticking out of the water. Color the sky and add details of the banks of the loch with other colors.

BADGES AND MOTTOES

Highland chieftains gave members of their clans a circular badge with a motto written in Latin, French, English, or Gaelic around the outside. The head of a clan had feathers on his badge. Some clans had animals on their badge while others had trees or other plants.

Motto Picture
Materials:

- Paper
- Crayons or colored felt-tip markers
- Scissors

Cut a circle from paper. Choose a symbol for your badge and then think of a motto to write around the outside of the badge.

IRELAND

Capital: **Dublin**
Government: **Republic**
Population: **3,494,000**
Area: **27,137 square miles**

Ireland is famed for its emerald beauty and magical legends. Once part of the British empire, the Republic of Ireland, which is mostly Catholic, has been independent since the 1940s. Northern Ireland is still part of Great Britain. Irish writers have had a profound influence on Western literature. Famous writers from Ireland include Jonathan Swift, William Butler Yeats, George Bernard Shaw, James Joyce, and Samuel Beckett.

IRISH ARCHITECTURE

Stone is plentiful in Ireland, so many buildings are constructed from that material. Ruins of ancient buildings dot the countryside.

Stone Cottages

Many farmers and crofters still live in stone cottages with thatched roofs.

Clay Stone Cottage
Materials:

- Small white pebbles
- Cardboard for base
- Modeling clay
- Dried grass or straw

Form the walls of a cottage from clay and set it on top of cardboard base. Press the pebbles into the clay. Top your model with a roof made of dried grass or straw.

3-D Cottage Picture

Materials:

- Small white pebbles
- Glue
- Dried grass or straw
- Heavy paper or cardboard
- Crayons

Glue the pebbles onto the paper in the shape of a stone cottage. Glue grass or straw on top to make the roof and add details with crayons.

Round Towers

These Irish towers, many of which are still standing today, were built for protection from attacks by the Vikings. Pictures of these towers can be found in *Now and in Time to Be: Ireland and the Irish* by Thomas Keneally.

Oatmeal Box Tower

Materials:

- Oatmeal boxes
- Small pebbles
- Gray construction paper
- Scissors
- Glue

Glue pebbles or torn pieces of paper to the sides of the oatmeal box. Cut a window into the top of the box. Add a spiked railing, cut from gray paper, at the very top.

IRISH ART

The Irish are fine artists and excellent craftsmen with a fine tradition of art that extends back thousands of years.

The Book of Kells

The *Book of Kells* is the most famous manuscript in the Library of Trinity College in Dublin. This Latin text of the four Gospels is accompanied by intricately painted and illuminated pages, as well as by brilliant decorations within the lines of the text itself. Only two of its 680 pages are without colors. Pictures of the Book of Kells can be found in *The Oxford Illustrated History of Ireland,* edited by R. F. Foster, and *The Book of Kells* by Peter Brown.

Illuminated Stories

Materials:

- White construction paper
- Poster paints
- Small paintbrushes or long quill feathers
- Black felt-tip markers

Write a folk tale or fairy tale (either a favorite old story or an original story that you've made up) on white paper with the black marker. Write in narrow columns, leaving wide margins, and paint delicate pictures in the margins.

Irish Lace

Irish lace is world famous for its quality, and the Irish are known for the intricate designs of their lace. The elite of Irish society call themselves the "Lace Curtain Irish."

Embroidered Fabric

Materials:

- Sheer white gauze fabric
- White thread
- Needles

Use white thread to embroider designs on gauze, creating the impression of lace.

Lace Picture

Materials:

- White paper
- Scissors

Cut intricate paper snowflakes from the white paper to simulate lace.

Weaving

Weaving is a major industry in Ireland. Irish linens are sold worldwide, and Ireland is also known for its fine tweeds and woven blankets.

Cardboard Loom

See the "Shoebox Loom" activity in chapter 7 (p. 96) for loom weaving techniques.

Celtic Cross

The Celts embraced Christianity and merged it with their own religious legends. The Celtic cross is a symbol of this merging of religions. It is a traditional Christian cross over a circle. Celtic crosses are some of the finest samples of Irish artwork. Pictures of Celtic crosses can be found in *Now and in Time to Be: Ireland and the Irish* by Thomas Keneally.

Clay Cross

Materials:

- Modeling clay
- Toothpicks

Form a cross from the modeling clay, making the ends of the arms wider than at the center. Add a circle behind the cross and use a toothpick to embellish the arms of the cross.

IRISH SYMBOLS

Ireland is a land of symbols. The country has adopted an entire color, green, as their own, and on St. Patrick's Day shamrocks and leprechauns pop up everywhere, even here in America.

Leprechauns

According to legend, Ireland is populated by the little people. Fairies and elves inhabit the fields and valleys, and the leprechauns, probably the most well known little people of Ireland, hide their pot of gold at the end of every rainbow.

Leprechaun Picture

Materials:

- Dark orange yarn
- Paper plates
- Green and black construction paper
- Crayons
- Scissors
- Glue

Draw a leprechaun face on the paper plate. Design a beard and hair from the red yarn and cut a green bowler hat with a black buckle from construction paper.

Rainbow Mural

Materials:

- White butcher paper
- Paint (bright colors)
- Black and white paper
- Gold glitter
- Paintbrushes
- Glue

Cut the butcher paper into a long arch. Paint a rainbow along the arch, using bright colors. Cut a kettle from the black paper and put it at one end of the rainbow. Fill the kettle with white paper coated with glitter.

The Shamrock

The shamrock is the national symbol of Ireland and of Saint Patrick, Ireland's patron saint. It is a symbol of good luck.

Shamrock Prints

Materials:

- Sponges
- Green paint
- Scissors
- Paper

Cut the sponges into shamrock shapes and use them to paint shamrocks onto the white paper.

Shamrock Picture

Materials:

- Green paper
- Shamrock pattern (see fig. 13.3)
- Scissors

Using the shamrock pattern as a guide, cut shamrock shapes from green paper.

REFERENCES

Abels, Harriette. *The Mystery of Stonehenge*. Mankato, MN: Crestwood House, 1987.

The Arts of Mankind: Painting, Architecture and Music. Englewood Cliffs, NJ: International Geographic Society, 1962.

Bain, Robert. *The Clans and Tartans of Scotland*. London: Collins, 1968.

Branley, Franklyn M. *The Mystery of Stonehenge*. New York: Thomas Y. Crowell, 1969.

Brown, Peter. *The Book of Kells*. New York: Alfred A. Knopf, 1980.

Digby, Ian. *Scotland*. England: W. H. Smith & Son, 1980.

Fisher, Leonard Everett. *The Tower of London*. New York: Macmillan, 1987.

Foster, R. F., ed. *The Oxford Illustrated History of Ireland*. New York: Oxford University Press, 1989.

Gaunt, William. *The Great Century of British Painting: Hogarth to Turner*. London: Phaidon Press, 1971.

Geis, Darlene, ed. *Let's Travel in England*. Chicago: Childrens Press, 1964.

Grant, James. *Tartans of the Clans of Scotland*. New York: Dover, 1992.

James, Ian. *Inside Great Britain*. New York: Franklin Watts, 1988.

Keneally, Thomas. *Now and in Time to Be: Ireland and the Irish*. New York: W. W. Norton, 1991.

Klamkin, Marian. *The Collector's Book of Wedgwood*. New York: Dodd, Mead, 1971.

Lyon, Nancy. *The Mystery of Stonehenge*. New York: Contemporary Perspectives, 1977.

Macauley, David. *Castle*. Boston: Houghton Mifflin, 1977.

———. *Cathedral*. Boston: Houghton Mifflin, 1973.

McSpadden, J. Walker. *Robin Hood*. New Jersey: Unicorn, 1990.

Miquel, Pierre. *The Days of Knights and Castles*. New York: Hamlyn, 1980.

Sutton, Ann, Richard Carr, and David Cripps. *Tartans, Their Art and History*. New York: Arco, 1984.

Turner, Dorothy. *The Man-Made Wonders of the World*. Minneapolis, MN: Dillon, 1986.

Unstead, R. J. *See Inside a Castle*. New York: Warwick Press, 1986.

FURTHER READING

Bauer, Henry H. *The Enigma of Loch Ness: Making Sense of a Mystery*. Urbana: University of Illinois Press, 1986.

Fox, Villa M. *Costumes and Customs of the British Isles*. Boston: Plays, 1974.

Langley, Andrew. *Passport to Great Britain*. New York: Franklin Watts, 1986.

Lye, Keith. *Take a Trip to Wales*. London: Franklin Watts, 1986.

McHenry, Robert, ed. *The New Encyclopaedia Britannica*, vols. 2–4, 6–8, 10–12. Chicago: Encyclopaedia Britannica, 1992.

Rowling, Marjorie. *Life in Medieval Times*. New York: G. P. Putnam's Sons, 1979.

Toy, Sidney, *Castles: Their Construction and History*. New York: Dover, 1984.

Weir, Alison. *The Princes in the Tower*. New York: Ballantine Books, 1992.

Fig. 13.3.

14
SCANDINAVIA

The Scandinavian countries are Denmark, Sweden, Norway, and Iceland. These countries are grouped together because of historical, cultural, and linguistic similarities. Finland is sometimes included on geological and economic grounds although it is not linguistically related to the other four countries. Scandinavia is the ancient home of Viking warriors, and the Scandinavians are a fiercely independent people. Their spirit of adventure can be seen in such modern day explorers as Thor Heyerdahl, who is best known for his ocean voyages on the Kon-tiki and the Ra in attempts to prove his theories about the migration of ancient peoples; and Roald Amundsen, who was the first person to reach the South Pole.

Given the harsh climate of Scandinavia, the people spend much of their energy exploring and adventuring. They do not have much time for art, but the winter months were often devoted to handicrafts and storytelling. A unit on Scandinavia will introduce students to a spirit of adventure and to a brave people.

THE VIKINGS

The Vikings lived in Scandinavia between 800 and 1100 and raided wide areas of Europe, England, and Russia. These raids were prompted by a combination of factors including overpopulation at home and the relative helplessness of their victims. More than simply warriors, the Vikings were explorers, tradesmen, and craftsmen. They valued cleanliness and health, and had laws protecting the rights of women to own property.

Vikings first set foot on the American continent in 986, more than 500 years before Columbus "discovered" the New World. Icelander Bjarni Herjulfsson was blown off course and landed on what was possibly Nova Scotia, a land he called Vinland. Fourteen years later, Leif Eriksson was a member of an expedition to Vinland that attempted, unsuccessfully, to establish a settlement.

Some good books about the Vikings are *Everyday Life in the Viking Age* by Jacqueline Simpson, *The Vikings* by Pamela Odjin, and *The Vikings* by Hazel Martell.

179

Viking Longhouses

A typical longhouse was constructed of wood; the roof and walls were covered with straw. Homes were usually situated at the foot of a high, grassy slope, and a bank of earth ran along the inside of each wall, serving as a bed at night and a bench during the day. An open fire in the middle of the hall provided light, warmth, and a means for cooking. Smoke escaped through a hole in the roof. Additional rooms in the back of the longhouse provided storage and workspaces for the women. Pictures of longhouses can be found in *The Art of the Vikings* by Shirley Glubok and *Everyday Life in the Viking Age* by Jacqueline Simpson.

Shoebox Longhouse

Materials:

- Shoebox
- Brown construction paper
- Straw or yellow construction paper
- Scissors
- Glue

Turn the shoebox upside down and glue strips of brown construction paper over the sides of the shoebox. Cut a door into the narrow end of the box. Glue straw or shredded yellow construction paper over top and sides of the longhouse.

Longships

The Vikings were mighty sailors, even crossing the Atlantic in their open boats. Their favorite boats were the longships that they used for war. These ships could be up to 180 feet long. They were carved to resemble a dragon—from the prows carved in the shape of a dragon's head to the striped broad sails that looked like a mighty dragon's wings unfurled to the oars protruding from the sides of the ship, looking like the dragon's legs (see fig. 14.1). Pictures of a longship can be found in *The Art of the Vikings* by Shirley Glubok and *Everyday Life in the Viking Age* by Jacqueline Simpson.

Longship Picture

Materials:

- Brown and blue construction paper
- Heavy tissue paper or paper towel
- Drinking straw
- Aluminum foil
- Scissors
- Glue

Cut a long, shallow boat from the brown paper. Make the bow and stern of the boat extend high while the middle of the boat dips low. Glue the ship onto the blue paper. Cut a dragon's head from the brown paper and glue it to the bow of the boat. Glue a drinking straw in the middle of the boat for a mast and glue a sheet of white tissue paper or paper towel to the mast as a sail. Line the sides of the boat with brown circles with aluminum foil centers. These represent the shields that the Viking warriors rested at their sides while they rowed the boat. Cut thin, rectangular oars from brown paper and extend these out the side of the boat into the blue paper water.

Fig. 14.1.

Viking Warriors

The strong warrior is the image most people have of the Viking. These warriors treasured their armor and weapons, giving them poetic names such as Eagle's Flight and Thor's Blade.

Viking Battle Helmets

Contrary to the popular image, Viking battle helmets did not have horns. They were actually constructed to protect the head and face in a design that was possibly borrowed from the Romans.

Foil Helmet

Materials:

- Aluminum foil
- Cardboard
- Scissors
- Glue

Mold a piece of aluminum foil to fit the crown of your head, building the top into a pointed peak. Cut a face plate with a noseguard from cardboard, leaving holes for your eyes. Cover the face plate with the aluminum foil and attach it to your helmet.

Ceremonial Helmets

Viking ceremonial helmets were lavishly decorated, often with horns, and it is this helmet that most people today envision the Viking wearing.

Paper Viking Helmet

Materials:

- Brown construction paper
- White paper
- Stapler
- Scissors
- Tape

Cut a circle from brown paper. Cut a slit from one edge to center of circle. Overlap cut edges and staple the edges together, making a domed hat. Cut two triangles from white paper and roll them into cone shapes. Attach the cones to the brown paper hat.

The Viking Shield

The Viking Shield was round and often decorated with geometric shapes or animals. Shields were made of wood or metal and covered with leather. In the center of the shield was a metal dome.

Posterboard Shield

Materials:

- Posterboard
- Aluminum foil
- Colored felt-tip markers
- Paints and paintbrushes
- Scissors
- Glue

Cut a large circle from posterboard to form your shield. Decorate it with paints or markers. Glue a foil circle in center.

Battle Ax

A hallmark of Viking weaponry was the long, two-bladed battle ax.

Cardboard Ax

Materials:

- Long wooden dowel
- Cardboard
- Aluminum foil
- Tape or yarn
- Scissors
- Glue

Cut a rectangle from the cardboard and cover it with foil. Attach the dowel to the center of the rectangle with the tape or yarn to create a two-headed battle ax.

Runic Alphabet

The Vikings had no paper, so their alphabet consisted of vertical and diagonal strokes that could be carved easily on wood and stones. Runes were also considered to have magical properties. Runes carved in small sticks were used for blessings, spells, and curses; some stones were completely covered with runes. Runic carvings have been found from Greenland to the Black Sea. The runic carvings were painted with bright colors and set by the road for passersby to read. Obtain copies of the Runic alphabet from the library for students to study. A copy of the Runic alphabet can be found in *The Vikings* by Pamela Odjin.

Viking Runes

Materials:

- White paper
- Paints
- Paintbrushes
- Copy of the Runic alphabet

Using different colors of paints, copy runic symbols onto the paper.

Woodcarvings

Vikings were excellent woodcarvers. Most of their everyday items were made from wood and were carved with intricate designs. Many of their carvings tell stories of Viking legends and battles.

Wood or Styrofoam Carving (ages 10 and older)

Materials:

- Styrofoam or soft wood
- Sharp carving knife
- Brown paint if Styrofoam is used
- Paintbrush

Carve a design in the wood or Styrofoam. If you use Styrofoam, paint your carving brown when you are finished.

Wood Carving Picture

Materials:

- Brown construction paper
- Black felt-tip marker
- Scissors

Cut figures resembling wood carvings from brown paper, adding details with the black marker. Read stories from Norse mythology, and choose a favorite figure to depict.

Metalcraft

Vikings made intricate ornaments by melting down gold and silver acquired through trade. Animals were a favorite motif. Pictures of Viking jewelry can be found in *The Art of the Vikings* by Shirley Glubok.

Clay Ornaments

Materials:

- Leather strings
- Beads with holes in center
- Modeling clay
- Silver or gold paint
- Pencils
- Paintbrushes

Study pictures of Viking jewelry, then form an ornament from the modeling clay. Poke a hole through the top with a pencil. Let the clay harden. Paint your ornament either silver or gold and let it dry. String the ornament on a leather string along with other colored beads. Hang the necklace around your neck.

DENMARK

Capital: Copenhagen
Population: 5,141,000
Area: 16,638 square miles

Although modern Danes are descended from the fierce Viking warriors, today they are a peaceful people. They enjoy one of the world's oldest and most extensive social welfare systems. Some great artists from Denmark include writer Hans Christian Andersen, philosopher Søen Kierkegaard, sculptor Bertel Thorvaldsen, and architect Arne Jacobsen.

Hans Christian Andersen

Hans Christian Andersen is one of the world's most beloved storytellers. His stories are still read today, the world over, and have been made into many popular movies. His fairy tales are among the most frequently translated works in literary history.

THE UGLY DUCKLING

Andersen wrote this story of an ugly little duckling who turns into a beautiful swan about his own life.

Paper Bag Swan

Materials:

- Paper lunch bags
- White construction paper
- Orange paper
- Crayons
- Scissors
- Glue

Cut 4 inches from the open end of the lunch bag. Glue small pieces of white paper over the surface of the bag, covering it completely. Cut a 1½-by-4 inch rectangle from white paper. Curve the top of the strip and glue the bottom to the top of one of the narrow ends of the sack. Color eyes onto the curl and attach a small triangular beak cut from orange paper. Cut two large triangles from white paper. Fringe the edges and glue them to the sides of the bag for wings.

THUMBELINA

This is the story of a beautiful girl, no bigger than a person's thumb, who marries a fairy prince.

Thumbelina Picture

Materials:

- Inkpad or paint with a paper towel blotter
- Paper
- Crayons

Dip one thumb into the paint or ink pad and press it onto paper. Decorate your thumbprint with colors so that it will look like a tiny girl.

THE LITTLE MERMAID

This is one of Andersen's most beloved tales. A statue of the little mermaid sits in the harbor at Copenhagen, looking out to sea.

Mermaid Picture

Materials:

- Green tissue paper
- Crayons
- Blue watercolors
- White construction paper
- Paintbrushes
- Scissors
- Glue

Draw the top half of a mermaid on the white paper with crayons. Cut a tail fin from the green tissue paper and glue it in place. Paint over the entire picture with a thin blue watercolor wash.

SWEDEN

Capital: Stockholm
Population: 8,529,000
Area: 173,732 square miles

Sweden is tucked away in the far northern corner of Europe, isolated by the Baltic Sea. Although today's Swedes are descended from the warlike Vikings, they are leaders in the movement for world peace. Famous Swedes include Jenny Lind, Bjorn Borg, Greta Garbo, Ingmar Bergman, and Ingrid Bergman.

St. Lucia's Day

This is one of Sweden's most joyous festivals. It is held on December 13, ushering in the long, dark night of Sweden's winter. On St. Lucia's Day, white-robed girls wear headdresses with lit candles. Accompanied by boys carrying wands tipped with stars, they take coffee and cakes to older people.

Cardboard Candle Headdress

Materials:

- White cardboard
- White paper
- Yellow paper
- Stapler (optional)
- Scissors
- Glue

Cut a strip from the white cardboard and measure it to fit around your head, cutting as necessary. Glue or staple the ends together. Cut four candles from the white paper. Top the candles with flames cut from yellow paper and then glue the candles to the headband.

Fir Trees

The Swedish mountain ranges are covered with luxuriant fir trees, the harvest of which makes valuable contributions to the Swedish economy.

Fir Tree Picture

Materials:

- Gray and blue construction paper
- Sponges cut into triangular shapes
- Dark green and white tempera, mixed thickly
- Squeeze bottles
- Scissors
- Glue

Cut tall mountains from the gray paper and glue them onto the blue paper. Pour white paint into the squeeze bottles and squeeze the paint onto mountain ranges, letting paint ooze down the sides for a snowcapped effect. Sponge-paint fir trees with the dark green paints on the slopes of the mountains.

Smorgasbord

Smorgasbords are said to have originated in the days of the Vikings when warriors would bring back food from their voyages. They only brought a small amount of each type of food, so the people at home only got a small taste of each.

Smorgasbord Picture

Materials:

- Magazines
- Paper
- Scissors
- Glue

Cut pictures of food from magazines and arrange them on paper to create a smorgasbord picture.

ICELAND

Capital: Reykjav'k
Population: 256,000
Area: 39,699 square miles

Icelanders are probably the most fiercely independent of the Scandinavians, no doubt because of the harshness and isolation of their country. Their remote island is the most volcanically active place in Europe, and it is continually ravaged by volcanoes and earthquakes.

Mudpots

These natural bubbling pots of mud bear witness to the seething geothermal activity beneath the surface of Iceland. Pictures of mudpots can be found in *Iceland* from the *Enchantment of the World* series by Emilie U. Lepthien.

Mudpot Picture

Materials:

- Paper
- Brown tempera paint (mixed 1:1 with glue)
- Spoons

Drop globs of paint from a spoon onto the paper, covering the paper completely. Cover with another piece of paper and press firmly pushing the paint beneath the paper. Remove the top paper and you will have two identical mud pot pictures.

Geysers

Geysers are formed when superheated water is blasted out of the earth. Geysers erupt when the pressure of the heated water grows too great, and hot water and steam are shot into the air.

Geyser Picture

Materials:

- Brown crayons
- Blue paper
- White paint
- Straws
- Candle

Light the candle and hold a brown crayon near the flame until it is soft. Color the bottom of the paper with the melted crayon, creating swirls and circles. Drop white paint on top of the brown surface and straw-paint a geyser's eruption upward.

NORWAY

Capital: Oslo
Population: 4,246,000
Area: 125,050 square miles

Norwegians are a rugged people, singularly adapted to a harsh environment. The country is formed of some of the oldest rocks on earth, rocks that are 1 to 2 billion years old. There are still approximately 1,700 glaciers in Norway, and the country is subject to frequent high winds and weather changes. The long, cold winters give storytelling enormous importance in the Norwegian culture, which has a rich folklore.

Twentieth-century Norwegian painters are excellent muralists. Norwegian artists are also known for multimedia art, pictorial weaving, and nonfigurative sculpture. Famous Norwegians include Edvard Munch, who is regarded as the founder of Expressionism, and the writer Henrik Ibsen.

Sol Dag

Much of Norway is located above the Arctic Circle, where the sun sets at the end of November and is not seen again for two months. The festival of *Sol Dag,* or Sun Day, is celebrated on January 21, when inhabitants welcome the reappearance of the sun by displaying paper suns.

Paper Suns

Materials:

- Construction paper
- Crayons
- Scissors
- Glue

Color a construction paper circle with bright yellow and orange crayons. Cut rays from paper, color them, and glue them around the edges of the circle. Hang your sun from the ceiling.

Trolls

Norwegian folklore is peopled with ugly trolls who live in trees and under bridges waiting to trap the unwary. Read *The Troll Book* by Michael Berenstain.

Life-Size Troll Picture

Materials:

- Butcher paper
- Collage items
- Crayons or colored felt-tip markers

- Pencils
- Scissors
- Glue

Have a classmate lie on a piece of butcher paper and trace around him or her. Then let someone trace you. Turn your outline into a troll by using crayons or markers and collage materials.

Giant Troll Picture

Materials:

- Construction paper
- Crayons or colored felt-tip markers

- Scissors
- Glue

Divide yourselves into groups of four or five. Each person in the group should draw a portion of the troll's body—head, legs, body, and so on. When you are finished, combine your troll part with those in your group to create one complete troll.

FINLAND

Capital: **Helsinki**
Population: **4,926,000**
Area: **130,559 square miles**

Finland is Europe's most forested country, and is one of the most northern countries in the world, with one third of its land lying within the Arctic Circle.

Finland's national epic, the *Kalevala*, was compiled in the nineteenth century by Elias Lönnvot from old Finnish ballads, lyrics, and incantations, setting off an upsurge in patriotic enthusiasm that has since been the chief motivating factor in almost all of Finland's cultural activities.

Reindeer

The Lapps moved into the Arctic regions of Finland about the year 100, when they began to hunt and keep small herds of reindeer. This gradually developed into a full-scale nomadic lifestyle a few centuries later, with the entire family group living and moving with their large reindeer herds. This nomadism has virtually disappeared in recent years. Now the families stay in permanent winter or summer homes while the herders travel with the animals.

Reindeer Picture

Materials:

- Brown, black, and gray construction paper
- Scissors and glue

Put your shoe on the brown paper and cut around it. This will be your reindeer's head. Cut antlers from the gray paper and cut a nose and eyes from the black paper, and glue these pieces to the head.

Snow

Scandinavians love the snow and relish getting out to play in it, though they also have a healthy respect for the cold and snow. Winter sports provide an important source of income from tourists.

Snow Picture

Materials:

- Construction paper
- Crayons or colored felt-tip markers
- Glue (watered down)
- Brushes for glue
- White cornmeal

Students draw a scene on white paper. Use a paintbrush to paint glue in desired areas, then sprinkle white cornmeal onto the wet glue to create snow. When the glue dries, shake off the excess cornmeal.

REFERENCES

Berenstain, Michael. *The Troll Book*. New York: Random House, 1980.

Glubok, Shirley. *The Art of the Vikings*. New York: Macmillan, 1978.

Lepthien, Emilie U. *Iceland*, Enchantment of the World series. Chicago: Childrens Press, 1987.

Martell, Hazel. *The Vikings*. New York: Warwick Press, 1986.

Odjin, Pamela. *The Vikings*. New York: Englewood Cliffs, 1989.

Simpson, Jacqueline. *Everyday Life in the Viking Age*. New York: G. P. Putnam's Sons, 1967.

FURTHER READING

Clayton, Robert, and John Miles. *Scandinavia*, Finding Out About Geography series. New York: Golden Press, 1967.

Hosford, Dorothy. *Thunder of the Gods*. New York: Holt, Rinehart & Winston, 1952.

Lepthien, Emilie U. *Iceland*, Enchantment of the World series. Chicago: Childrens Press, 1987.

Magnusson, Magnus. *Hammer of the North*. London: Orbis, 1976.

McHenry, Robert, ed. *The New Encyclopaedia Britannica*, vols. 1, 4, 6, 8, 10, 11. Chicago: Encyclopaedia Britannica, 1992.

Orton, Gavin. *Scandinavia*. Morristown, NJ: Silver Burdett, 1979.

Pendlesonn, K. R. G. *The Vikings*. New York: Windward, 1980.

Scandinavia, Library of Nations series. Amsterdam: Time-Life, 1985.

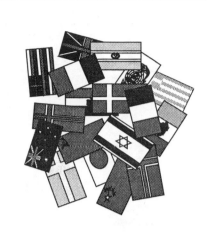

15
MEXICO

Capital: Mexico City
Government: Federal Republic
Population: 82,659,000
Area: 756,066 square miles

Mexico is a land of bright colors, with one of the richest cultures in North America, a blend of Native American and Spanish cultures. The first people to arrive in Mexico were nomadic hunters who crossed the Bering Strait from Asia during the Ice Age. By 20,000 years ago, these prehistoric peoples had crossed into Mexico. By 5,000 B.C. the settlers in the valleys and coastal plains had begun to cultivate maize, beans, and pumpkins.

By the time Hernán Cortés landed at Vera Cruz in 1519, a thriving Aztec city existed at Tenochtitlán, site of today's Mexico City. The Spanish conquistadors destroyed the city; betrayed and murdered the Aztec emperor, Montezuma; and destroyed the Aztec Empire, which had been comparable in size and scope to the Roman empire. Mexico then came under Spanish rule until their War of Independence in 1821.

Religious beliefs have always been a fundamental part of Mexican culture. The Spanish conquistadors brought Christianity to the country, but they grafted it onto the established beliefs of the native peoples so they would not reject the new religion. Christian worship was carried out in the shrines of the old gods, and many of the older rituals were incorporated into the Christian ceremonies.

A basic theme of Mexican art has always been adoration of either the ancient deities or the Christian ones. The Native American peoples had a highly developed sense of color and applied these techniques to Christian artwork. Hence we see many religious paintings with brightly colored fruit and flowers intermingled with religious subjects.

Although toward the end of the colonial period European trends somewhat stifled the creativity of Mexican artists, after the revolution, there was a return to the ancient traditions, incorporating new ideas and beliefs. A unit on Mexico will introduce students to a people that have blended two very different cultures into one that is diverse, unique, and beautiful.

THE OLMECS

The Olmecs developed one of the earliest civilizations in Mexico. They reigned from about 1200 B.C. to A.D. 250 and used their keen astronomical observations to create a precise calendar. Succeeding civilizations were heavily influenced by their science and philosophy. Their chief deity took the form of a jaguar. The most impressive artistic creations of the Olmecs were enormous stone heads, many of which have survived to today. These stone heads weighed as much as 40 tons, stood 8 to 9 feet tall and may have been portraits of Olmec rulers. Pictures of the Olmec heads can be found in *Mexico: Land of the Plummed Serpent* by Clara Louise Grant and Jane Werner Watson and *Mexico: The Land and Its People* by John Howard.

Olmec Stone Head

Materials:

- Butcher paper
- Crayons or colored felt-tip markers

Cover a section of a wall with several large sheets of butcher paper. On each sheet of paper, draw a huge head.

THE TOLTECS

Between 1000 and 1150, the Toltec empire controlled Mexico. They worshipped many of the same gods as the Olmecs, who had come before, and practiced human sacrifice. They were a fierce, warlike people who built great pyramids and temples of worship, and they were also great mathematicians and astronomers. The Toltec capital was Tula and some of their chief artifacts are columns representing Toltec warriors which served as supports for temple colonnades. Pictures of the Toltec columns can be found in *Let's Travel in Mexico*, edited by Darlene Geis, and *Mexico: The Land and Its People* by John Howard.

Refrigerator Box Columns

Materials:

- Refrigerator box or other long, narrow box
- White paper
- Gray paint
- Paintbrushes
- Glue

Cover the box with white paper and stand it up on one end. Paint the figure of a warrior on the box with gray paint.

THE MAYA

The Mayan civilization lasted from about 300 B.C. to A.D. 900. The Maya built upon previous civilizations, such as the Toltec, to create one of the greatest civilizations to ever inhabit the earth. They developed a system of writing, built temples and pyramids, and used their knowledge of astronomy to predict eclipses. They were also warriors and practiced human sacrifice to appease their gods. Books about the Mayas include *The Maya* by Patricia C. McKissack and *The Ancient Maya* by Barbara L. Beck.

Glyph Writing

The Maya created a system of picture writing, called glyphs. Some of the glyphs stood for sounds in the Mayan language. Mayan books, called codices, were long strips of paper made from bark or skin and folded like an accordion. Mayan writings record the history of ruling families and wars, laws, and taxes. Obtain as many examples of Mayan glyph writing from the library as you can to study. See *The Ancient Maya* by Barbara L. Beck and *The Maya* by Patricia C. McKissack for examples of glyph writing.

Paper Codices
Materials:

- Paper
- Colored felt-tip markers
- Samples of Mayan glyphs
- Tape

Study samples of Mayan glyph writing. Copy glyphs onto your paper. Tape several sheets of paper together and fold them accordion-style to make codices.

Stelae

Stelae, or stone slabs, were covered with glyph carvings and were erected to commemorate important events in a leader's life. Stelae could be as much as 30 feet tall.

Clay Stele
Materials:

- Modeling clay
- Toothpick

Form clay into a rectangular pillar. Using toothpicks, scratch small pictures and markings into the pillar.

Maize Necklaces

The Maya made lovely necklaces from colored corn.

Corn Kernel Necklace
Materials:

- Ears of Indian corn
- Saucepan
- Nylon fishing thread
- Needles

Remove colored kernels from the cob and boil until soft. String kernels with needle and thread. Tie the ends of the string together to form a necklace and hang it to dry. Use shorter lengths of string to make bracelets.

Mayan Masks

The Maya created elaborate wooden masks for spiritual purposes. These were worn by Mayan priests during ceremonies and represented the Mayan deities.

Papier-Mâché Mask
Materials:

- Balloon
- Glue (mix 1:1 with water) and glue
- Feathers
- Newspaper
- Crepe paper and streamers
- Paint and paintbrushes

Inflate the balloon. Cover half of the balloon with several layers of strips of newspaper dipped in the glue mixture. Let the papier-mâché dry thoroughly. When it is dry, peel off the balloon, and paint and decorate the mask with crepe paper, streamers, and feathers.

THE AZTECS

The Aztec empire began as a small nomadic tribe who took refuge from other warlike tribes on a swampy island in Lake Texoco in the early fourteenth century. Their god gave them a sign to show them where to build their village, an eagle sitting on a cactus eating a snake. From the muddy swamp, the Aztecs created a city, Tenochtitlán, which became the most powerful city in Mexico. The seemingly unstoppable Aztec conquest brought the Valley of Mexico completely under Aztec control until Cortés and his Spanish conquistadors entered the valley in 1519. Within two years, the Aztec empire was completely destroyed. To learn more about this people, read *The Aztecs* by Jacqueline Dineen.

The Great Temple

The Great Temple was the main religious building in Tenochtitlán, where the Aztecs carried out their rituals of human sacrifice. It was rebuilt six times, with each new building using the materials of the previous version, because each Aztec ruler wanted to build a bigger, more improved Great Temple than that of his predecessor. See *The Aztecs* by Jacqueline Dineen for pictures of The Great Temple.

Cardboard Box Temple

Materials:

- Two half-pint milk cartons
- Construction paper
- Glue
- Four stationery boxes from packaging store, decreasing sizes
- Cardboard
- Colored felt-tip markers
- Scissors

Set the stationery boxes one atop the other to form a pyramid. Cut out the two front corners of each box, creating square impressions, and cover the holes with paper. Glue the boxes securely. Have a sheet of cardboard lead from the bottom box to the top, drawing lines on it with markers to represent the steps. Cut the tops off the two milk cartons, cover them with paper, and set at the back of the top layer. Decorate the milk cartons with pictures of jaguars and serpents.

Shields

The Aztecs were a warrior race and used any excuse to go to war. Soldiers were not paid, but if they performed bravely enough in battle, they were rewarded with gifts of land, slaves, or clothing. It was even possible to attain the rank of nobleman through distinction in battle. Shields were made from wicker, covered with leather, and decorated with feathers.

Cardboard Shield

Materials:

- Cardboard
- Feathers
- Paints
- Paintbrushes
- Scissors
- Glue

Cut a circle from the cardboard to make your shield. On the surface, paint a design, perhaps of a fierce eagle or jaguar. Glue feathers around the edge of the shield.

Featherwork

The Aztecs made beautiful objects of art from feathers, which were also used to make mosaic pictures. The feathers came from an aviary in Tenochtitlán where thousands of birds were kept. As the birds molted, the feathers were collected and taken to the featherworkers.

Feather Picture

Materials:

- Cardboard
- Feathers
- Crayons
- Scissors

Draw a simple design on a piece of cardboard. Lay the feathers over the design and glue them into place.

MEXICAN CLOTHING

Sombreros

The word sombrero is derived from the Spanish word *sombra*, meaning shade. These practical hats help protect the wearer from Mexico's hot sun, and the brims can be up to 2 feet wide. In the United States, the sombrero has been modified to become the very popular cowboy hat.

Cardboard Sombrero

Materials:

- Styrofoam cup
- Yarn
- Scissors
- Colored tissue paper
- Cardboard (14 by 14 inches)
- Hole punch

Cut a 12-inch circle from the cardboard. Cut a hole in the center the same size as the diameter of the cup. Punch holes around the outside edge of the circle. Cover the outside of the cup with tissue paper and stick the cup through the hole from the bottom, pushing until it can go no farther. Lace yarn around the edges of the cardboard circle.

Serapes and Rebozos

These colorful blankets and shawls serve as head coverings, protection from the cold, and ornamental dress.

Cloth Serape

Materials:

- Strip of muslin (12 by 36 inches)
- Crayons
- Iron

Color a geometric design on the muslin and run a hot iron over drawing to set the design (be sure to keep a piece of cloth between the design and the iron). Boys drape the serape over one shoulder while girls wear the rebozo over their heads.

FIESTAS

El Dia del Muerte

On this day in early November, Mexicans honor their dead family members. As a popular treat during this festival, they make cookies and candy in the shape of small skulls.

Paper Skeleton
Materials:

- Brass paper fasteners
- White construction paper (8 by 12 inches)
- Scissors

Fold one sheet of paper in half. Cut bones from the folded paper for upper and lower arms, upper and lower legs. Cut feet, hands, neck, backbone and ribs, and skull from a flat sheet of white paper. Attach all pieces together with brass paper fasteners.

La Posada

At Christmas, Mexican children re-enact the Biblical story of Mary and Joseph's search for a room at an inn. They dress up and parade through the streets, knocking on doors and asking for a place to sleep. At last they are allowed inside, where they celebrate with a piñata.

Papier-Mâché Piñata
Materials:

- Cones, cardboard tubes, paper cups, etc.
- Newspaper
- Colored tissue paper
- Balloon
- Glue mixed with water (1:1)
- Glue

Blow up the balloon and cover it with strips of paper dipped in the glue and water mixture. Let each layer dry thoroughly before applying another. Use papier-mâché to attach cones, cardboard tubes, and cups to your piñata to give it the desired shape. When the piñata is completely dry, pieces of colored tissue paper may be glued onto the piñata.

Paper Bag Piñata
Materials:

- Paper grocery bags
- Colored construction paper
- Yarn
- Crepe paper streamers
- Scissors
- Stapler
- Glue

Put candy and prizes inside doubled paper bags. Roll the top down and staple the bags shut. Decorate as desired with colored construction paper and streamers. Suspend from ceiling with yarn.

Easter Cascarones

These empty, painted eggshells are filled with confetti and hidden for children to find and throw at each other.

Painted Eggshells

Materials:

- Hollowed-out eggshell (made by poking a hole in each end of a raw egg and blowing out the contents)
- Small pieces of torn construction paper
- Colored felt-tip markers or paints
- Paintbrushes

Fill eggshells with torn paper and decorate with markers or paints.

Cinco de Mayo

Cinco de Mayo means the fifth of May in Spanish, which is the date when Mexicans commemorate the Battle at Puebla of 1862, at which the Mexican army defeated French forces sent by Napoleon III, who wanted to establish a French satellite state in Mexico. Today Mexicans celebrate Cinco de Mayo by decorating piñatas with large, colorful paper flowers and holding dances with mariachi bands.

Tissue Paper Flowers

Materials:

- Colored tissue paper (size depends on how big a flower is desired)
- Twist ties

Layer six pieces of tissue paper and fold them together fan-style. Wrap a twist tie around the center and pull the layers apart on each side.

Maracas

These gourd rattles are a staple of traditional Mexican mariachi bands. The word *mariachi* comes from the Spanish word for "marriage," because these bands frequently perform at weddings.

Papier-Mâché Maracas

Materials:

- Small balloons
- Newspaper
- Glue (mixed 1:1 with water)
- Dried beans
- Paint
- Paintbrushes

Insert several dried beans into uninflated balloons. Inflate the balloons, then cover them with layers of newspaper strips dipped into the glue mixture. Allow each layer to dry thoroughly. Extend newspaper strips out at bottom to form a handle. When your maracas are dry, paint them with bright designs.

ANIMALS IN MEXICO

Many types of animals live in Mexico, including more than 40 types of snakes, alligators, lizards, and thousands of insects.

Tarantulas

Tarantulas are common in Mexico. There are many varieties of tarantulas. Some varieties are poisonous, and some are even bigger than a man's hand.

Paper Spider

Materials:

- Black construction paper
- Black yarn
- Scissors
- Glue

Cut two circles from the black paper, one smaller than the other, and glue them together, end to end. Attach eight black construction paper legs to the larger circle. Cover the paper spider with short pieces of black yarn to represent the tarantula's hair.

Burros

These beasts of burden were less expensive and hardier than horses, making them very valuable to Mexican peasants.

Sawdust Clay Burro

Materials:

- 4 cups sawdust
- 1 cup wheat paste
- 2½ cups water

Mix all the materials together to make sawdust clay. Roll two balls, a large one for the body and a smaller one for the head, reserving some clay for the legs and tail. Attach four legs rolled from clay and a thinner roll for a tail. Shape your burro with your fingers. Finally, pinch two triangles for ears.

Butterflies

Mexico is home to many beautiful butterfly species, including the monarch butterfly, which migrates to Mexico in the winter. For more information about this butterfly, read *The Monarch Butterfly* by Ivah Green.

Marble-Painted Butterfly

Materials:

- Orange construction paper
- Black paint
- Marbles
- Scissors

Cut orange paper into butterfly shapes. Dip a marble into black paint, then roll it across the surface of your butterfly to create the markings of a monarch butterfly.

Plastic Bag Butterfly

Materials:

- Gallon-size plastic zip-locking bags
- Colored construction paper, cut into small pieces
- Pipe cleaners

Put two handfuls of paper pieces in the bag and seal, squeezing most of the air out. Clinch the bag at middle with pipe cleaner, spreading out sides to form the wings of the butterfly.

Ink Blot Butterfly

Materials:

- Large sheets of white paper
- Colored tempera, mixed thickly
- Spoons
- Scissors

Fold the paper in half and cut out half of a large butterfly shape. Unfold the paper and drop globs of paint from a spoon onto one side of butterfly. Fold the paper again, pressing firmly to create a matching, symmetrical design.

THE PLANTS OF MEXICO

Cactus

There are many varieties of cactus growing in Mexico. Native Americans eat the fruit of one variety, the prickly pear, and make a drink from its fermented juice. Aztecs used to punish their children by pricking them with cactus needles.

Cactus Picture

Materials:

- Green construction paper
- Toothpicks
- Scissors
- Glue

Cut various shapes of clumped cactus from the green paper and cover with toothpick spines.

Paper Bag Cactus

Materials:

- Paper grocery bags
- Green paint and paintbrushes
- Toothpicks
- Red tissue paper
- Newspaper
- Glue

Paint a grocery bag green and cover it with toothpicks for prickles. Paste crumpled pieces of tissue paper on the bag to represent cactus flowers. Fill the bag with crumpled newspaper so it will stand up. For an added touch, display several of these cacti on top of each other along the wall and use brown paper lunch bags, decorated in a similar manner, to form arms of a saguaro cactus.

Poinsettia

In the nineteenth century, America's ambassador to Mexico, Joel Robert Poinsett, brought back this beautiful flower he had learned of in Cuernavaca, a city in south-central Mexico. Since then, this flower, named in English after Poinsett, has become a traditional symbol of Christmas.

Poinsettia Picture

Materials:

- Sponges
- Red tempera, mixed thickly
- Paper
- Green paint
- Paintbrushes
- Scissors

Paint a stem and broad leaves using green paint and paintbrush. Cut the sponge into broad, triangular petal shapes. Sponge-paint petals around the top of the stem, creating the poinsettia plant.

Construction Paper Poinsettia

Materials:

- Yellow and red construction paper
- Glue
- Scissors

Cut 10 to 12 petals (4 inches long) from red paper and glue them, overlapping slightly, around a yellow 1-inch circle.

CRAFTS IN MEXICO

Mexico has been called "the land of handicrafts" and is famous worldwide for its distinctive products.

Basket Weaving

Mexican baskets are used for everything from storage to decoration to tableware.

Yarn Basket

Materials:

- Plastic margarine tubs
- Yarn
- Heavy-duty scissors

Cut slits about 1 inch apart from the rim of the tub to the bottom all the way around. Take a 2-yard piece of yarn and fold it in half. Slip loop behind one of the spokes of the margarine tub. Cross the ends of the yarn over each other in front of spoke and twine around next spoke, continuing in this manner until you run out of yarn or want to change colors. Tie a knot with the two loose ends, changing colors as many times as desired.

Murals

From the time of the Maya, Mexican people have painted beautiful murals depicting scenes from battles, the lives of famous people, or scenes from everyday life. Some twentieth-century muralists are Diego Rivera, José Clemente Orozco, and David Alfaro Siqueiros. Pictures of Mexican murals can be found in *Mexico: A History in Art* by Bradley Smith and *Mexico: The Land and Its People* by John Howard.

Butcher Paper Mural

Materials:

- Butcher paper
- Brightly colored paints
- Paintbrushes
- Pencils

Hang the butcher paper on the wall. Choose a subject to paint, sketching on the paper before painting.

Pottery

When the Spaniards arrived in Mexico they were amazed by the beautiful pottery created by the Native Americans. Today, Mexican pottery is still famous worldwide.

Clay Pottery

Materials:

- Modeling clay
- Paints and paintbrushes

Use modeling clay to form a bowl, pot, or figure. Let the pottery harden and then paint using bright colors—flowers are a popular design.

Papier-Mâché Pottery

Materials:

- Margarine tubs
- Newspapers
- Bright paints and paintbrushes
- Brown paper bags
- Glue (mixed 1:1 with water)
- Clear shellac or varnish

Tear the newspaper and brown paper bag into thin strips. Dip newspaper in glue mixture and cover the margarine tub. Let each layer dry. Finally, apply a top layer with the paper bag strips to simulate the clay used in Mexico. When your papier-mâché pot is dry, paint it with bright colors. When the paint is dry, coat the pot with a clear layer of varnish.

Ojo de Días

These beautiful yarn pictures come in many different designs and colors. The name means "eye of God" in Spanish.

Yarn Ojo de Días

Materials:

- Craft sticks
- Colored yarn
- Glue

Glue two craft sticks together at the center into a cross and then weave yarn over and under the sticks, wrapping the yarn around each stick once before going to the next stick.

REFERENCES

Beck, Barbara L. *The Ancient Maya*. New York: Franklin Watts, 1983.

Dineen, Jacqueline. *The Aztecs*. New York: Macmillan, 1992.

Geis, Darlene, ed. *Let's Travel in Mexico*. Chicago: Childrens Press, 1965.

Grant, Clara Louise, and Jane Werner Watson. *Mexico: Land of the Plumed Serpent*. Champaign, IL: Garrard, 1968.

Green, Ivah. *The Monarch Butterfly*. Chicago: Encyclopaedia Britannica Press, 1964.

Howard, John. *Mexico*, The Land and Its People series. Morristown, NJ: Silver Burdett, 1977.

McKissack, Patricia C. *The Maya*. Chicago: Childrens Press, 1985.

Smith, Bradley. *Mexico: A History in Art*. Garden City, NY: Doubleday, 1968.

FURTHER READING

Caso, Alfonso. *The Aztecs: People of the Sun*. Norman: University of Oklahoma Press, 1958.

Fisher, Leonard Everett. *Pyramid of the Sun, Pyramid of the Moon*. New York: Macmillan, 1988.

Kopper, Philip. *The Smithsonian Book of North American Indians: Before the Coming of the Europeans*. Washington, DC: Smithsonian Books, 1986.

Leonard, Jonathan. *Ancient America*. New York: Time, 1967.

McHenry, Robert, ed. *The New Encyclopaedia Britannica*, vols. 1, 7–9, 11, 13. Chicago: Encyclopaedia Britannica, 1992.

Schobinger, Juan. *The First Americans*. Grand Rapids, MI: William B. Eerdmans, 1994.

16 NATIVE AMERICANS

The many peoples that lived in North America before the coming of the Europeans after Columbus, were descended from prehistoric peoples who migrated across the Bering Strait 20,000–35,000 years ago from Asia. At the time of the first European contact, it is estimated that there were 10 million Native Americans in what would become America, 90 million Native Americans total on the North and South American continents. This population was decimated by the European settlements through war, famine, forced labor, social upheaval, and epidemics.

The term "Native American" refers to people from many different cultures and ways of life; each culture was unique and distinct, and it would be inaccurate to lump the cultures all together. Generally speaking, though, American Indians altered their technologies based on local resources, living conditions, and tribal needs. Major technologies were flint-knapping, pottery, basketry, and weaving. Art was utilitarian and ornamental, and folklore and learning were transmitted orally and through dances and chants. Distinctive crafts and artistic styles characterize the different tribal cultures.

Native Americans have much to teach Western culture about living in harmony with one's environment, about the careful use and preservation of natural resources, and about adapting to one's surroundings. A unit on Native Americans will help students develop an appreciation for the first people to inhabit our land and lead to an understanding of a different lifestyle and belief system.

HOME AND FAMILY LIFE

The Native American style of homes varied according to the tribe and the part of the country in which the tribe lived. Nomadic tribes depended heavily upon the tipi, which was easy to put up and take down, whereas farming tribes lived in more permanent homes.

Tipis

Indians of the Great Plains—the Blackfoot, Cheyenne, Crow, Dakota, and Sioux, among others—lived in tipis which, more than simple tents, were sophisticated dwellings in keeping with the nomadic lifestyle of those tribes. Made from animal skins, the tipi provided shelter from the elements, warmth in the winter, and coolness in the summer. Pictures of tipis can be found in *First Houses: Native American Homes and Sacred Structures* by Jean Guard Monroe and Ray A. Williams and *The Tipi: A Center of Native American Life* by David and Charlotte Yue.

Paper Tipi

Materials:

- Brown construction paper
- Craft sticks
- String or twist ties
- Crayons
- Scissors
- Glue

Tie three craft sticks together at the top, spreading them out at the bottom and standing them upright. Cut the brown paper into a semicircle with a radius of 7 inches. If you wish, study Native American art and draw similar symbols on the paper. Wrap the paper around the craft sticks and glue them securely.

Bedsheet Tipi

Materials:

- Bedsheet or butcher paper
- String
- Three broomsticks or other long poles about the same height
- Safety pins or tape
- Crayons

Tie the three poles together at the top. Decorate the butcher paper or sheet with Native American designs and drape it around the poles, fastening with tape, pins, or string.

Pueblos

The Native Americans of Arizona and New Mexico—such as the Hopi, Zuni, and Tewa—took advantage of their desert surroundings by forming their homes from the dirt and clay that surrounded them. They shaped mud into lumps and plastered them into a wall, allowing each layer to dry before adding the next layer, constructing them into multistoried tenement homes modeled after the cliff dwellings of the Anasazi. When the Spaniards came, they taught the Native Americans how to use molds to cast the mud into large adobe bricks and dry them in the sun. Pictures of pueblos can be found in *First Houses: Native American Homes and Sacred Structures* by Jean Guard Monroe and Ray A. Williams.

Shoebox Pueblos

Materials:

- Shoeboxes
- Manila or light brown construction paper
- Toothpicks
- Crayons
- Glue
- Smaller boxes of various sizes
- Craft sticks
- Other found materials
- Scissors

Cover the shoeboxes with paper and stand them on end. Draw lines to represent the bricks. Cut holes for windows and doors. Cover and cut smaller boxes for a varied effect. Make ladders out of craft sticks and toothpicks to lead up to windows. Add details with other found materials.

Iroquois Longhouse

The Iroquois were a woodland hunting tribe on the East Coast who lived in settled villages that were occupied year round. Extended families lived together in a longhouse, a rectangular building with a domed roof, made by extending saplings from one side of the house to the other and tying bark over the frame. The longhouse was extended as necessary to make room for new family members. Some were up to 150 feet long, although most were less than 70 feet long. There were no windows, only a door at either end of the house. Pictures of the longhouse can be found in *First Houses: Native American Homes and Sacred Structures* by Jean Guard Monroe and Ray A. Williams and *The Iroquois Indians* by Victoria Sherrow.

Appliance Box Longhouse

Materials:

- Large appliance box
- Orange construction paper
- Crayons or paints and paintbrushes
- Butcher paper (brown corrugated if possible)
- Two dowels the same height as the width of the box
- Several sticks
- Ears of Indian corn
- Scissors and glue

Have your teacher cut a door at each end of the appliance box. Use brown paper to make an arched roof over the top of the box and support it with strings or sticks. Draw or paint brown lines on the sides of the box to represent logs. Make a roofed porch at the front of the longhouse by propping a piece of paper up on the two dowels at one end and attaching the other end to the front of the box. Hang the ears of corn from the roof of the box. Make a pretend fire by piling some sticks in the center of the box and cutting a flame from orange paper.

Shoebox Longhouse

Materials:

- Shoebox
- Toothpicks or sticks
- Glue
- Brown corrugated paper
- Scissors

Cut a door into each end of the shoebox. Cover the shoebox with brown corrugated paper. Make a roof by arching a sheet of heavy construction paper over the top of the box and gluing toothpicks or sticks onto the paper. Make a porch at the front end by extending a piece of construction paper out and propping it up with toothpicks.

Igloos

Contrary to popular belief, this domed snowhouse was rare in Alaska. It was much more common in the northern parts of Canada, where igloos were built large enough to hold dancing parties of 60 people. Like Native Americans everywhere, the Inuit (or Eskimo) peoples of the far north made their homes and tools from what was available: snow, driftwood (which was rare), dirt, stone, and even frozen fish!

Igloo Cutout Picture

Materials:

- White and blue construction paper
- Crayons
- Scissors
- Glue

Study details of Inuit life, then create cutout igloos by arranging squares of white paper on the blue paper. Add details with crayons.

Eggshell Igloo

Materials:

- Empty eggshell halves
- Colored felt-tip markers
- Cotton
- Glue

Draw lines on each eggshell half to represent snow blocks. Color a door at the bottom. Dip the bottom edge of the shell in glue and place it on the cotton.

Hogans

The Navajo of Arizona, New Mexico, and Utah lived in *hogans*. These were dome-shaped homes, covered with bark and mud. Pictures of a hogan can be found in *First Houses: Native American Homes and Sacred Structures* by Jean Guard Monroe and Ray A. Williams.

Clay Hogans

Materials:

- Modeling clay
- Cardboard
- Cedar litter (such as that used for small animal cages)

Form domes from the modeling clay, using the cardboard as a base. Carve out a door for the home. Cover the surface of the clay with cedar chips.

NATIVE AMERICAN CLOTHING

As with the homes they lived in, the clothing of Native Americans varied according to the materials available to them and the climate of their part of the country.

Medicine Bundle

The people of the Plains tribes each wore a medicine bundle on a thong around their necks. These medicine bundles contained objects with special personal or spiritual significance—items that were sacred to the bearer, often given by their spirits or guardians.

Leather Medicine Bundle

Materials:

- Leather scraps (cut into 4-inch circles)
- Hole punch or awl
- Leather thong

Punch holes all the way around the circle of leather 1 inch from the edge. Thread the leather thong through these holes, leaving the same length at each end of the thong. Tie the ends and draw tight, creating a drawstring pouch. If you want, choose special items to put in your pouch.

Feather Headdresses

Plains Indians were awarded feathers for achievement in battle, which were largely fought to show bravery and skill, not to kill opponents. However, many wars were fought with extreme violence and loss of life. After horses and guns were introduced, the idea of "counting coup," or touching your opponent was made commonplace. There were many ways to "count coup," or show bravery and skill in battle, therefore earning feathers. Once a warrior had earned a feather, he could wear it for the rest of his life.

Paper Headdress

Materials:

- Scissors
- Construction paper, brown and other colors (or real feathers)
- Glue

Cut a band from construction paper to fit around your head. Cut feathers from colored paper and glue them to the band. Use real feathers if you have them available. If you like, study alterations made by certain tribes to the feathers for various achievements and try to imitate those.

Armor

The Tlingit of the Northwest are one of the few Native American tribes that wore armor to protect themselves in battle. They made breastplates and leg guards from wooden rods and wore helmets that looked like a bizarre human head. Read *The Tlingit* by Alice Osinski.

Corrugated Paper Armor

Materials:

- Corrugated paper (if available)
- Craft sticks (if corrugated paper not available)
- Paper grocery bags
- Construction paper scraps
- Glue
- Scissors

Cut holes for your arms and head in one grocery bag. Glue corrugated paper (set so the stripes run vertically) or craft sticks all the way around the bag. Cut a second bag in half and cut a rectangle out of the front for seeing. Use construction paper scraps to design a face for the helmet.

Shields

Plains Indians carried leather shields in battle.

Cardboard Shield

Materials:

- Cardboard
- Scissors and glue
- Paints and paintbrushes
- Feathers

Cut a circle from cardboard. Decorate it with paints and glue feathers to the bottom.

Quiver

Many Native Americans tribes used quivers to hold their arrows and sometimes their bows. Quivers were usually made of leather and decorated with beads, feathers, or fur.

Cardboard Quiver

Materials:

- Lid from spray can
- Colored felt-tip markers
- Leather or cloth strip, 36 inches long
- Glue
- Beads and feathers
- Scissors and glue
- Cardboard (wide enough to fit around the circumference of the lid and at least 12 inches tall)

Curve the cardboard to fit inside the spray can lid. Staple it, making a tube with the spray can lid at one end. Decorate your quiver with markers, beads, and feathers. Cut arrows from cardboard and stick them inside the quiver. Attach the cloth or leather strip to the top and bottom of the quiver to create a shoulder strap.

NATIVE AMERICAN ART

Native Americans were great artists, using the materials they found around them to express their reverence for nature, their people, and their deeds in battle.

Animal Skins

Curing animal skins was a lengthy process, but it was well worth the effort. Cured hides, or leather, was used to create clothing, footwear, tipis, saddles, ropes and thongs, carrying sacks, and blankets. These hides were often painted with symbols from Indian legends or pictures of animals.

Leather Picture

Materials:

- Brown construction paper or paper cut from brown grocery bag
- Crayons

Crumple paper several times then spread it out again to simulate the texture of leather. Cut the paper into a shape such as an animal skin would have. Draw Native-American symbols on the paper, telling a story or showing an everyday activity.

Masks

Among the Native Americans who wore masks were the Iroquois members of the False Face Society. Their elaborately carved masks were sculpted while still part of the living tree and were not removed until the mask was finished. If the mask were created from dead wood, it would have no life in it. Pictures of false face masks can be found in *The Iroquois* by Barbara A. McCall.

Paper Mask

Materials:

- Construction paper
- Found materials, especially yarn
- Glue
- Scissors

Cut an oval from construction paper. Decorate it with found materials and construction paper. Use yarn for hair.

Totem Poles

Totem poles, tall carved poles created from a single tree trunk, were often erected as a memorial to the chief by his heir. The carvings on the pole recited his ancestry and deeds. *Whale in the Sky* by Anne Siberall is a charming book with illustrations and a story from a totem pole legend. Another book with many pictures of totem poles is *The Totem Pole Indians of the Northwest* by Don E. Beyer.

Paper Bag Totem Pole

Materials:

- Paper grocery bags
- Newspaper
- Masking tape
- Construction paper scraps
- Glue
- Scissors

Study pictures of totem poles. Then stuff the paper bags with crumpled pieces of newspaper. Fold the top of the bags over and tape securely. Make faces of animals or people with construction paper scraps. Stack the bags one on top of another to make totem poles.

Paper Totem Pole

Materials:

- Construction paper
- Tape, stapler, or glue
- Scissors

Roll a sheet of construction paper into a cylinder and tape, staple, or glue securely. Create a column of faces on one side of the cylinder with construction paper scraps.

Oatmeal Box Totem Pole

Materials:

- Oatmeal boxes, coffee cans, other round boxes
- Construction paper
- Scissors and glue

Decorate each box with a face made from construction paper, then stack them on top of each other.

Beads

Depending on what was locally available, Native Americans used porcupine quills, shells, small rocks, teeth, claws, and clay beads to decorate their clothing and ornaments. Many tribes traded such beads and decorations with other tribes to obtain materials unavailable in the surrounding areas.

Bead Necklace

Materials:

- Colored beads (available at craft store)
- Thin wire for stringing

String beads on wire to make necklaces or bracelets.

Kachinas

The *kachinas* were Hopi spirits that were a part of all ceremonies from July until January. Men wore kachina costumes and masks, and when the costumed men were present, so were the actual spirits. Kachinas came in many guises. The *koshare*, or clowns, had black and white stripes all over their bodies, while the mudheads represented the men who first emerged from a hole in the earth. These were covered all over with mud and had round circles over their eyes and mouth. Pictures of kachinas can be found in *The Hopi: A New True Book* by Ann Heinrichs Tomchek, *Kachina Dolls: The Art of Hopi Carvers* by Helga Teiwes, and *Hopi Katcinas* by Jesse Walter Fewkes.

Kachina Picture

Materials:

- Construction paper
- Glue
- Crayons

Study pictures of kachinas, then using pieces of construction paper, design your own kachina.

Signs and Symbols

Native Americans used picture symbols to communicate with each other, scratching designs in dirt or tree trunks, and painting on animal skins or pieces of bark or rock. Pictures of Native American symbols can be found in *Indian Picture Writing* by Robert Hofsinde and *Coffee in the Gourd* by J. Frank Dobie.

Symbol Picture

Materials:

- Colored felt-tip markers
- Paper
- Samples of Native-American symbols (obtainable from library)

Study Native-American symbols and then copy the designs onto the paper. Try to use the symbols to write an actual message or story.

Sand Paintings

Sand paintings, created with different colors of sand, were an essential part of the Navajo religion. Each picture was created especially for a particular ceremony and destroyed after the ceremony ended.

Sand Painting

Materials:

- White sand or corn meal
- Stiff paper
- Glue or rubber cement
- Powdered tempera
- Spoons

Mix a spoonful of powdered tempera with a cup of sand or cornmeal, one for each color. Make a design with glue on the stiff paper or draw a simple design and fill in areas of design with rubber cement. Sprinkle desired color of cornmeal over the glue or cement. Shake off excess and repeat with another color.

Whale Tooth Necklaces

These beautifully carved necklaces were made by the Native Americans of Alaska and northwest Canada from the teeth of killer whales.

Styrofoam Necklace

Materials:

- White Styrofoam meat trays
- Yarn
- Black felt-tip markers (thin point)

Cut a long, pointed tooth about 4 inches long from the meat tray. Draw a design on the tooth with black marker. Poke a hole in the top and string on yarn to create a necklace.

NATIVE AMERICAN CRAFTS

Flint-Knapping

Native Americans were experts at this craft, using flint and obsidian to create arrowheads, spears, knives, and cooking utensils. Some of their achievements in flint-knapping have not been duplicated to this day.

Plaster-of-Paris Flint-Knapping

Materials:

- Plaster of paris, poured into cupcake tins (younger children may prefer a flat bar of soap)
- Rocks, with a straight or sharp edge

Students can practice chipping at the plaster-of-paris or soap "rocks" with their rocks and see if they can form arrowheads.

Pottery

Today, the Pueblo Indians still make beautiful pottery to sell to tourists. Most Pueblo potters use the same pinched-coil method their ancestors have used for generations.

Clay Pottery

Materials:

- Modeling clay
- Paints and paintbrushes

Study samples of Pueblo pottery. Roll several "snakes" from the clay and coil them on top of each other. Pinch these clay rolls together to smooth and give the desired shape. When your pot is dry, paint it with Pueblo designs.

Weaving

Navajo women are some of the most famous weavers in the world, producing blankets of extraordinary beauty. The Pueblo, however, were the only North Americans to use a loom.

Paper Weaving

Materials:

- Construction paper, various colors
- Scissors
- Tape

Cut several different colored sheets of paper into strips, 9½ inches long. Take a sheet of uncut paper, 9½ by 18 inches. Fold the paper widthwise and cut slits from the folded edge to within 1 inch of the open end. Weave the paper strips through these slits, taping them at the ends to keep the strips in place. When you are finished, you might want to go a step further by cutting zigzag strips of a third color and weaving them through the paper loom.

Nylon Net Weaving

Materials:

- Nylon net from onion or potato sacks
- Colored yarn
- Glue

Prepare for this activity a day ahead of time by cutting the yarn into 12-inch lengths and dipping each end in glue. The next day, cut a section of net from an onion or potato sack. Then weave the yarn through the net. When your weave is complete, tie the ends of the yarn together.

Dolls

Just like children the world over, Native-American children loved playing with dolls.

Corncob doll

Materials:

- Corncob
- Black yarn
- Beads and feather
- Black felt-tip marker
- Tan cloth or leather
- Stiff paper

Dry the corncob for several days. On the large end of the cob, color facial features with a marker. Cut a rectangular strip from cloth or leather, leaving a hole in the center for the head. Decorate the cloth or leather with beads. Fit this over the doll, securing it at the waist with a strip of cloth. Tie a cloth strip around the doll's head and glue a feather to the band. Cut hands and feet from stiff paper.

MUSICAL INSTRUMENTS

Native-American music is used mainly during their celebrations and religious ceremonies. Most of their instruments are rhythm instruments to help dancers keep the tempo.

Leg Rattles

Leg rattles were strapped to the legs and worn during ceremonial dances.

Bell Rattles

Materials:

- String, yarn, or elastic
- Small jingle bells, shells with a hole for stringing, pasta, etc.

Cut enough string, yarn, or elastic to fit around your ankle. Thread bells and other items on the string and tie securely.

Indian Drums

These were essential for keeping the beat during ceremonial dances.

Tin Can Drum

Materials:

- Manila paper
- Brown construction paper
- Large cans or cylindrical containers (e.g. tin cans, oatmeal box, salt boxes)
- Paint and paintbrushes or colored felt-tip markers
- Scissors
- Glue

Cut the brown paper to a length equal to the height of the can. Glue the paper around the can. Cut a large circle from the manila paper and glue it to the top of the can, pulling the overhanging edges down and gluing to the sides of the can. Paint or draw Native-American symbols or scenes on the sides of the drum.

REFERENCES

Beyer, Don E. *The Totem Pole Indians of the Northwest.* New York: Franklin Watts, 1989.

Dobie, J. Frank. *Coffee in the Gourd.* Dallas: Southern Methodist University Press, 1969.

Fewkes, Jesse Walter. *Hopi Katcinas.* Glorieta, NM: Rio Grande Press, 1969.

Hofsinde, Robert. *Indian Picture Writing.* New York: William Morrow, 1959.

Monroe, Jean Guard, and Ray A. Williams. *Native American Homes and Sacred Structures*, First House series. Boston: Houghton Mifflin, 1993.

Osinski, Alice. *The Tlingit.* Chicago: Childrens Press, 1990.

Sherrow, Victoria. *The Iroquois Indians.* New York: Chelsea House, 1992.

Siberall, Anne. *Whale in the Sky.* New York: E. P. Dutton, 1982.

Teiwes, Helga. *Kachina Dolls: The Art of Hopi Carvers.* Tucson: University of Arizona Press, 1991.

Tomchek, Ann Heinrichs. *The Hopi: A New True Book.* Chicago: Childrens Press, 1987.

Yue, David, and Charlotte Yue. *The Tipi: A Center of Native American Life.* New York: Alfred A. Knopf, 1984.

FURTHER READING

Bancroft-Hunt, Norman. *People of the Totem: The Indians of the Pacific Northwest.* London: Orbis, 1979.

Brooks, Barbara. *The Seminole*, Native American People series. Vero Beach, FL: Rourke, 1989.

Fenton, William N. *The False Faces of the Iroquois.* Norman: University of Oklahoma Press, 1987.

Kopper, Philip. *The Smithsonian Book of North American Indians: Before the Coming of the Europeans.* Washington, DC: Smithsonian Books, 1986.

Leonard, Jonathan. *Ancient America.* New York: Time, 1967.

Liptak, Karen. *Indians of the Pacific Northwest.* New York: Facts on File, 1991.

McCall, Barbara A. *The Iroquois.* Vero Beach, FL: Rourke, 1989.

McHenry, Robert, ed. *The New Encyclopaedia Britannica*, vols. 4, 6, 8, 11, 13, 25. Chicago: Encyclopaedia Britannica, 1992.

Samachson, Dorothy, and Joseph Samachson. *The First Artists.* Garden City, NY: Doubleday, 1970.

Schobinger, Juan. *The First Americans.* Grand Rapids, MI: William B. Eerdmans, 1994.

Scully, Vincent. *Pueblo Architecture of the Southwest.* Austin: University of Texas Press, 1971.

Shemie, Bonnie. *Houses of Snow, Skin and Bone.* Plattsburgh, NY: Tundra Books, 1989.

Snow, Dean R. *The Iroquois.* Cambridge, MA: Blackwell, 1994.

Walker, Lester. *American Shelter: An Illustrated Encyclopedia of the American Home.* Woodstock, NY: Overbrook Press, 1981.

17 HAWAII

Capital: **Honolulu**
Population: **1,115,000**
Area: **6,471 square miles**

Hawaii is the most racially and ethnically diverse state in the United States. People first came to Hawaii from Polynesia in about 400. There they lived in isolation, clustered in coastal villages without knowledge, or need, of metal. They worshipped four major gods and a host of minor deities, constructing their places of worship from lava rock. The Hawaiian culture transmitted legends and traditions through songs, dances, chants, and stories.

The islands were discovered by Europeans when Captain James Cook came there in 1778. Despite the influx of Europeans, and the attempts made by European missionaries to "civilize" the native islanders—who had a sophisticated civilization of their own—native Hawaiians were more influenced by Japan, which continues to be a major influence on the islands today. However, Americans who had settled in Hawaii succeeded in overthrowing the Hawaiian monarchy and making Hawaii a part of the United States.

Nearly everyone dreams of a Hawaiian vacation, and no wonder. The islands that make up this great state are a lush, tropical paradise. A unit on Hawaii will help students realize that our United States houses people of many cultures.

HAWAIIAN CLOTHING

Grass Skirts

These skirts are worn today during the traditional hula dance.

Paper Grass Skirt
Materials:

- Green butcher paper
- Paper clips
- Scissors

Measure a piece of green paper to fit around your waist. Cut strips from the bottom up, stopping just below the waistline. Fasten the skirt around your waist with paper clips.

Paper Lunch Bag Hula Dancer
Materials:

- Paper lunch bags
- Seed catalogs
- Crayons
- Scissors
- Glue

Color the open end of your lunch bag green and cut a fringe along the open end. Draw a face on the top of the sack. Cut small flower pictures from seed catalogs and glue under the face to make a necklace, or *lei*. Add another flower for the hair.

Royal Standards (Kahili)

The Hawaiian king's attendants carried these staffs wherever he went as a symbol of his office. They were covered with brightly colored feathers and looked like tall feather dusters.

Styrofoam Cup Standard
Materials:

- Tissue paper
- Straws
- Glue
- Styrofoam cups
- Tape

Turn the cup upside down and tape the bottom of the cup to the top of a drinking straw. Cover the cup with crumpled pieces of tissue paper.

Feathered Capes

Kings and queens of Hawaii wore full-length cloaks made of thousands of feathers. It could take up to 100 years to make just one of these elaborate cloaks.

Butcher Paper Cape
Materials:

- Butcher paper
- Scissors
- Tissue paper
- Glue

Cut a trapezoid from the butcher paper, big enough to drape around your shoulders. Cover your cape with torn pieces of tissue paper so that it will look like feathers.

SYMBOLS

Ukuleles

The ukulele was developed in Hawaii from the Portuguese machete in the nineteenth century. The gentle sound of the ukulele has become a symbol of sunny beaches and crashing waves.

Cardboard Ukulele

Materials:

- Heavy cardboard
- Brass metal fasteners
- Brown paint
- Scissors
- Pencils
- Rubber bands
- Paintbrushes
- Glue

Cut two identical ukulele shapes from heavy cardboard and glue the two pieces together. Attach a pencil to the neck to serve as a support. Paint the ukulele brown. Use brass metal fasteners to make the tuning keys and cut rubber bands to use for strings.

Leis

These necklaces are woven from bright flowers. Hawaiians give them to friends to say hello and good-bye. Before you leave Hawaii, drop your lei into the ocean. If your lei is washed back to land, you will return one day.

Tissue Paper Lei

Materials:

- Colored tissue paper (size depends on how big a flower is desired)
- Twist ties
- Needles
- Thread

Create tissue paper flowers by layering four pieces of tissue paper (cut into 4-by-4 inch squares) and folding them together fan-style. Wrap a twist tie around the center and pull the layers apart on each side. When you have created several flowers, string them together in a necklace.

NATURE IN HAWAII

Hawaii is a land filled with natural wonders; there are more native plant and animal species here than anywhere else in the United States. However, many plants and animals have become extinct or are endangered. The islands are also subject to the violence of nature, such as volcanoes, earthquakes, and monsoons.

Volcanoes

Hawaii was actually created by volcanoes. The ancient Hawaiian goddess Pele was the goddess of fire and volcanoes, and had a quick and violent temper. Two of the biggest volcanoes in Hawaii, Mauna Loa and Kilauea, are still active. Most of the other volcanoes are classified as dormant, although geologists say they could become active again at any moment. Pictures of volcanoes can be found in *Hawaii in Words and Pictures* by Dennis B. Fradin, *Hawaii Volcanoes* by Lewann Sotnak, *Ring of Fire and the Hawaiian Islands and Iceland* by Alice Thompson Gilbreath, *Volcanoes and Earthquakes* by Pierre Kohler, *Volcanoes* by Helen J. Challand, and *Volcanoes* by James Carson.

Volcano Picture

Materials:

- Blue and brown construction paper
- Orange tempera, mixed thickly
- Glue
- Drinking straws
- Scissors

Cut a volcano from brown paper and glue it onto the blue paper. Spoon orange paint on the peak of the volcano and blow the paint through a straw to make it seem to erupt upward and down the sides of the volcano.

Magma

Materials:

- White glue (not school glue)
- Black tempera
- Liquid starch
- Waxed paper

Mix two parts glue with one part liquid starch. Add black tempera. If the mixture is too sticky to handle, add a little more starch. Shape the magma into rocks and set them on a piece of waxed paper. They will harden over several days.

Palm Trees

The coconut palm was introduced into Hawaii by Polynesian settlers 1,500 years ago and is now a symbol of this lush, tropical land. Anthropologists believe that the coconut was a source of food on the long ocean voyage to the islands.

Paper Palm Tree

Materials:

- Brown and green paper
- Scissors and glue

Tear strips of brown paper and arrange them on the wall to form the trunk of the tree. Cut palm leaves from green paper, fringing the edges. Attach these leaves to the top of the tree.

Red Hibiscus Picture

The red hibiscus is the state flower of Hawaii. Originally a rosy red in color, it has been bred in many other shades. It is often woven into leis or worn in the hair for decoration.

Materials:

- White or blue construction paper
- Glue or tape
- Crayons or colored pencils
- Tissue paper (red preferred)
- Scissors

Draw several green stems and leaves on the construction paper. Cut a 4-inch circle from the tissue paper for each flower. Pinch the circle together at the center and tape around the center. With scissors, cut four lines from the outer edge almost to the center. Glue or tape the center of the circle to the top of the stem for a three-dimensional hibiscus picture.

Hawaiian Products Painting

Sugar cane, pineapples, and macadamia nuts are principal products of Hawaii. The state is one of the largest pineapple producers in the world.

Materials:

- White construction paper
- Stalks of sugar cane
- Macadamia nuts
- Paint—any color, mixed thickly
- Fresh pineapple (uncut)

Create a Hawaiian picture by pressing the Hawaiian products in paint and then on paper. Try rolling the uncut pineapple in the paint and then across the paper. Then ask your teacher to cut the pineapple into chunks and paint with the chunks. Try using the stalk of sugar cane as a paintbrush and then cutting it to print with sections of the stalk.

THE OCEAN AND HAWAII

Whales

Whaling as an industry hit the islands in the 1820s and was a major source of additional income for several decades. However, as whales became scarce and people turned to other, cheaper products, whaling went into a decline. Today, people around the world are struggling to restore whale populations and bring them back from the near-extinction brought on by excessive whaling. Two books about whales for children are *The Sea World Book of Whales* by Eve Bunting and *Whales* by Helen Hoke, Valerie Pitt, and Thomas R. Funderburk.

Whale Picture
Materials:

- Butcher paper
- Paint and paintbrushes
- Crayons
- Newspaper
- Scissors
- Stapler

Layer two pieces of butcher paper and draw a whale shape on the top layer. Cut the shape out. Paint whale features on both outside surfaces and let dry. Lay crumpled newspaper inside and staple around edges. Hang your whale from the ceiling.

3-D Whale Picture
Materials:

- Styrofoam meat tray
- Plastic wrap (blue or clear)
- Glue
- Aquarium gravel or sand colored with tempera
- Scraps of paper
- Crayons or colored felt-tip markers
- Scissors

Color a meat tray blue or green. Glue the aquarium gravel or colored sand to the bottom of the tray. Cut a whale shape from paper. Cut out other shapes such as fish or plants. For each underwater object, accordion fold a small strip of paper and glue one end to the back of the object and the other end to the meat tray. Cover the entire model with plastic wrap.

Beaches

Today, Hawaiians have turned their broad white beaches into a major tourist attraction. Read *Beach Patterns: The World of Sea and Sand* by Stella Snead.

Beach Picture
Materials:

- Blue paper
- Construction paper scraps
- Brushes for glue
- White sand (or cornmeal mixed with powdered white tempera)
- Small shells
- Glue (mixed 1:1 with water)
- Scissors

Brush glue across the bottom of the blue paper and sprinkle sand on the glue, shaking off the excess. Add shells, palm trees, beach balls, the sun, and other details cut from construction paper.

Beach in a Jar
Materials:

- Baby food jar
- Sand or cornmeal colored with powdered tempera
- Small shells

Layer different colors of sand in a jar. Arrange shells on top and put the lid on the jar. Don't shake your jar!

Plaster-of-Paris Footprints
Materials:

- Sand
- Plaster of paris
- Pie tins
- Paints and paintbrushes

Pour the sand into the pie tin. Moisten the sand, then take off your shoe and sock and make a footprint in the damp sand. Fill in your footprint with plaster of paris. When the plaster of Paris is dry, remove it and paint it if you wish.

Undersea Life

The seas around Hawaii abound with brightly colored fish, seaweeds, and other sea life. Divers take great delight in exploring the many varieties of life there. Read *The Pacific* by Pat Hargreaves or *Pacific: An Undersea Journey* by David Doubilet.

Undersea Picture
Materials:

- Blue construction paper
- Shell-shaped pasta
- Construction paper scraps
- Sand or cornmeal
- Crepe paper
- Scissors and glue

Glue sand and shell-shaped pasta across the bottom of the paper. Twist strips of crepe paper and glue them in place to create seaweed. Add fish cut from colored paper.

Chalk Undersea Picture

Materials:

- Blue construction paper
- Chalk fixative (available at craft stores)
- White glue
- Bright chalk pastels

Using squeeze bottles, squirt lines and shapes of glue onto paper, forming shapes of fish, seaweed, and other underwater life. Decorate with squiggly lines and dots. Allow to dry for a day. When dry, color over raised glue with pastel chalks. You can color on top of the glue or inside the boundaries, or just rub over the page. When you are finished, spray your picture with fixative.

Shells

Shells of all shapes and sizes can be found on Hawaiian beaches.

Plaster-of-Paris Shell Casts

Materials:

- Pie tins
- Sea shells, various shapes and sizes
- Paints
- Sand
- Plaster of paris
- Paintbrushes

Fill the pie tins with damp sand. Press shells in the sand then carefully remove. Fill depressions with plaster of paris. When dry, remove the shell molds and paint.

Seashell Picture

Materials:

- Paper
- Paint
- Shells

Make a picture by dipping shells in paint and then pressing on paper.

Tropical Fish

The fish that inhabit the waters around Hawaii come in every imaginable color and in many different shapes and sizes.

Tropical Fish Picture

Materials:

- White construction paper
- Pans
- Scissors
- Colored chalk
- Water

Cut white paper into fish shapes. Scrape different colors of chalk into a pan of water. Blow surface of water gently to mix the colors. Dip fish-shaped paper into water to pick up designs.

REFERENCES

Bunting, Eve. *The Sea World Book of Whales*. San Diego, CA: Sea World Press, 1980.

Carson, James. *Volcanoes*. New York: Bookwright, 1983.

Challand, Helen J. *Volcanoes*. Chicago: Childrens Press, 1983.

Doubilet, David. *Pacific: An Undersea Journey*. Boston: Little, Brown, 1992.

Fradin, Dennis B. *Hawaii in Words and Pictures*. Chicago: Childrens Press, 1980.

Gilbreath, Alice Thompson. *Ring of Fire and the Hawaiian Islands and Iceland*. Minneapolis, MN: Dillon, 1986.

Hargreaves, Pat. *The Pacific*. Morristown, NJ: Silver Burdett, 1981.

Hoke, Helen, Valerie Pitt, and Thomas R. Funderburk. *Whales*. New York: Franklin Watts, 1973.

Kohler, Pierre. *Volcanoes and Earthquakes*. New York: Barron's, 1987.

Snead, Stella. *Beach Patterns: The World of Sea and Sand*. Barre, MA: Barre, 1975.

Sotnak, Lewann. *Hawaii Volcanoes*. New York: Crestwood House, 1989.

FURTHER READING

McHenry, Robert, ed. *The New Encyclopaedia Britannica*, vol. 5. Chicago: Encyclopaedia Britannica, 1992.

Penisten, John. *Honolulu*, A Downtown America Book series. Minneapolis, MN: Dillon, 1989.

Tabrah, Ruth. *Hawaii: A Bicentennial History*. New York: W. W. Norton, 1980.